Step 2: Practice

"Before everything else, getting ready is the secret of success."

— Henry Ford

Thank you for pursuing excellence in your coding education! As coding becomes a more complex and specialized career, it is extremely important that we coders stay at the top of our coding game. That's why, as a lifelong coder and educator, I know that tools for more advanced learning and practice are crucial for today's top coders. *Thank you for being committed to being one of the best and rising to the top of our career.*

— Carol J. Buck, MS, CPC-I, CPC, CPC-H, CCS-P

Track your progress!

**See the checklist in the back of this book
to learn more about your next step toward coding success!**

2010

THE NEXT STEP

ADVANCED MEDICAL CODING

2010
THE NEXT STEP

ADVANCED MEDICAL CODING

Carol J. Buck
MS, CPC-I, CPC, CPC-H, CCS-P
Program Director, Retired
Medical Secretary Programs
Northwest Technical College
East Grand Forks, Minnesota

Jacqueline Klitz Grass
MA, CPC
Coding Specialist
Grand Forks, North Dakota

SAUNDERS
ELSEVIER

evolve
learning system

3251 Riverport Lane
Maryland Heights, Missouri 63043

WORKBOOK FOR THE NEXT STEP: ADVANCED MEDICAL CODING, 2010 EDITION

ISBN: 978-1-4377-0675-8

NOTE: *Current Procedural Terminology, 2010,* was used in updating this text.

Current Procedural Terminology (CPT) is copyright 2009 American Medical Association. All Rights Reserved. No fee schedules, basic units, relative values, or related listings are included in CPT. The AMA assumes no liability for the data contained herein. Applicable FARS/DFARS restrictions apply to governement use.

ISBN: 978-1-4377-0675-8

Acquisitions Editor: Michael S. Ledbetter
Development Editor: Jenna Johnson
Publishing Services Manager: Pat Joiner-Myers
Senior Project Manager: Mary Pohlman
Senior Designer: Amy Buxton

Printed in the United States of America

Last digit is the print number: 9   8   7   6   5   4   3   2   1

CONTENTS

Evaluation and Management Services

Make sure to check
evolve learning system
for the latest content updates

CASE 1-1

The patient in Case 1-1 presents to the emergency department with trauma due to a cow stomping on her. Code the emergency physician's E&M service.

1-1A EMERGENCY DEPARTMENT SERVICES

LOCATION: Hospital Emergency Department

PATIENT: Fran Green

PHYSICIAN: Paul Sutton, MD

CHIEF COMPLAINT: Level 3 trauma

SUBJECTIVE: A 44-year-old female was treating a sick calf when a cow attacked her and stomped her. She presents to the emergency room via ambulance complaining of an open ankle dislocation. She also is complaining of some abrasions on her chin and under her left leg. She specifically denies loss of consciousness or headache. No neck, back, chest, abdomen, or pelvic pain. She is quite stoic.

PAST MEDICAL HISTORY: Remarkable for some hypertension, depression, and migraine.

MEDICATIONS:
1. Premarin
2. Question Xanax

ALLERGIES: None

FAMILY HISTORY: Deemed noncontributory

SOCIAL HISTORY: She is married, I believe a nonsmoker, and is a laborer.

REVIEW OF SYSTEMS: As above. She says her foot is cold.

PHYSICAL EXAMINATION: Preliminary survey is benign. Secondary survey: Alert and Oriented × 3. Immobilized in a C-collar and long spine board. Head is normocephalic. There is no hemotympanum. Pupils are equal. There is an abrasion under her chin. Trachea is midline. She does have a C-collar in place. Air entry is equal.

Lungs are clear. Chest wall is nontender. Abdomen is soft. Pelvis is stable. Long bones are remarkable for an obvious open dislocation of the right ankle. The toes are all dusky, she has a strong posterior tibial pulse, and the nurse thinks she felt a faint dorsalis pedis. She has an abrasion under her left leg.

HOSPITAL COURSE: We did give her a tetanus shot and 1 g of Ancef. I immediately gave her some parenteral Fentanyl and Versed, and we were able to reduce the dislocation without difficulty. Postreduction film looks surprisingly good. There is perhaps a subtle fracture noted only on the lateral projection. C-spine shows some degenerative change, is of poor quality, but is negative; and upon re-examination she is not tender in that area. However, it was done because she had such a severe distracting injury and given the mechanism. Chest x-ray and left femur look fine.

ASSESSMENT: Level 3 trauma with an open right ankle dislocation, multiple abrasions.

PLAN: Plan to call Dr. Almaz, who graciously agreed to assume care. The patient is kept n.p.o.

1-1A:

SERVICE CODE(S): _____

ICD-9-CM DX CODE(S): _____

ICD-10-CM DX CODE(S): _____

CASE 1-2

The patient in Case 1-2 is an 86-year-old female who is seen by her physician, Dr. Green, in the emergency department and admitted the patient to the hospital. Report Dr. Green's service.

1-2A INITIAL HOSPITAL CARE

LOCATION: Inpatient, Hospital

PATIENT: Margaret A. Mann

ATTENDING PHYSICIAN: Ronald Green, MD

CHIEF COMPLAINT: Excessive coughing.

HISTORY OF PRESENT ILLNESS: Ms. Mann is an 86-year-old-lady with past medical history of hypertension, hypothyroidism, abdominal aortic aneurysm, chronic obstructive pulmonary disease, and history of laryngeal carcinoma, status postlaryngectomy. She presented to the emergency room with complaint of excessive coughing for the past 4 days. She stated that the cough is productive of greenish and occasionally blood-stained sputum. She has also been having associated shortness of breath at rest and a feeling of heaviness on the right side of the chest. She has taken over-the-counter medications without relief. She denies having fever, nausea, or vomiting, and her appetite has been good. No recent weight loss. No exertional chest pain or pleuritic chest pain.

REVIEW OF SYSTEMS: CARDIAC: No PND, no orthopnea, no palpitations. CHEST: As in the history. GASTROINTESTINAL: No constipation, no abdominal pain, no nausea or vomiting. GU: No dysuria, no hematuria, no frequency of micturition. NEUROLOGIC: No headache, no blurring of vision, no diplopia. She has a history of cataracts.

MEDICATIONS:
1. Synthroid 0.088 mg daily.
2. Multivitamin 1 tablet daily.
3. Tylenol 500 mg daily.
4. Enalapril 20 mg bid.
5. She was started on azithromycin yesterday by her primary doctor.

ALLERGIES: Demerol-reaction uncertain.

SOCIAL HISTORY: She is a retired bookkeeper. She is widowed and lives alone. She has two sons and three daughters. One of her daughters has multiple sclerosis. She remains quite active.

PHYSICAL EXAMINATION: She is alert and oriented to place, time, and person. She is not in any acute distress. VITAL SIGNS: BLOOD PRESSURE: 155/81. PULSE: 91 per minute. RESPIRATORY RATE: 18 per minute. O_2 saturation 93% on room air. She is not pale, not jaundiced, not cyanosed, and no peripheral edema. No finger clubbing. The stoma of her tracheostomy is noted; it looks clean and no signs of surrounding inflammation. No cervical lymphadenopathy. CVS: Pulse is regular and of good volume. No jugular venous distention. First and second heart sounds are normal. No cardiac murmur. No gallop rhythm. CHEST: She had good air entry bilaterally, has crackles at both lung bases, more on the right. She has no rhonchi. GASTRO-INTESTINAL: Abdomen is soft and nontender; no hepatosplenomegaly, no ascites.

EXTREMITIES: No abnormalities detected. CNS: Neck is supple. No cranial nerve deficits. Normal tone, power, and reflexes in all extremities.

LABORATORY DATA: CBC – WBC 11.22, hemoglobin 11.1, hematocrit 32.6, MCV 90.8, platelets 415; WBC differential—neutrophils 78.6, lymphocytes 11%. Basic metabolic profile—sodium 133, potassium 4.5, chloride 95, bicarbonate 23.1, BUN 19, creatinine 1.3, calcium 8.9, and glucose 77. Sputum culture showed less than 10 squamous epithelial cells by low power field and 10 to 25 white blood cells by low power field; no organisms seen.

Chest x-ray: The right heart border is indistinct. There is questionable infiltrate in the right middle lobe. I am yet to get the official report of the chest x-ray.

ASSESSMENT & PLAN:
1. R/O right middle lobe pneumonia. Will start the patient on moxifloxacin 400 mg daily. The patient will be on oxygen by nasal cannula 2 liters per minute. If the patient fails to improve, we may consider getting a CT scan of the chest to rule out an underlying reason for the chest infection, more so as this patient has a history of laryngeal CA.
2. Hypertension. I will continue the patient on Enalapril 20 mg bid. If blood pressure is uncontrolled with this, I may add another agent, preferably a beta blocker.
3. Hypothyroidism. Will continue with the Synthroid 0.088 mg.
4. Peptic ulcer disease. I will start the patient on Ranitidine 150 mg daily.
5. Chronic obstructive airway disease. The patient will be on Albuterol and Atrovent nebulizers prn q 12 hours.
6. DVT prophylaxis. Will start the patient on subcutaneous heparin 5,000 units q 12 hours.

1-2A:

SERVICE CODE(S): _____

ICD-9-CM DX CODE(S): _____

ICD-10-CM DX CODE(S): _____

CASE 1-3

Dr. Pleasant has been the attending physician in Case 1-3. Report Dr. Pleasant's service.

1-3A PROGRESS REPORT

LOCATION: Inpatient, Hospital

PATIENT: David R. Harris

ATTENDING PHYSICIAN: Timothy L. Pleasant, MD

SUBJECTIVE: The patient is doing very good today. His lower back pain is much better after he has had the epidural pump. He complains of increased secretions in the trachea and some rattling noise and pain in his chest when he breathes. He is not coughing up any secretions, and he has no other chest pain. He is not having any fever. No other complaints.

REVIEW OF SYSTEMS: Complete and negative other than what is mentioned above.

OBJECTIVE: He looks okay, in no acute distress. Vitals are stable and he is afebrile, temperature just for one time was 37.9° C, otherwise afebrile. Blood pressure this morning was 96/41. Ears, nose, and throat are unremarkable. Neck is supple, no JVD. Lungs clear to auscultation with a few rhonchi and no wheezing. The abdomen is benign. Extremities: There is trace edema, peripheral pulses palpated.

BLOOD WORK FOR TODAY: Gram stain of the pleural fluid showed a lot of RBCs, no growth. Bedside glucose was 108. Blood cultures are negative. Cell count, on the pleural effusion nucleated cells, were 520 and RBCs 2,800. Sputum culture is pending.

ASSESSMENT:
1. Pleuritic chest pain, likely related to metastatic nonsmall cell carcinoma of the lungs and pain medication withdrawal
2. Lower back pain and lower extremity pain, resolved right now with epidural pain pump
3. Non-small cell carcinoma, lung
4. History of chronic smoking, and he is still smoking. He is on the nicotine patch.
5. Malnutrition
6. Hepatitis C
7. Depression
8. History of coronary artery disease
9. Hypertension
10. COPD

PLAN: Waiting for permanent pain pump, hopefully tomorrow morning. I will add Combivent and Allegra to help with secretions. Continue other management.

1-3A:

SERVICE CODE(S): _____

ICD-9-CM DX CODE(S): _____

ICD-10-CM DX CODE(S): _____

CASE 1-4

Dr. Pleasant provides a follow-up service to a patient he admitted to the hospital for congestive heart failure.

I-4A PROGRESS REPORT

LOCATION: Inpatient, Hospital

PATIENT: Donald Harris

ATTENDING PHYSICIAN: Timothy L. Pleasant, MD

The patient is doing relatively well in general. I believe the sodium of 152 that was done yesterday morning was wrong since it has dropped down to 132 in 6 hours, which is impossible to happen.

He continues to need oxygen and he continues to be hypoxic. His V/Q scan showed intermediate probability, but his ABGs were not suggestive of respiratory alkalosis.

PHYSICAL EXAMINATION: Blood pressure seems to be stable. Heart rate is 70 per minute, paced. He is afebrile. He had decreased air entry bilaterally in the bases. I did not hear any crackles. Abdomen is negative. Extremities show no edema.

Chest x-ray shows bilateral pleural effusions, more on the right side.

Creatinine was 0.8. Basic metabolic panel was normal today with a sodium of 139.

IMPRESSION:
1. Severe congestive heart failure
2. Hypoxia probably related to the bilateral pleural effusions
3. Pleural effusion

PLAN: Keep the patient in ICU. We will involve Physical Therapy with him today. I will consult the pulmonologist on call in the morning to check on him and see if we could do a therapeutic and diagnostic thoracentesis, and whether we need to do a pulmonary angiogram to make sure he doesn't have pulmonary emboli. I believe that most of his hypoxia is related to his severe CHF and his pleural effusions. I discussed this with the patient. He agrees with the plan.

I-4A:

SERVICE CODE(S): _____

ICD-9-CM DX CODE(S): _____

ICD-10-CM DX CODE(S): _____

CASE 1-5

Report Dr. Lauer's professional service.

1-5A CONSULTATION

LOCATION: Inpatient, Hospital

PATIENT: Shawn Peterson

PRIMARY CARE PHYSICIAN: Leslie Alanda, MD

CONSULTANT: Elmer Lauer, MD

The patient is a 60-year-old male who was transferred from Franklin Hospital for further management. He was admitted earlier today for what later was shown to be diabetic ketoacidosis. However, while he was there, he was noted to have some GI bleeding, having a black emesis and having passed black tarry stools. Because they did not have the facilities for endoscopy, the patient was subsequently transferred here.

The patient apparently presented to the Emergency Room over at Franklin Hospital complaining of nausea and vomiting for the past 2 days. This was associated with some epigastric pain and tenderness and some coughing. He denies any dark stools or blood in his emesis prior to being seen in the Emergency Room. On admission to the ICU here, he was hemodynamically stable. He did not appear to be in any acute distress.

REVIEW OF SYSTEMS: He denies any other constitutional symptoms. He denies any recent fevers, chills, or night sweats. He also denies any recent dyspnea or chest pain even on exertion. Other than the abdominal pain that is associated with his nausea and vomiting for the past 2 days, he said he has not noticed any changes in his bowel habits. He also denies any changes in his voiding or urinary habits.

PAST MEDICAL HISTORY:
1. Diabetes, which he has had for more than 30 years now. When asked about his diabetes care, he did admit to not following up with any physician in particular. He would often just follow up when he runs out of his medications. At home he says his blood sugar in the last several weeks has actually been consistently above 300 mg percent. Despite this, however, he has never sought any medical attention.
2. Hypertension, which he has also had for several years.
3. Hypothyroid.

MEDICATIONS:

Prior to transfer, the patient was on the following medications:
1. Arthrotec 50 mg twice a day.
2. Thiamine 100 mg twice a day.

The patient was on the following medications on transfer:
1. Arthrotec 50 mg twice a day.
2. Thiamine 100 mg twice a day.
3. Ecotrin 325 mg daily.
4. Maxzide 75/30 mg daily.
5. Tamsulosin 0.4 mg twice a day before meals.
6. Synthroid 0.125 mg daily.
7. Lisinopril 10 mg daily.
8. Multivitamins one tablet daily.

9. KCL 10 mEq three times a day.
10. Tylenol 325 mg as needed for pain.
11. Benadryl 25 mg as needed for sleep.
12. Prilosec 20 mg daily.
13. Lantus insulin 10 units in the morning and regular insulin four times a day as a sliding scale.

ALLERGIES: He has no known drug allergies.

FAMILY HISTORY: Significant for diabetes. The patient's father and brother both carry the disease. Both his brother and his mother are hypertensive. His mother also had cerebrovascular disease. Mother also was diagnosed with lung cancer after smoking for several decades. The patient is a widower and has four children, all of whom are alive and well.

SOCIAL HISTORY: He denies any recent tobacco or alcohol intake. He said he quit smoking last December of 2003 primarily for financial reasons. He does have about a 50 to 60 pack per year smoking history though. He did admit to significant alcohol use. He said that he is a binge drinker. He has had several problems with alcohol in the past. His last binge was about 4 or 5 months ago. During these binges the patient would often pass out. He is not aware of any liver complications from his alcohol intake.

PHYSICAL EXAMINATION: He was lying down in bed. He did not appear to be in any acute pain or distress. His blood pressure was 117/60, pulse rate 99, breathing about 16 to 18 times per minute on room air and was saturating 100%. HEAD/NECK: Showed pink palpebral conjunctivae with anicteric sclerae. He did not have any active nasal or ear discharge. His oropharynx was otherwise clear of any exudates or any lesions. His neck was supple and was nontender. He did not have any cervical or submandibular lymphadenopathy. His carotid upstroke was normal. CHEST: Shows lung fields to be essentially clear to auscultation bilaterally; however, he did have some decreased breath sounds towards both bases. There were no distinct rales or wheezes. CARDIAC: Shows a regular rate and rhythm without any rubs. ABDOMEN: Showed it to be soft, slightly tender to deep palpation particularly in the epigastric area. He did have normoactive bowel sounds. There were no palpable masses or any bruits appreciated. EXTREMITIES: Showed fair and equal pulses without any significant edema.

LABORATORY DATA: Today's hemoglobin is 16 with a white count of 17.6 and a platelet count of 320,000. Sodium is 134, potassium 5.3, chloride 92, and bicarb 19. His anion gap was 22 to 23. BUN 42, creatinine 1.9, glucose 605. His stool guaiac was positive for occult blood. He also had a blood gas that showed a pH of 7.29. His serum ketones were positive, but was not quantified.

ASSESSMENT:
1. Diabetic ketoacidosis. I am not sure what the initiating or precipitating event was. The patient does not appear to have any clear focus of infection, however, we will need to rule out the more common causes including pneumonia, urinary tract infection, and possible gastroenteritis.
2. GI bleeding. The patient currently is hemodynamically stable despite the bleeding episode.

PLAN:
1. Hydrate the patient with 0.9 normal saline. Switch the normal saline to D5 normal saline once his Accu-Cheks have dropped below 200.
2. Start on insulin drip. Accu-Cheks and adjustments of the drips per protocol.
3. Keep the patient NPO for now.
4. Keep the patient on IV proton pump inhibitors.
5. Start the bowel prep with magnesium citrate and Dulcolax in preparation for possible endoscopy tomorrow.

6. Will consult GI in the morning to evaluate the patient for possible endoscopic evaluation.

7. Will keep the patient on serial compression device boots for DVT prophylaxis.

8. Follow the patient's BMP and anion gap. Continue the insulin until the patient's anion gap acidosis has resolved.

Total time spent with patient tonight was 2 hours and 20 minutes.

1-5A:

SERVICE CODE(S): _____

ICD-9-CM DX CODE(S): _____

ICD-10-CM DX CODE(S): _____

CASE 1-6

Report Dr. Pleasant's service.

1-6A CONSULTATION

LOCATION: Hospital Inpatient

PATIENT: Will Phelps

ATTENDING PHYSICIAN: Alma Naraquist, MD

CONSULTANT: Timothy L. Pleasant, MD

CHIEF COMPLAINT: Hypoxia, renal failure, and previous bypass.

Mr. Phelps is a 54-year-old Caucasian male I was asked to see by Dr. Naraquist after the patient had an episode of shortness of breath and his oxygen sats went down to 85% in room air. At the time when I saw him he was actually not in any respiratory distress, his SATS in the 85% range, his ABGs not PO_2 in the 50s. He went up to the mid 90s with four liters of nasal cannula. He looked well. He did not complain of any chest pain. He had actually no shortness of breath. I did a chest x-ray on him, which showed some left basilar atelectasis, possible infiltrates, but he was not in any pulmonary edema, his cardiac silhouette was borderline. His CBC that I did stat showed no elevation in white count, but his creatinine on admission last night was 1.5 and went up to 1.8.

The patient is known to have coronary artery disease. He has an extensive cardiac history. He had bypass surgery to the posterior descending artery and the LAD. His postoperative course was complicated with congestive heart failure and atrial fibrillation.

Unfortunately, the patient was admitted last night because of renal colic and a left ureteral stone that was found on CT today. He had this 6 years ago, and it has been quiet for that long. His CT scan today showed two stones, one of them blocking the left ureter with hydronephrosis.

He complained of hematuria and dysuria, but he had no urine symptoms in the past six years. He had decreased urine output. He received almost 3 liters of IV fluids with minimal urine output, and that was what concerned Dr. Schultz and the nursing staff.

PAST MEDICAL HISTORY: Significant for the following:
1. Coronary artery disease, five cardiac catheterizations, myocardial infarction, totally occluded right coronary artery, ejection fraction of 53% preop and 18% postop. He had multiple angioplasties in the past.
2. Kidney stone as mentioned.
3. Hyperlipidemia.
4. Bilateral eye surgeries.
5. Thyroid nodule, which has been aspirated multiple times. He has normal TSH in the past 2 months.

MEDICATIONS:
1. Lorazepam at night.
2. Coreg b.i.d.
3. Digoxin, Zocor, and Coumadin for atrial fibrillation.
4. Toradol.
5. Anzemet p.r.n.

ALLERGIES: No known drug allergies.

SOCIAL HISTORY: He is married. He does not smoke or drink. He enjoys playing with his grandson who is 7 years old and has muscular dystrophy.

FAMILY HISTORY: No diabetes, heart disease, or coronary artery disease.

REVIEW OF SYSTEMS: Complete review of all 12 systems has been completed, and all are negative except for RESPIRATORY: Hypoxia but no cough or shortness of breath. GENERAL: He had no fever or chills, but has been complaining of easy fatigability and being tired all the time. GI: The patient has been nauseated since he started Coreg, and he threw up a few times today; we don't know whether this is related to the Coreg or the morphine PCA he is on. CARDIOVASCULAR: The patient complains of chest pain at least twice a week, heaviness that stays for a couple hours and resolves by itself.

PHYSICAL EXAMINATION: On examination the patient was not in any respiratory, cardiac, or neurological distress. His sats were 94% on 4 liters per nasal cannula. He was awake, alert, and oriented times three without any focal neurological deficits. VITAL SIGNS: TEMPERATURE: 35.4° C. BLOOD PRESSURE: 102/62. HEART RATE: 73 radially but 104 by EKG earlier in the day. HEAD and NECK: Normal oropharyngeal mucosa. No cervical lymphadenopathy. He has right-sided thyroid nodule inferiorly. It was firm and nontender and moves with swallowing. LUNGS: Good air entry bilaterally, except in the bases but no crackles. CARDIAC EXAM: Distant heart sounds but regular. He was tachycardic. ABDOMEN: Scar of previous bypass surgery, well-healed. Soft and slightly tender in the left flank, no organomegaly, palpable femoral arteries. INTEGUMENTARY: No pallor, jaundice, or cyanosis. EXTREMITIES: Very trace edema, adequate pulses.

IMPRESSION:
1. Acute renal failure secondary to intravascular volume depletion and unilateral left-sided hydronephrosis.
2. Atelectasis with hypoxia.
3. Severe congestive heart failure, probably ischemic cardiomyopathy.
4. Recent chest pains at home but not since admission, possible angina.

PLAN:
1. Decrease IV fluids to 75 cc/hour and change the IV to normal saline since his potassium was 5.
2. Incentive spirometry.
3. Discontinue Toradol to prevent kidney function from getting worse.
4. Discontinue Anzemet, and use Zofran 4 mg IV q.4h. Anzemet did not work for him.

I discussed kidney stone, hydronephrosis, atelectasis, and hypoxia, in addition to coronary artery disease and congestive heart failure with atrial fibrillation with the patient. We went over everything. I think eventually he needs to see a cardiologist again to decide whether he needs another angiogram to figure out why his cardiac function deteriorated after his bypass surgery. Time spent with the patient today was 120 minutes; 100 minutes was spent on counseling and coordination of care. I also discussed the case with the urologist, and he agrees with the above plan. He will try to take the stone out tomorrow if the OR schedule allows him to do that.

Thank you for allowing me to participate in the care of Mr. Phelps. I will continue to follow.

1-6A:

SERVICE CODE(S): _____

ICD-9-CM DX CODE(S): _____

ICD-10-CM DX CODE(S): _____

1-6B PROGRESS REPORT

Report Dr. Pleasant's service.

LOCATION: Hospital Inpatient

PATIENT: Will Phelps

ATTENDING PHYSICIAN: Alma Naraquist, MD

CONSULTANT: Timothy L. Pleasant, MD

Mr. Phelps had no major event during the night. He denies any chest pain or shortness of breath. He feels well. He has some pain on his left flank. He continues to have a Foley catheter with urine that looks turbid with a blood tinge to it. His heart rate has been in the 60s and sinus rhythm. His blood pressure has been in the 80s, which is his baseline. He is making 25 to 35 cc of urine an hour.

PHYSICAL EXAMINATION: On examination, he is afebrile. No increase in jugular venous pressure. He is on nasal cannula maintaining his sats in the mid 90s. He was not in any respiratory, cardiac, or neurological distress. Blood pressure was 87/60. Lungs have good air entry bilaterally except in the bases but no crackles. Regular rate and rhythm. No murmurs or pericardial friction rub. He is slightly tender on the left flank. No leg edema.

IMPRESSION:
1. Severe ischemic cardiomyopathy.
2. Bradycardia and hypotension secondary to spinal anesthesia.
3. Coronary artery disease.
4. Left kidney stone with left-sided hydronephrosis.
5. Acute renal failure secondary to hydronephrosis and intravascular volume depletion.
6. Atrial fibrillation but currently in sinus rhythm.
7. Severe bradycardia with asystole, recovered.

PLAN:
1. Foley will be discontinued today.
2. The patient will be transferred out of the ICU to regular floor on telemetry.
3. We will continue to watch his kidney function and his urine output.
4. Meanwhile, I will continue holding his Digoxin and Coreg.

The patient agrees with the above plan.

1-6B:

SERVICE CODE(S): _____

ICD-9-CM DX CODE(S): _____

ICD-10-CM DX CODE(S): _____

1-6C PROGRESS REPORT

Report Dr. Pleasant's service.

LOCATION: Hospital Inpatient

PATIENT: Will Phelps

ATTENDING PHYSICIAN: Alma Naraquist, MD

CONSULTANT: Timothy L. Pleasant, MD

The patient was seen after Dr. Elhart successfully placed a dual-chamber pacemaker/AICD. The patient was hypoxic during the procedure. He could not lay flat. His sats were in the high 80s, low 90s. He was on a non-rebreather mask when he came up here. He did not complain of shortness of breath, but his sats were 90%.

EXAMINATION: His heart rate was 72 per minute, paced. Blood pressure was 115/55. He had decreased air entry in both bases and with crackles bilaterally. Abdomen is soft and nontender. Extremities show trace edema and are warm bilaterally.

His creatinine this morning came down to 1.5. His magnesium was normal.

IMPRESSION:
1. Post dual chamber pacemaker/AICD placement.
2. Hypoxia secondary to congestive heart failure and bilateral pleural effusions.
3. Ischemic cardiomyopathy.
4. Post cardiac arrest with asystole in OR while placing a left ureteral stent.
5. Left kidney stone.
6. Acute renal failure, improving.
7. Unilateral left-sided hydronephrosis.

PLAN:
1. We will get ABGs as a baseline to make sure and to check his pH.
2. We will give him 2 mg of IV Bumex, since that worked on him last night very well.
3. We will continue to observe him in the intensive care unit.
4. We will continue to monitor his urine output.
5. Repeat labs in the morning, including basic met panel and magnesium.
6. Repeat chest x-ray in the morning.

I will continue to follow along with Dr. Elhart at this point.

1-6C:

SERVICE CODE(S): _____

ICD-9-CM DX CODE(S): _____

ICD-10-CM DX CODE(S): _____

CASE 1-7

Report Dr. Naraquist's service.

1-7A ICU REPORT

LOCATION: Hospital Inpatient

PATIENT: Robert Jones

ATTENDING PHYSICIAN: Alma Naraquist, MD

The patient was seen multiple times today. He was seen early in the morning and was still complaining of some abdominal discomfort and distention but he had some flatus. He was also evaluated today by a general surgeon. There was no acute abdomen obviously. We did x-rays, which showed a few air fluid levels.

The patient had what looked like dark old blood in his mouth. Because of the tympanitic abdomen and because of whatever he had in his mouth we placed an NG tube. We had 300 mL of dark liquid that appears like coffee grounds.

Overnight, the heart rate went to the 80s and 90s. Occasionally it went up to the 100s. He was on a Cardizem drip.

He is on CAPD-4.255, 2 liter fill volumes. He had almost 850 mL so far today.

During the day and while I was in the ICU, the patient developed wide complex tachycardia with a heart rate of 168 per minute.

An echocardiogram was done and his ejection fraction was around 20%, but the official report is still pending. I did ask Dr. Elhart to see him on consultation, and I do appreciate his help on the case.

I reviewed his chest x-ray, which looks better than yesterday. Yesterday's x-ray had air below the right diaphragm. We thought this was related to peritoneal dialysis, and this is why the general surgeon was involved. His pulmonary edema has improved.

His troponin has been climbing and was at 0.56 this afternoon.

The patient still looks well. He has no complaints. This afternoon he had no abdominal pain.

PHYSICAL EXAMINATION: Blood pressure is up to the 120s/60s. It was hanging around 90s to 100 systolic. Respirations are 18–20 per minute. SATS are maintained in the mid 90s. He is not making any urine. He was on a Cardizem drip at 5 mg and heparin. He had crackles in the bases. He was not in any respiratory, cardiac, or neurological distress. Afebrile. He had a distended abdomen that was tympanitic. No rebound tenderness. Extremities have declining edema. It is probably 3+ bilaterally.

LABORATORY FINDINGS: INR was 1.1. White count 8400, hemoglobin 8.7, MCV 93.6, platelets 185,000. Sodium 136, potassium 3.4, chloride 97, bicarb 29.7, glucose 163, BUN 41, creatinine 4.8, calcium 7.4, and magnesium 2.1.

IMPRESSION:
1. Acute respiratory failure.
2. Pulmonary edema requiring oxygen.
3. Acute non-Q-wave myocardial infarction.
4. Atrial fibrillation.

PLAN:

1. The patient will remain in the Intensive Care Unit.
2. He is code level I.
3. Repeat flat and decubitus abdominal x-rays in the morning.
4. Repeat labs in the morning, including comprehensive panel, phosphorus, magnesium, CBC, and troponin-I.
5. Check potassium again at 6 o'clock and will replace it if it is less or equal to 3.4.
6. Keep NPO at this time.
7. NG under intermittent suction.
8. Repeat chest x-ray in the morning.
9. Hold Coumadin.
10. Continue with heparin.
11. Continue with IV Protonix.
12. Will change his Digoxin to IV 0.125 mg daily.
13. Will hold all his PO medications.
14. Cardizem has been discontinued.
15. IV metoprolol will be given.
16. Amiodarone will also be initiated.

I discussed all of the above with the patient. He seems to understand and agree with the plan. Total time spent on this patient today was 70 minutes.

I-7A:

SERVICE CODE(S): _____

ICD-9-CM DX CODE(S): _____

ICD-10-CM DX CODE(S): _____

CASE 1-8

The services in 1-8A, B, and C were all provided by the same physician.

1-8A CRITICAL CARE

LOCATION: Hospital Inpatient

PATIENT: Debbie Murphy

ATTENDING PHYSICIAN: George Orbitz, MD

Mrs. Murphy is a 53-year-old lady with severe pulmonary hypertension, significant hypoxic hypercarbic respiratory failure. The patient's PCO_2 is generally in the 80s. This morning the patient got out of bed when her husband got out of bed. He has a mail route, so he was up at 3:30. She fell on the bathroom floor, an ambulance was summoned, and the patient was then taken to the hospital in her hometown. There she was found to have a broken leg. She is a complicated patient with severe underlying diseases so she was sent here. Here it was found she was somewhat hypoxemic. She had a PCO_2 of 109, and she was then transferred to ICU because they thought her chest x-ray represented a "pneumonia." The patient has no fever, sweats or chills. No nausea, vomiting, or diarrhea. No change in weight or appetite. No sputum production, no cough, no hemoptysis. Obviously she is very short of breath with just minimal exertion. She was given a shot, probably for the pain of the broken leg, and I think that has caused the trouble with the elevated PCO_2 and some of the confusion although the patient's confusion is intermittent and seems to be getting better.

PAST MEDICAL HISTORY:
1. Severe chronic obstructive pulmonary disease.
2. Fractured leg. She broke her left leg twice last year.
3. History of a silent heart attack many years ago.
4. Type 2 diabetes mellitus.
5. History of congestive heart failure.
6. Severe pulmonary hypertension.
7. History of anemia.

PAST SURGICAL HISTORY:
1. Status post cholecystectomy.
2. Three cesarean sections.
3. Incidental appendectomy.
4. Tonsillectomy.
5. Repair of left humeral fracture.
6. Comminuted displaced supracondylar left femoral fracture.

She is steroid dependent and oxygen dependent.

FAMILY HISTORY: Difficult to get from the patient because she is so sleepy. She says her father had cancer of the prostate. I could not tell whether he was still living or not. Mother died at age 70-something with cancer all over. One brother has diabetes. She has no other brothers or sisters.

SOCIAL HISTORY: The patient is still smoking. She still sneaks occasional cigarettes. Married and lives with her husband close to Edmonton. She has two children who are well. She has no specific diet and has no exercise capacity at all. She does not get out of the house to socialize much at all. She says she drinks occasional tequila, but she does not remember when the last one was. It is several months ago she said.

REVIEW OF SYSTEMS: The patient is too sleepy to really get a good one. What is present in the history of present illness is that she has no fever, sweats, or chills. No trouble with her appetite. No trouble with weight change. She is no more short of breath now than she has been. She is severely short of breath with minimal exertion. No cough, PND, orthopnea, or pedal edema. She says she is using her BiPAP at home. The last settings here are 12/4 with 5 liters, so we will start there and titrate her to see where we have to end up. She has no chest pressure, no GERD, no heartburn. GI: No diarrhea. She has a little bit of trouble with constipation. GU: No blood in her urine. No kidney stones. MUSCULOSKELETAL: She does not really have much in the way of ache or pains, at least that she complained of now other than her leg. This is her third fracture of an extremity, so I imagine she has underlying osteoporosis. HEMATOLOGY: She said she has had trouble with low blood, i.e., anemia. She has never had a transfusion that she remembers at least at this point. PSYCHIATRIC: She does not have any specific complaints there. DERMATOLOGY: No chronic rashes or skin cancers. ALLERGIES: She cannot remember any but the chart does describes an allergy to cephalosporins. The reaction is not specified in the chart and she does not remember that.

PHYSICAL EXAMINATION: HEENT: Benign. No blood in the posterior pharynx or the nose. Eyes are equal, round, and react to light. On conjugate gaze she just appears sleepy. Neck is supple with JVD. Thyroid is not palpably enlarged. Trachea midline. I did not notice any head trauma. CHEST: Very distant breath sounds. I do not hear any regular rhythm with rate of about 105 without S3 or S4. No diastolic sounds, clicks, or rubs. No murmurs. Abdomen is benign without hepatosplenomegaly. Normal bowel sounds are present. No bruits heard in either flank; no masses palpable; nontender. Extremities showed no edema, rashes, clubbing, cyanosis, or tremor. LYMPHATIC SYSTEM: No nodes in neck, cervical, or axillary area.

IMPRESSION: Hypercarbic hypoxic respiratory failure. I do not get a feeling for acute pneumonia at this point, but at this time I do not have a good x-ray because the last one we got is rotated is difficult to compare, so I will repeat that. We will keep her in the ICU for the time being just to see if she wakes up from the medication. I think she does not get along well with any kind of sedation drugs, mainly because her PCO_2 is so high and she is quite sensitive to that.

We will use Avelox 400 mg once a day. Will try range of motion and what activity is allowed by the orthopedist. For the BIPAP 12/4 and 5 liters O_2, adjust it accordingly, and check the cardiac enzymes to make sure she has cultures (as best we can get) anyway. This took 1 hour to go over this case at the bedside to try to discern just how acutely ill this patient was. I think most of it is her chronic illness with the acute fracture. I talked to the husband by phone, examined the patient and talked to the patient, reviewed her lab, old records, charts, whatever I can get a hold of, examined the patient, try to get a plan together, and dictate the note, and get things settled in the ICU for her. I did talk to the patient about code level, and she does not want to be on a ventilator nor does she want to be resuscitated if things go poorly. I actually do not expect that. I think she will just get around the sedation and do fine.

1-8A:

SERVICE CODE(S): _____

ICD-9-CM DX CODE(S): _____

ICD-10-CM DX CODE(S): _____

I-8B PROGRESS REPORT

LOCATION: Hospital Inpatient

PATIENT: Debbie Murphy

ATTENDING PHYSICIAN: George Orbitz, MD

She was admitted yesterday with a fractured lower leg and noted to be hypoxemic, difficult to control. After we compared all chest x-rays, it became obvious the patient does have pneumonia on the right lower lobe at least. She has a lot of chronic changes, so it made it somewhat difficult to try to follow that. The tibia and fibula show mildly comminuted fracture of the proximal right fibula shaft and a fracture of the proximal shaft of the right tibia with mild impaction of the fracture fragment. This was from a fall in the bedroom, she had pneumonia and fell because she was weak and may have actually been a little bit septic. This is superimposed in a patient with rather severe COPD/emphysema, oxygen dependent, actually uses BiPAP at home because of it.

PHYSICAL EXAMINATION
1. Cardiac: Blood pressure 120/50, sinus rhythm rate of 80. No S3 or S4. No diastolic sounds, clicks, rubs, or murmurs.
2. Pulmonary: PO_2 of 62 on 65% with BiPAP of 15/5, PCO_2 of 107, pH of 7.35. The patient keeps taking the mask on and off and letting the gas escape, so it is probably less than totally effective. Her breath sounds are quite distant, so I don't really hear anything except faint breath sounds.
3. GI: A little distended abdomen, nontender, no hepatosplenomegaly. She has a PO diet. She can use nasal oxygen while she is eating but she desaturates fairly quickly, which we will have to work around.
4. GU: BUN of 7, creatinine of 0.5 with 1600 in yesterday, 275 out. No edema noted.
5. Endocrine: Glucose is 108, there are some that go up higher than that, one at 151.
6. Electrolytes: Sodium 146, potassium 4.7, chloride 98, CO_2 greater than 42, calcium 8.2, magnesium 1.5, phosphorus is low at 2.1 with ionized of 4.9.
7. Hematology: White count of 7530, hemoglobin 10, platelets of 124,000.
8. Infectious Disease: I have no organisms to shoot at. Her highest temp was 37.6° C yesterday, and she is on Avelox as a single agent for presumed community-acquired pneumonia right lower lobe.
9. Neurologic: The patient is awake and alert and able to give some history. Does get confused intermittently, but obviously has been her pattern for as long as I have known her.

PLAN: We will try to replace her phosphorus. Try to get her a little more free water so she can dilute herself and mostly it is time. We will let her sit in the chair, but she will have to use her BiPAP when she is doing it. She needs to move around a little bit. I will have OT and PT work with her for range of motion, and I will see if we can get a PIC line put in.

I-8B:

SERVICE CODE(S): _____

ICD-9-CM DX CODE(S): _____

ICD-10-CM DX CODE(S): _____

I-8C PROGRESS REPORT

LOCATION: Hospital Inpatient

PATIENT: Debbie Murphy

ATTENDING PHYSICIAN: George Orbitz, MD

Mrs. Murphy is here because of pneumonia. I am assuming that she developed pneumonia, became weak, and then when she was walking to the bathroom, her leg gave out and had a right proximal tib-fib fracture. She has been casted and has been doing well. Overnight, she has been doing well. Of course, she is short of breath with minimal exertion.

PHYSICAL EXAMINATION/DATA REVIEW

1. Cardiac: Blood Pressures are reasonable. I have 110s to 130s over diastolics of 40s to 50s. Sinus rhythm rate of 80. No S3, S4, diastolic sounds, clicks, or rubs. No murmurs.

2. Pulmonary: PCO_2 is coming down. It was greater than 115 for a while. It is now down to 95. PO_2 was 63 on the BiPAP of 15/5 and 70%; pH is 7.38, PO_2 of 63. Chest x-ray shows probably an increasing density in the right base. Basically, no change. Cardiomegaly has increased indistinctness of the pericardial markings and some Kerley B lines, suggesting a congestive heart failure pattern, atelectatic left lung base with some decreasing aeration. She needs to get out of bed more and a confluent density, right base, which is where we think her pneumonia is. Actually, her chest looks worse on x-ray than it sounds.

3. GI: She is eating well as per the nursing personnel but she desaturates quite quickly when she is off the BiPAP.

4. GU: BUN is 6. Creatinine of 0.6 with 3,865 in, 2,783 in. I don't really pick up much edema.

5. Endocrine: Glucoses are good. She is on an insulin drip at low levels. I think I have 2 units an hour at this point.

6. Electrolytes: Sodium is 146. Potassium is 3.7. Chloride is 96, CO_2 is greater than 41.8. Calcium is 7.9. Magnesium is 1.4. Phosphorus is 3.2.

7. Hematology: White count is 6,480. Hemoglobin is 10.2. Platelets are 126,000, which have been about the same since yesterday.

8. Infectious Disease: She is on Claforan and Zithromax. She is afebrile. The highest temp was 37.6° C. She is on Avalox at this time, but I don't have any organism to treat. The microbiology is negative. She didn't cough up any sputum for me.

9. Neurological: The patient is awake and able to give some history, although she is confused. But I think this is her baseline.

DISPOSITION: I would get her out of bed a little bit more. Continue with the present program. I think this could be a long-term problem with this patient. I don't know if we are going to be able to handle this all at the hospital. She may have to go to a nursing home for a while.

1-8C:

SERVICE CODE(S): _____

ICD-9-CM DX CODE(S): _____

ICD-10-CM DX CODE(S): _____

CASE 1-9

Report Dr. Naraquist's services for this case.

1-9A OFFICE VISIT

LOCATION: Outpatient, Clinic

PATIENT: Andrew Vetter

PRIMARY CARE PHYSICIAN: Alma Naraquist, MD

CHIEF COMPLAINT: Recheck Diabetes

He has started doing PT to get his strength back and has noted improvement. He has not been having any chest pain or SOB. Past History of CAD.

His DM has been variably controlled. He is taking Lantus 28 units in the evening and Humalog 12 units with meals. He is testing 2–4 times per day. He is having reactions around 3 PM about once a week. He does get a warning with the reactions. His sugars are highly variable at all testing times with high and low sugars. His evening sugars tend to be high, and he may overeat after supper.

He continues to have numbness in the feet. There is no edema. His depression seems to be ok.

EXAM: Vitals: Weight is 180. Blood Pressure is 120/70. Patient is alert and conversant. He is near his ideal weight. There is no edema. The foot pulses are normal. The ankle and knee reflexes are normal. There is a slight decrease in the vibratory sensation. The chest is clear. Cardiac: The heart is regular with no murmur or S3. The abdomen is soft and nontender with no masses. The prostate is a little enlarged with no masses. The rectum is normal, and there are some small hemorrhoids noted. The stool is hemoccult negative.

IMPRESSION: 1) DM Type I with variable control, 2) Hemorrhoids, 3) CAD, stable.

PLAN: Anusol suppository bid prn and tub soaks. He may need to cut the noon Humalog by 2 units. See in 4 months with a HgbA1c.

1-9A:

SERVICE CODE(S): _____

ICD-9-CM DX CODE(S): _____

ICD-10-CM DX CODE(S): _____

CASE 1-10

Report Dr. Naraquist's service.

1-10A OBSERVATION

LOCATION: Hospital Observation Unit

PATIENT: Lloyd Hanson

ATTENDING PHYSICIAN: Alma Naraquist, MD

REASON FOR ADMISSION: Exacerbation of COPD.

HISTORY OF PRESENT ILLNESS: The patient is a 74-year-old male who comes in tonight complaining of progressive shortness of breath over the past 4 days. He had upper-respiratory tract symptoms a week ago with nasal discharge and cold-like symptoms. It progressed to shortness of breath over the past 4 days. I was called by a family member of his earlier tonight and I advised him to come to the Emergency Room, which he did. In the ER, he was wheezy and had oxygen saturation of 92%. He received a nebulizer treatment. A chest x-ray was done, which I reviewed myself and showed no evidence of infiltrates. He has a large heart. The patient was admitted to the 6th floor. I proceeded by doing ABGs on him. His pH was 7.46, PCO_2 94, bicarb 33.5 on 2 liters per nasal cannula.

The patient has some cough with clear phlegm. No fever or chills now. He had some chills a week ago.

The patient recently had an angiogram for his abdominal aortic aneurysm. He also had a stress test that apparently was positive.

The patient is known to have chronic renal failure with a baseline creatinine of 2 to 2.2 with creatinine clearance of 32 ml per minute with a serum creatinine of 2.0 back in December.

He does have severe congestive heart failure with ejection fraction less than 20%.

PAST MEDICAL HISTORY:
1. Chronic renal failure as mentioned.
2. Coronary artery disease, post two myocardial infarctions.
3. Post AICD placement.
4. Atrial fibrillation with rapid ventricular response, controlled.
5. Congestive heart failure with ejection fraction of less than 20%.
6. Abdominal aortic aneurysm, which is infrarenal measuring 6.2 cm.
7. Bilateral common iliac aneurysm, approximately 3.5 to 3.6 cm.
8. Left internal iliac artery aneurysm, questionably coiled lately.
9. COPD/asthma.
10. History of gouty arthritis with a recent gouty attack in his right first metatarsal phalangeal joint.
11. History of diverticulitis.
12. Hyperlipidemia.
13. Status post cholecystectomy, inguinal hernia repair, appendectomy.
14. Chronic renal failure, post PD catheter placement.

ALLERGIES: No known drug allergies.

MEDICATIONS:
1. Nebulizer at home.
2. Bumex 2 mg in the morning and 1 mg in the evening.
3. Coumadin 2 mg on Monday, 1 mg on other days.
4. Digoxin 0.125 mg po daily.
5. Potassium chloride 20 mEq po b.i.d.
6. Zocor 10 mg po q hs.
7. Coreg 25 mg po b.i.d.
8. Allopurinol 100 mg po daily.
9. Ranitidine 150 mg po q hs.

FAMILY HISTORY: Mother died of pancreatitis. Father died at age 71. Otherwise family history is noncontributory.

SOCIAL HISTORY: Lives here in town with his wife. She was not available today. He quit smoking 16 years ago.

REVIEW OF SYSTEMS: CONSTITUTIONAL: No fever, chills, or night sweats. ENT: Resolved upper-respiratory tract symptoms. RESPIRATORY: As mentioned. CARDIO-VASCULAR: Exertional dyspnea. No chest pain. GI: Questionable dark stool but no diarrhea, nausea, or vomiting. He had some abdominal discomfort with coughing. MUSCULOSKELETAL: History of gouty arthritis, but seems to be controlled. SKIN: Trace edema. NEURO: Negative. PSYCHIATRIC: Negative.

PHYSICAL EXAMINATION: The patient was in mild respiratory distress. He was awake, oriented times three without any focal neurological deficits. His heart rate is in the 70s range, blood pressure has been 120s/80s, sats 92% when he came in, 98% on 2 liters per nasal cannula. Slightly increased jugular venous pressure. No cervical lymphadenopathy. LUNGS: Good air entry bilaterally but expiratory wheezes bilaterally. No crackles. No sacral edema. ABDOMEN: Soft and nontender, no masses. He has PD catheter in the left lower quadrant. Small hematoma in the right inguinal area from his recent aortogram. LOWER EXTREMITIES: Very trace edema.

LABORATORY STUDIES: CBC tonight shows a white count of 8.6 thousand, hemoglobin 12.3, platelets 140,000, BUN 29, sodium 139, potassium 3.6, chloride 98, bicarb 31, creatinine 2.2, calcium 8.5. BNP 536 picogram/ml. INR 1.5 with a pro-time of 14.3. Digoxin 0.6. Troponin-I less than 0.04. His last uric acid level was 7.4.

IMPRESSION:
1. Exacerbation of COPD/asthma with wheezes.
2. Abdominal aortic aneurysm.

PLAN:
1. Albuterol MDI 2 puffs t.i.d.
2. Atrovent MDI 2 puffs t.i.d.
3. Azmacort MDI 2 puffs b.i.d.
4. Solu-Medrol 80 mg IV q 8 hours.
5. Continue the current po medications.
6. Zithromax 500 mg IV daily.
7. The patient is code level I.

Discussed all of the above with the patient. He seems to understand and agrees with the plan. Will discuss further issues to his abdominal aortic aneurysm and further plans with his positive stress test when the rest of the family is available in the next couple of days.

1-10A:

SERVICE CODE(S): _____

ICD-9-CM DX CODE(S): _____

ICD-10-CM DX CODE(S): _____

1-10B OBSERVATION DISCHARGE SUMMARY

LOCATION: Hospital Observation Unit

PATIENT: Lloyd Hanson

ATTENDING PHYSICIAN: Alma Naraquist, MD

DISCHARGE DIAGNOSIS: Acute Exacerbation of COPD.

The patient came in with wheezing. Oxygen saturations were 92%. He had no pulmonary edema. He had no infiltrates. Was given steroids, nebulizer therapy. He did well. His PO_2 was 94 on 2 liters. We walked him the next day. He was doing much better without any major complaints. He was discharged in reasonable general condition.

CODE LEVEL: I

DISCHARGE MEDICATIONS:
1. Albuterol inhaler two puffs three times a day p.r.n.
2. Allopurinol 100 mg p.o. daily.
3. Bumex 1 mg in the evening and 2 mg in the morning.
4. Coreg 25 mg p.o. b.i.d.
5. Digoxin 0.125 mg p.o. daily.
6. Zantac 150 mg p.o. daily.
7. Atrovent three times a day.
8. Potassium chloride 20 mEq p.o. b.i.d.
9. Zocor 10 mg p.o. daily.
10. Triamcinolone inhaler (Azmacort) two puffs three times a day.
11. Coumadin 2 mg every Monday and 1 mg on other 6 days a week.
12. Prednisone 10 mg he will take six pills for 3 days, then five pills for 3 days. He will go down by 10 mg every 3 days until off.
13. Zithromax 500 p.o. daily for 8 more days.

DISCHARGE PLAN: The patient will be scheduled in my clinic in three weeks with a basic panel, CBC, and protime/INR.

Discussed all of the above with the patient. He seems to understand. I gave him the plan. Issues related to his aneurysm and cardiac status will be discussed in the clinic.

1-10B:

SERVICE CODE(S): _____

ICD-9-CM DX CODE(S): _____

ICD-10-CM DX CODE(S): _____

CASE 1-11

Report Dr. Ortez's services for Case 1-11.

1-11A HOSPITAL SERVICES

LOCATION: Hospital Inpatient, Delivery Room and Neonatal Intensive Care Unit.

PATIENT: Dale Everest

ATTENDING PHYSICIAN: Roland Ortez, MD

CHIEF COMPLAINT: Respiratory distress and rule out sepsis.

SUBJECTIVE: This is a 31-week AGA male who was born to a 20-year-old gravida 2, para 1, now para 2, mom. Mom had adequate prenatal care. Maternal blood type A positive. Antibody negative. Rubella immune. Serology nonreactive. Hepatitis B surface antigen negative. Group B strep negative. GC negative. Chlamydia negative. Mom also had a urinary tract infection and was treated. Mom was admitted to the hospital on April 22-25 for threatened preterm labor. She was given steroids at that time. She was discharged home on April 25 on bed rest. On April 29, mom had spontaneous rupture of membranes at 01:00 and was admitted. After admission, mom was placed on ampicillin and erythromycin IV for two days. After the two days on IV ampicillin and erythromycin, mom was placed on the oral form of the drugs for the past five days. Because of the suspected chorioamnionitis, mom was induced with Pitocin earlier today. Mom was also given one dose of penicillin G at 10:15 today and one dose of penicillin G at 14:45 today. Mom was also given one dose of Nubain and one dose of Stadol prior to delivery. The patient delivered at 18:30 today via spontaneous vaginal delivery. No complications were reported. Apgar score at one minute was 7, and at five minutes was 8. The patient required some blow-by oxygen after delivery. Birth weight is 1,579 grams. The patient was admitted to the NICU for respiratory distress and rule out sepsis.

OBJECTIVE: TEMPERATURE: 36.7. HEART RATE: 156. RESPIRATIONS: In the 60s–80s. BLOOD PRESSURE: Systolic 51/diastolic 24–29. Mean pressure 32–36. O_2 SATS on 26% Oxy-Hood is 97–99%. WEIGHT: 1579 grams. OFC: 29 cm. LENGTH: 43 cm. On examination, the patient is awake, active, and crying. HEENT: Anterior fontanel is flat. Eyes: Conjunctivae clear. Red reflex exam deferred. Nose is clear. Oropharynx shows no cleft. Both ear canals are clear. NECK: No palpable mass. HEART: Regular rhythm and rate. No murmurs. LUNGS: Good air movement bilaterally. The patient has tachypnea. No retractions. ABDOMEN: Soft and nontender. EXTREMITIES: Normal movement of all four extremities. NEUROLOGICAL: Normal tone for his gestational age. GENITALIA EXAMINATION: Normal external male. Testes are not descended.

INTEGUMENTARY: No cyanosis. No clubbing. No edema. Capillary refill less than two 2 seconds. Creases on the anterior one-third of the soles. Skin is well-perfused, no rash.

LABORATORY DATA: Chest x-ray shows adequate inflation bilaterally. Initial capillary blood gas: pH 7.28, PCO_2 50, PO_2 51, HCO_3 23, O_2 sat 97% on 28% FiO_2 on the Oxy-Hood. ABG: After 1 fluid bolus, pH was 7.36. PCO_2 105. HCO_3 22 on 26% FiO_2 on the Oxy-Hood. CBC with differential is pending.

ASSESSMENT & PLAN:

1. This is a 31-week AGA male admitted to the NICU for prematurity, respiratory distress, and rule out sepsis.

2. RESPIRATORY: Mild tachypnea, probably secondary to TTN. We will continue the oxygen supplement as needed. We will continue to monitor the respiratory status closely.

3. CARDIOVASCULAR: Cardiovascular status is stable at this point. No murmur. We will continue to monitor.

4. GI: We will keep the patient NPO tonight.

5. HEMATOLOGIC: We will follow hematocrit.

6. INFECTIOUS DISEASE: Because of the PROM and suspected chorioamnionitis in mom, blood cultures were obtained and the patient was started on antibiotics, ampicillin, and gentamicin. We will follow the blood cultures.

7. RENAL: We will monitor urine output.

8. HEALTH CARE MAINTENANCE: Hearing screen, newborn metabolic screen, and hepatitis B will be given at the appropriate time.

9. NEUROLOGIC: The patient's tone is appropriate for his gestational age.

10. SOCIAL: Plan was discussed with mom and she agrees with the plan.

I-I IA:

SERVICE CODE(S): _____

ICD-9-CM DX CODE(S): _____

ICD-10-CM DX CODE(S): _____

I-I IB NICU PROGRESS NOTE

LOCATION: Hospital Inpatient, Neonatal Intensive Care Unit.

PATIENT: Dale Everest

ATTENDING PHYSICIAN: Roland Ortez, MD

SUBJECTIVE: Baby boy is a 1-day-old, 31-week gestation infant who was born yesterday. The infant's mother had prolonged rupture of membranes and started to develop uterine tenderness and foul-smelling vaginal fluid so the baby was induced due to presumed maternal chorioamnionitis.

OBJECTIVE: Weight today is 1558 grams, which is down 21 grams from birth. OFC is 29.25 cm, which is unchanged. He is currently on D-10-W at 80 mL/kg/day. He is NPO. His urine output has been adequate at 3.72 mL/kg/hour. He has had no stools since birth. Review of vital signs shows heart rates between 124 and 160, respiratory rates between 52 and 100, mean blood pressures between 32 and 47. Axillary temperatures have been stable under the radiant warmer. He currently is on 23% FiO_2 per Oxy-Hood. He did have two desaturation episodes since birth that have been fleeting. No apnea.

PHYSICAL EXAMINATION: He appears comfortable under the open warmer. HEENT exam is unremarkable other than he is placed under an Oxy-Hood, and he has an OG in place and he is sucking on the OG. NECK is supple. LUNGS are clear to auscultation bilaterally with good breath sounds bilaterally. He does have some very mild subcostal retractions. His current respiratory rate is in the low 50s. S1–S2 regular. There is a soft systolic ejection murmur heard. ABDOMEN is soft and nontender without hepato-splenomegaly or masses. He has good bowel sounds. There is a UAC in place. GU exam reveals normal external premature male genitalia. He has good femoral pulses. Cap refill is 2 seconds. EXTREMITY exam reveals no decreased range of motion, joint deformity, or abnormality. SKIN is warm and well-perfused, and pink.

MEDICATIONS:
1. Ampicillin 78.95 mg IV q. 12 hours.
2. Gentamicin 7.11 mg IV q. 48 hours.
3. He did receive a 15 mL bolus of normal saline.

ASSESSMENT & PLAN:
1. Day of life 1 for 31-week gestation male whose birth was induced due to maternal prolonged rupture of membranes and presumed chorioamnionitis.
2. RESPIRATORY: He seems to be doing well from a respiratory standpoint. His oxygen needs have decreased, and he has become less tachypneic since birth. His arterial blood gas determinations have been acceptable. We will plan on continuing to monitor him closely with serial clinical examinations, and arterial blood gas determinations and chest x-rays as needed. We will plan on weaning his oxygen as tolerated.
3. CARDIOVASCULAR: He has been hemodynamically stable with acceptable mean arterial blood pressures. He dose have a soft murmur. We will continue to watch this closely.
4. INFECTIOUS DISEASE: Blood cultures are pending at this time. Because of the maternal chorioamnionitis, he will be kept on ampicillin and gentamicin for at least 48 hours. We will continue to monitor him closely for any signs of any ongoing infectious process.
5. GI: He is currently NPO. His abdominal exam remains benign. We will plan on starting some enteral feedings today.
6. FLUID/ELECTROLYTES/NUTRITION: His calcium is a little bit low this morning. We will plan on adding some calcium in his IV fluid. We will increase his IV fluids today and also start some enteral feedings. So far his urine output has been acceptable as well.
7. HEMATOLOGIC: His hematocrit on his CBC was acceptable at 42.8%.
8. NEUROLOGIC: He does have diffuse hypotonia, consistent with his prematurity; otherwise no focal deficits. Given his prematurity, close neurodevelopmental follow-up will be important and enrollment in a tracking system will be recommended.
9. HEALTH CARE MAINTENANCE: Newborn metabolic screen, hearing screen, and hepatitis B vaccination will be performed/given when appropriate.
10. SOCIAL: His family is being kept up-to-date as to his progress.

I-11B:

SERVICE CODE(S): _____

ICD-9-CM DX CODE(S): _____

ICD-10-CM DX CODE(S): _____

I-11C NICU PROGRESS NOTE

LOCATION: Hospital Inpatient, Neonatal Intensive Care Unit

PATIENT: Dale Everest

ATTENDING PHYSICIAN: Roland Ortez, MD

SUBJECTIVE: Baby boy Everest is a 2-day-old, 31-week gestation infant who was born via induction due to maternal prolonged rupture of membranes who developed presumed chorioamnionitis. He continues to be stable.

OBJECTIVE: Weight today is 1476 grams, which is down 103 grams from yesterday. He is down 6.5% from his birth weight. OFC is 29.25 cm, which is unchanged. He currently is on D-10 with electrolytes and a small amount of Pregestimil, and took in 95 mL/kg/day, 36 kcal/kg/day. Urine output was 172 mL, which is 4.6 mL/kg/hr. He has had one 1 stool in the last 24 hours. Review of VITAL SIGNS show heart rates between

124 and 152, respiratory rates between 32 and 60, mean blood pressures between 42 and 52. Axillary temperatures have been stable in his Isolette. He has had a couple of desaturation episodes in the last 24 hours. He is currently on oxygen between 1/16 and 1/32 liter to keep his sats in the mid 90s.

PHYSICAL EXAMINATION: He appears comfortable in his Isolette, in no acute distress. HEENT exam is unremarkable other than nasal cannula and NG in place. NECK is supple. LUNGS are clear to auscultation bilaterally with good breath sounds to the bases. I do not appreciate any retractions. His current respiratory rate is in the low 50s. S1 and S2, regular. I do not appreciate a murmur today. He has good femoral pulses. Capillary refill is 2 seconds. ABDOMEN is soft and nontender without hepatosplen-omegaly or masses. He has good bowel sounds. GU exam reveal normal external premature male genitalia. EXTREMITY exam reveals no decreased range of motion, joint deformity, or abnormality. SKIN is warm and mildly jaundiced.

MEDICATIONS:
1. Ampicillin 78.95 mg IV q. 12 hours.
2. Gentamicin 7.11 mg IV q. 48 hours.

LABORATORY DATA: Sodium 139, potassium 4.2, chloride 106, BUN 11, creatinine 0.9, glucose 77, calcium 9.6, magnesium 2.1, phosphorus 8.0, bilirubin 6.8.

ASSESSMENT & PLAN:
1. Day of life 2 for 31-week gestation male whose birth was induced due to maternal prolonged rupture of membranes and presumed chorioamnionitis.
2. RESPIRATORY: He has been stable from a respiratory standpoint. He does continue to require a small amount of oxygen to keep his sats in the mid 90s. His chest x-ray did show granular opacities within the lungs bilaterally consistent with hyaline membrane disease. The radiologist also noted patchy lower-lung-zone opacities. We will wean his oxygen as tolerated and continue to monitor him clinically.
3. CARDIOVASCULAR: He has been hemodynamically stable with acceptable mean arterial blood pressures. He does have a history of an intermittent murmur.
4. INFECTIOUS DISEASE: Blood cultures continue to be pending at this time. Because of the maternal chorioamnionitis, he will be kept on ampicillin and gentamicin for at least 48–72 hours. Will continue to monitor closely for any signs of any ongoing infectious process.
5. GI: He is currently tolerating some small feedings of Pregestimil. Will plan on advancing his feedings slowly. His bilirubin is elevated to 6.8. Will plan on starting phototherapy.
6. FLUID/ELECTROLYTES/NUTRITION: He did have some hypocalcemia yesterday, which corrected with the addition of calcium in his IV fluid. The rest of his electrolytes are acceptable. We will plan starting TPN today and advance his fluids.
7. HEMATOLOGIC: His hematocrit on his CBC was acceptable at 42.8%.
8. NEUROLOGIC: He does have diffuse hypotonia consistent with his prematurity, otherwise no focal deficits. Given his prematurity, close tracking system will be recommended.
9. HEALTH CARE MAINTENANCE: Newborn metabolic screen, hearing screen, and hepatitis B vaccination will be performed/given when appropriate.
10. SOCIAL: His family is being kept up-to-date as to his progress and are in agreement with the above outlined plan.

1-11C:

SERVICE CODE(S): _____

ICD-9-CM DX CODE(S): _____

ICD-10-CM DX CODE(S): _____

CASE 1-12

Report Dr. Alanda's service.

I-I2A OFFICE VISIT

LOCATION: Outpatient, Clinic

PATIENT: Maria Zans

PRIMARY CARE PHYSICIAN: Leslie Alanda, MD

REASON FOR VISIT: Annual exam; routine gynecologic

SUBJECTIVE: The patient is a 59-year-old married white female gravida 2, para 3-0-0-3 who is postmenopausal. Here for her annual gynecologic exam. No complaints except she thinks there is a small lump over her mastectomy site.

ROS: Negative for chest pain, shortness of breath, headaches, dizziness, visual changes, problems with hearing. No problems with bowel or bladder function. Negative for pelvic or vaginal symptoms, negative for depression. No problem with allergies at this time.

PAP: Last pap smear was performed 1 year ago.

MAMMOGRAM: Last mammogram was preformed 3 months ago. Right breast negative. Left breast absent.

PAST MEDICAL HISTORY: Positive for left breast cancer; status post mastectomy. Seasonal allergies.

SOCIAL HISTORY: Negative for tobacco use. Occasional social alcohol use.

FAMILY HISTORY: Positive for colon cancer in her mother at age 59.

OBJECTIVE: Blood pressure is 110/60. Height $61\frac{1}{2}$ inches. Weight is 195. Neck is supple, no palpable thyroid. The patient's left chest wall is flat except there is a thumbnail-sized palpable mobile lump at the base of the incision (approximately the medial $\frac{1}{3}$). Right, negative for masses, discharge, or tenderness. Abdomen: Soft, bowel sounds audible. No hepatosplenomegaly, lymphadenopathy, or inguinal hernias noted. Pelvic exam reveals adult female genitalia, marital, clean vagina. Cervix is multiparous. Uterus is normal in size and shape, benign. Adnexa: Negative. Rectal confirms. Stool guaiac pending. BUS within normal limits.

IMPRESSION: Annual gynecologic exam. Palpable mass chest wall status post mastectomy.

PLAN: Pap done. Patient was counseled on seatbelt use, importance of regular exercise, and preventive screening tests including colonoscopy due to family history. Colonscopy will be scheduled with general surgery. The patient is referred to general surgery for evaluation of this mass. The patient will follow up p.r.n. for her annual exam.

I-I2A:

SERVICE CODE(S): _____

ICD-9-CM DX CODE(S): _____

ICD-10-CM DX CODE(S): _____

CASE 1-13

Report Dr. Alanda's service.

1-13A OFFICE VISIT

LOCATION: Outpatient, Clinic

PATIENT: Julia Fry

SUBJECTIVE: The patient is a 67-year-old female who presents for an annual physical.

PROBLEM LIST:
1. Atelectasis right lower base, stable.
2. Osteoporosis with old compression fracture of the thoracic spine.
3. Anxiety.
4. Depression.
5. Recent abnormal Cardiolite stress test showing ischemia at the periapical lateral anterior wall with recent angiogram showing no evidence of coronary artery disease, but showing evidence of bridging.
6. Hypertension.
7. Nicotine habituation.
8. Chronic obstructive pulmonary disease.
9. History of pneumothorax.
10. History of hemoptysis, resolved, and not recurrent.
11. History of gastroesophageal reflux disease.
12. Atrophic vaginitis.
13. Rhinitis.
14. Degenerative joint disease of the thoracic spine.
15. Hyperlipidemia, on Baycol therapy.

The patient states she is doing well. She saw a cardiologist in August for follow-up regarding her heart disease and hypertension. He states that she has myocardial purging, and this has been stable with Covera. Her hypertension has been better. Blood pressure is still slightly elevated, and he did recommend low-salt diet. The patient states that she has not been adding any salt to her cooking. She uses "lite" salt for table salt. She avoids any processed foods, canned vegetables, or soups. She denies symptoms of headache, dizziness, lightheadedness, and nausea. She had a DEXA scan performed in May for osteoporosis. There was osteoporosis noted of the thoracic spine that stated was in the severe range, but none noted on the hips. The radiologist thought that the severity of the osteoporosis was probably due to degenerative change of the spine and not necessarily all osteoporosis. She does have a history of compression fractures of the thoracic spine, which show up on x-ray. She is taking 1500 mg of calcium a day and vitamin D biweekly. She has never been on hormone replacement therapy. She has been menopausal for several years. She had a complete hysterectomy for a benign tumor. She states that she was on male hormone therapy following her surgical menopause and never has been on estrogen therapy. She does not know why she was put on male hormones versus estrogen. The patient stopped taking the Paxil and the Buspar for depression and anxiety. She states that she takes the Buspar on a p.r.n. basis, if she really needs to. She feels that she needs to work on her depression without medication and does not feel that her depression is consuming. She has no other concerns or complaints.

PAST MEDICAL HISTORY: See problem list.

PREVIOUS SURGERIES:
1. Total abdominal hysterectomy with bilateral salpingo-oophorectomy for benign tumor.
2. Cataract removal.
3. Insertion of chest tube for pneumothorax.
4. Exploratory laparotomy for malformation of the uterus.

CURRENT MEDICATIONS:
1. Azmacort 3 puffs b.i.d.
2. Atrovent 3 puffs q.i.d.
3. Atrovent nasal spray 2 sprays each nostril daily.
4. Multivitamin daily.
5. Aspirin 1 daily.
6. Baycol 0.4 mg 1 daily.
7. Covera HS 240 mg 1 daily.
8. Zestoretic 20/25 1 daily.
9. Tums 500 mg 1 t.i.d.
10. Vitamin D biweekly.

ALLERGIES: No known drug allergies.

FAMILY HISTORY: Reviewed and remains unchanged from November of 1999.

SOCIAL/OCCUPATIONAL: Reviewed and remains unchanged from November of 1999.

REVIEW OF SYSTEMS: The patient denies any fevers, sweats, or chills. She denies any headaches, light-headedness, or dizziness. She does not have a history of migraine headaches. No visual disturbances, loss of vision, double vision, or blurred vision. No hearing deficits or tinnitus. She denies any dysphagia or choking. She is not having any episodes of chest pain, chest pressure, or shortness of breath. No hemoptysis. She continues to smoke 1 pack of cigarettes per day. She has known coronary artery disease affecting the left anterior descending artery, currently under a cardiologist's care and is stable. She had hypertension, which has been stable. No abdominal pain. Heartburn and indigestion are infrequent. No dysuria, polyuria, or polydipsia. She has no history of diabetes. No vaginal discharge. She denies any change in bowel habits or hematochezia. No constipation. No musculoskeletal complaints or focal neurological deficits. Psychiatric: see above.

OBJECTIVE: On physical exam, weight is 16¾ pounds. Blood pressure is 140/84. Pulse is 62. Oxygen saturation is 96%. Patient is alert and oriented and she is in no acute distress. HEENT: Head normocephalic. Face is symmetrical. Eyes clear. EOMs intact. PERRLA. Fundoscopic exam reveals well-defined disc margins and normal basculature bilaterally. Ears: Canals clear. TMs clear. Oropharynx is clear. No erythema or lesions. Neck is soft and supple without lymphadenopathy. No thyromegaly. No JVD or bruits on auscultation. Chest: Heart rate and rhythm are regular. She has a grade ⅙ systolic murmur heard along the apex. No S3 or S4. Lungs are clear to auscultation without adventitious sounds. No rales, rhonchi, or wheezing. Breasts are symmetrical. Nipples are everted without discharge. No retraction or dimpling. No palpable masses or nodules. There is no adenopathy of the chest. Abdomen is soft and nontender to palpation. Bowel sounds are normoactive. No bruits. No masses or organomegaly. Female GU exam: Normal external genitalia noted. No cystocele. Vaginal mucosa shows severe atrophic changes. Cervix is absent. There is no discharge. Bimanual exam is performed noting absence of fundus. No palpable pelvic masses. Rectal exam is performed noting normal sphincter tone. No palpable masses. Stool for guaiac is obtained and sent to the lab for processing. Extremities all four are without clubbing, cyanosis, or edema. She does have brawny discoloration of the lower extremities. No loss of hair. Pedal pulses are regular, strong, and equal bilaterally.

IMPRESSION:
1. Coronary artery disease with myocardial purging, controlled on conservative therapy.
2. Hypertension, stable.
3. Osteoporosis with old compression fractures of the thoracic spine.
4. Anxiety.
5. Depression.
6. Hyperlipidemia, currently on Baycol therapy.
7. Nicotine habituation.
8. Chronic obstructive pulmonary disease, stable.
9. History of pneumothorax.
10. History of hemoptysis, resolved, and not recurrent.
11. History of gastroesophageal reflux disease.
12. Atrophic vaginitis.
13. Rhinitis.

PLAN:
1. We will get a hemogram and acute care panel performed today. The patient also had a mammogram performed today.
2. We will start E-Vista 60 mg 1 tablet daily to avoid further loss because she has osteoporosis.
3. We will start Fosamax 10 mg daily for treatment of osteoporosis. The patient was instructed to take this 30 minutes prior to eating on any empty stomach and then not to lay down for 30 minutes after taking her medication. The patient was also informed of side effects of both E-Vista and Fosamax.
4. She will need a follow-up DEXA scan in 1 year.
5. We will see her back in April. She will need an AST, ALT, and a fasting lipid panel for her hyperlipidemia. If she has any problems, I can see her sooner.

1-13A:

SERVICE CODE(S): _____

ICD-9-CM DX CODE(S): _____

ICD-10-CM DX CODE(S): _____

Medicine

Make sure to check
evolve
learning system
for the latest
content updates

CASE 2-1

Report the services provided by Dr. Naraquist's nurse.

2-1A CHART NOTE

LOCATION: Outpatient, Clinic

PATIENT: Ronald House

PHYSICIAN: Alma Naraquist, MD

AGE: 58

COVERAGE: Blue Cross Blue Shield

Patient presents for administration of an IM injection of Hepatitis B vaccine administered by Dr. Naraquist's nurse.

2-1A:

SERVICE CODE(S): _____

ICD-9-CM DX CODE(S): _____

ICD-10-CM DX CODE(S): _____

CASE 2-2

Steve Meyer is an inpatient for whom Dr. Nelson provided an inpatient psychiatry service.

2-2A PSYCHOLOGICAL EVALUATION

LOCATION: Inpatient, Hospital

PATIENT: Steve Meyer

PHYSICIAN: Jerome Nelson, MD

HISTORY: Mr. Meyer is a 48-year-old, divorced, white male who was admitted after he was found lying on the floor in his apartment. Evidently, he had taken a fall, and he had some bruises on his face and tongue. Later, during the hospitalization, he developed delirium tremens and required to go on the ventilator. Earlier this week, I also came to see this patient, but at that time, he was given a dose of Haldol, and he was quite drowsy and sleepy.

Today, I reviewed his medical records and also met with the patient for a full evaluation. He was fairly cooperative. According to the nursing staff, the patient was just transferred to the rehab hospital, but there he became non-responsive and was transferred back yesterday. During this meeting, actually, he was pretty awake, although his concentration was still somewhat poor, but he seemed a fairly good historian. As I approached the patient, he was immediately able to recognize me, saying that I saw him many years back for "mental capacity" for social security benefits. At that time also, the patient had a history of auditory and visual hallucinations. The patient still talks about the same symptoms, saying he is seeing different animals from the side of his eyes and that it becomes quite scary, he will see elephants, people being hanged, and when he sees these things, he gets very nervous. He also talks about having auditory hallucinations. Again, the patient corroborated that it is nothing new and it has been going on for a number of years. He has been treated with Trazodone and then with some other medication like Mellaril, but all it did was make his mouth dry. Surprisingly, related to these psychotic symptoms, he never has had any psychiatric hospitalizations.

Today, the patient also admitted that he is feeling quite depressed, and he does not feel good. He has hopelessness and worthlessness feelings, but did add that he will not hurt or kill himself. Because of pain, he complains of sleep difficulties. He does get angry and irritable because the staff tries to be smart with him; like yesterday, he was talking about not eating and still they would keep on bringing food to him. However, the patient denies if he is physically aggressive to anyone. Then I also confronted the patient about his drinking habits, but the patient said it is just a rumor, saying he is not using any alcohol or street drugs, and he has no idea who is putting it in his records. He does complain of significant anxiety symptoms also.

PAST MEDICAL HISTORY: Significant for hypertension, gout, hypercalcemia and now general debility. His previous coronary angiogram was negative.

MEDICATIONS: At the time of admission, the patient was on numerous medications, but now they had been cut down significantly.

PAST PSYCHIATRIC HISTORY: As above. He does have a history of psychosis, but questionable treatment.

FAMILY HISTORY: The patient tells me he comes from a very large family. There were 11 kids. Some of his brothers are deceased. He could not really tell me if any other brother or sister has a diagnosis of psychosis. Both of his parents are deceased. The patient has two children, both of them are doing very well, one is a teacher and another technician in a hospital.

PERSONAL AND SOCIAL HISTORY: The patient was married. His marriage lasted for about 9 years. For many years, he worked on trenches. The patient minimizes if he abuses alcohol and denies using any street drugs.

MENTAL STATUS EXAMINATION: This is a heavyset male. He was pretty cooperative. He was able to recognize the undersigned right away. He remembered the name. His mood is quite depressed. He is close to tears often. Affect is flat. He also seems quite nervous. His voice is somewhat shaky. The patient was able to give his birthday month and the year correctly and knew he was 48 years old. The patient knew he was in the hospital and who the president of the United States is. He was off on current time with the serial 7's. He was not able to spell the word money and had quite a hard time spelling it backwards. He continues to have both auditory and visual hallucination and some paranoid behavior. No acute agitation or aggression.

ASSESSMENT:
1. Psychotic disorder, NOS. It does seem functional, especially with such a long history, and possibly, there is worsening of the symptoms with underlying delirium earlier.

RECOMMENDATIONS: Today, I tried to go into my old files, but I was unable to find the evaluation that I completed for the social security office. Looking at his current picture, the patient does seem quite psychotic, and I think it is reasonable to treat him with any antipsychotics. Probably, he could benefit from a trial with antidepressants also, but I would hold using too many medications suddenly at this point, especially, as his physical status is so unclear. It does not seem there is any explanation why he was so unresponsive just yesterday. Targeting his psychosis, we will start him on Risperdal small dose and slowly got up on the dose tolerated.

Thank you for asking me to see this interesting patient in consultation.

2-2A:

SERVICE CODE(S): _____

ICD-9-CM DX CODE(S): _____

ICD-10-CM DX CODE(S): _____

CASE 2-3

This patient carries a diagnosis of membranoproliferative glomerulonephritis. He has become acutely sick with nausea and vomiting and was found to have a high BUN reading. He is admitted to the hospital by Dr. Orbit for treatment of the patient's acute and chronic renal failure and the complications that have set in. Assign the codes for the H&P, daily dialysis and progress notes, and discharge management.

2-3A HISTORY AND PHYSICAL EXAMINATION

LOCATION: Inpatient, Hospital

PATIENT: Ken Fossen

PHYSICIAN: George Orbitz, MD

HISTORY OF PRESENT ILLNESS: Mr. Fossen is a 20-year-old male. I was called by his family physician earlier today informing me that he showed up in the clinic with nausea and vomiting for the past 2 weeks, was found to have a BUN in the 150 range, a creatinine in the 19 range.

The patient is known to have ADHD and is mentally disabled. Most of the history was taken from some of the records he had along and from his dad, who also receives dialysis.

Ken carries a diagnosis of membranoproliferative glomerulonephritis, the same diagnosis as his dad. He has not had any follow-up care for the past couple of years. Ken stopped his medications a few months ago, which included blood pressure medication, in addition to Zoloft, and Wellbutrin.

Over the past couple of months, he has been having nausea and vomiting, generalized weakness, fatigue. His social skills, according to his family, are not the greatest. He spends time playing video games. He has no interest in working.

I accepted the patient in transfer, and I admitted him to the intensive care unit.

LABORATORY DATA: His BUN was 152 with sodium of 138, potassium 3.8, chloride 96, glucose 92, creatinine 18.9. His calcium is 7.4, albumin 3.3, CO_2 22.2. Liver functions were normal. His CPK was 773 with CK-MB less than 0.5. White count was 15.6 thousand, hemoglobin 8.6, platelets 283,000. His LDH was 424, magnesium 2.2, and phosphorus 8.7. Troponin-I was slightly elevated at 0.19.

The patient feels that he is dehydrated. He is still making some urine. He denies any chest pain or shortness of breath. On admission to the intensive care unit, his blood pressure was in the 180s/100s, heart rate was in the 130s.

MEDICATIONS: None. The patient has been taking Advil for the past 2–3 weeks because of headaches.

ALLERGIES: None.

PAST MEDICAL HISTORY: Significant for
1. Membranoproliferative glomerulonephritis.
2. ADHD.
3. Mentally disabled.
4. Aortic dysplasia with aortic stenosis and mild aortic insufficiency.

FAMILY HISTORY: Significant for membranoproliferative glomerulonephritis in his father who is on hemodialysis and is well known to me.

REVIEW OF SYSTEMS: No fever or chills. ENT: Negative. RESPIRATORY: Negative. GI: Nausea and vomiting, as mentioned. GU: He still has urine output; otherwise, negative. NEUROLOGIC: Negative. SKIN: Negative. MUSCULOSKELETAL: Negative.

PHYSICAL EXAMINATION: Ken appeared very quiet. He is not very interactive. He is slightly pale. No jaundice or cyanosis. He is not in respiratory, cardiac, or neurological distress. Blood pressure 185/105, heart rate 130s per minute. He had no increased jugular venous pressure. No cervical lymphadenopathy. Thyroid was not palpable. LUNGS: Clear bilaterally. As he was in tachycardia, I could not hear any pericardial friction rub. HEART: He had no murmurs, but his dad told me that he had a murmur. I could not hear a murmur probably because of his tachycardia. ABDOMEN: Soft with dry skin. Intact hernial orifices. EXTREMITIES: No edema. Pallor obvious of the nail beds.

IMPRESSION:
1. Acute on top of chronic renal failure.
2. Chronic renal failure, probably end-stage renal disease.
3. Metabolic acidosis.
4. Anemia, secondary to chronic renal failure and possible iron deficiency.
5. Nausea and vomiting, secondary to uremia.

PLAN:
1. The patient has been already admitted to the intensive care unit.
2. Code Level I.
3. We will check iron studies.
4. Start heparin 20,000 units subcu daily.
5. Repeat labs in the morning.
6. We will give him 1 liter of saline bolus and run it at 500 mL/hr.
7. We will put him on renal diet.
8. EKG.
9. Chest x-ray.
10. Nephrocaps 1 po daily.
11. We will eventually start him on Renagel.

I had a long discussion with the patient and mainly his family in his room. We discussed options for renal replacement therapy, including hemodialysis, peritoneal dialysis, and kidney transplantation. He is a good candidate for peritoneal dialysis. His father agrees with that. I did discuss the advantages, disadvantages, risks, and benefits of hemo and peritoneal dialysis.

I did call the surgeon on call who is kind enough to accept seeing him in consultation for PD catheter placement in the morning.

I see no reason why this patient needs to have hemodialysis done tonight.

I discussed blood transfusion with the risks and benefits with the patient's dad, and he gave me consent. Blood transfusion we give probably should be irradiated in case he gets a kidney transplant in the future.

2-3A:

SERVICE CODE(S): _____

ICD-9-CM DX CODE(S): _____

ICD-10-CM DX CODE(S): _____

2-3B CAPD PROGRESS NOTE

The general surgeon has placed the peritoneal dialysis catheter and the patient is now receiving dialysis, due to acute and chronic renal failure.

LOCATION: Inpatient, Hospital

PATIENT: Ken Fossen

PHYSICIAN: George Orbitz, MD

CAPD PROGRESS NOTE: The patient was seen on CAPD due to acute and chronic renal failure after his PD catheter was placed earlier today. He has had –800 so far on dialysis due to acute and chronic renal failure. It is yellow, clear. No fibrin, no clots. Because of pulmonary edema, I will switch him to 4.25%, 1500 mL fill volumes every 4 hours. When I came and saw him, he was sleeping and snoring, and his sats were down to the high 80s. I think he looks like he has sleep apnea in addition to some of his pulmonary edema. I will get ABGs on him and continue with the dialysis prescription as above.

2-3B:

SERVICE CODE(S): _____

ICD-9-CM DX CODE(S): _____

ICD-10-CM DX CODE(S): _____

2-3C DIALYSIS PROGRESS NOTE

LOCATION: Inpatient, Hospital

PATIENT: Ken Fossen

PHYSICIAN: George Orbitz, MD

DIALYSIS PROGRESS NOTE: The patient was seen on CAPD due to acute and chronic renal failure. We are using 4.25%, 1500 mL fill volumes every 4 hours. In the last two exchanges, he had 800 out. He continues to have pulmonary edema on physical examination, with hypoxia, but he is not in distress. Will give him Bumex 2 mg IV x 1, then Bumex at .25 mg/hr. Fluid restriction at 1.5 liters a day. For his abnormally high blood pressure, will use labetalol p.r.n. but will start him on p.o. labetalol 100 mg p.o. b.i.d. We will start him on a high-protein diet. I discussed this with the patient. He seems to be in agreement.

2-3C:

SERVICE CODE(S): _____

ICD-9-CM DX CODE(S): _____

ICD-10-CM DX CODE(S): _____

2-3D DIALYSIS PROGRESS NOTE

LOCATION: Inpatient, Hospital

PATIENT: Ken Fossen

PHYSICIAN: George Orbitz, MD

DIALYSIS PROGRESS NOTE: The patient is on CAPD due to acute and chronic renal failure. We are using 4.25% 1.5 liter full volumes with heparin. He seems to be tolerating that well. His potassium was a little low at 3.3 and we will replace it. He is getting Bumex drip and he made 550 mL in the past 8 hours, and 800 overnight. I will give him 2 mg more of IV Bumex in a drip 2.5 mg/hour. He is hypoxic but he is totally asymptomatic. On his x-ray it looks like pulmonary edema, but he is asymptomatic without any shortness of breath, I will just continue with the current dialysis prescription. I will not investigate this any further. We might have to do an echocardiogram. The patient agrees. He has been playing with his game and we are going to try and get him ambulating.

2-3D:

SERVICE CODE(S): _____

ICD-9-CM DX CODE(S): _____

ICD-10-CM DX CODE(S): _____

2-3E DIALYSIS PROGRESS NOTE

LOCATION: Inpatient, Hospital

PATIENT: Ken Fossen

PHYSICIAN: George Orbitz, MD

DIALYSIS PROGRESS NOTE: The patient is on CAPD due to acute and chronic renal failure. Unfortunately, was not able to drain today. I took a KUB and we could not see his dialysis catheter in the pelvis. It was overlying the spine most likely and probably up. He has lost fluid but had good ultrafiltration. His weight is not consistent on the chart. It shows that he gained 5 lbs and that is probably his run because we have been having good ultrafiltration on him.

His BUN is down to 117, potassium was 3.3. Creatinine is down to 17.1. He was not in any distress. RESPIRATORY: chest is clear, CARDIAC: regular rate and rhythm, NEUROLOGICAL: alert and oriented × 3. His oxygenation was much better on Venti mask and we are tapering this down. We are putting him on nasal cannula.

For today I am going to hold his dialysis and tomorrow will have Interventional Radiology reposition the temporary dialysis catheter.

I had a chance to talk to his father and sister today and we discussed all the issues related to peritoneal dialysis and where he is at right now. Will plan for discharge soon.

2-3E:

SERVICE CODE(S): _____

ICD-9-CM DX CODE(S): _____

ICD-10-CM DX CODE(S): _____

2-3F DIALYSIS PROGRESS NOTE

LOCATION: Inpatient, Hospital

PATIENT: Ken Fossen

PHYSICIAN: George Orbitz, MD

DIALYSIS PROGRESS NOTE: The patient was seen on CAPD due to acute and chronic renal failure. I held his dialysis yesterday because it was not draining. We drained him through Interventional Radiology manipulation and I do appreciate their help on that. He had 2000 cc draining. We will currently use CAPD, 2.5%, 2-liter fill volumes every 4 hours. He does not have edema. His oxygen saturation is much better.

His hemoglobin is 7.6. I discussed with him risks and benefits of blood transfusion. He agreed with the transfusion but I will wait one more day and check it again tomorrow to see where his hemoglobin goes. Meanwhile, because of the high phosphorus we will start him on Renagel 800 mg p.o. t.i.d. with meals. He is already on Nephrocaps. We will start also Rocaltrol 0.25 micrograms p.o. three times a week.

The patient agrees with the plan. His sister was available at the time of discussion.

2-3F:

SERVICE CODE(S): _____

ICD-9-CM DX CODE(S): _____

ICD-10-CM DX CODE(S): _____

2-3G DIALYSIS PROGRESS NOTE

LOCATION: Inpatient, Hospital

PATIENT: Ken Fossen

PHYSICIAN: George Orbitz, MD

DIALYSIS PROGRESS NOTE: The patient was seen during CAPD due to acute and chronic renal failure. He is tolerating that well. We are using 2.5%, 2-liter fill volumes every 4 hours. So far today he had 160 mL out. Yesterday he had a total of 1800 mL out. His dialysis is clear and yellow.

He has no complaints. He is afebrile. Blood pressure has been in the 130s to 140s over 80s. Heart rate is down to the 90s. Weight is 238 lbs. Still making urine but we discontinued his Foley catheter.

His BUN is down to 104, his potassium is up to 3.6.

At this time we will change his CAPD to five exchanges a day at the same prescription. Will plan discharging him in the morning.

Start KCl 40 mEq p.o. b.i.d.

The patient agrees with the plan.

2-3G:

SERVICE CODE(S): _____

ICD-9-CM DX CODE(S): _____

ICD-10-CM DX CODE(S): _____

2-3H DISCHARGE SUMMARY

LOCATION: Inpatient, Hospital

PATIENT: Ken Fossen

PHYSICIAN: George Orbitz, MD

DIAGNOSES:
1. Chronic renal failure.
2. Metabolic acidosis secondary to renal failure.
3. Anemia of chronic renal failure.
4. Nausea and vomiting secondary to uremia.
5. Acute respiratory failure secondary to pulmonary edema.
6. Pulmonary edema secondary to acute overload state.

HOSPITAL COURSE: Ken is 20-year-old male known to have membranoproliferative glomerulonephritis who was admitted with uremia. His BUN was above 150 and creatinine was in the 19 range. He was hypoxic with pulmonary edema findings on the physical examination and chest x-ray, however, he was not complaining of any shortness of breath or chest pain. His blood pressure was elevated as well.

After discussions with family, specifically his dad who also suffers with the same condition and is currently on hemodialysis and after discussion options for renal replacement therapy including hemodialysis and peritoneal dialysis we preceded with peritoneal dialysis catheter placement. The patient was initiated on peritoneal dialysis successfully. A few days later he had problems with drainage. We manipulated his catheter in interventional radiology. He drained nicely. We started with 4.25% 1500 mL fill volumes every 4 hours and we progressed to the point that he was doing five exchanges a day to liter fill volumes with 2.5% dialysate.

The patient was originally on Venti-mask and was discharged on room air. Was discharged with sats in the 100% and high 90s point on room air.

CODE LEVEL: I

DISCHARGE MEDICATIONS: include the following:
1. Bumex 2 mg p.o. b.i.d.
2. Rocaltrol 0.25 mcg Monday, Wednesday, Friday.
3. EPO 10,000 units three times a day.
4. Nephrocaps one p.o. daily.
5. Labetalol 100 mg b.i.d.
6. Megace 100 mg b.i.d.
7. Protonix 40 mg daily.
8. Potassium chloride 40 mEq p.o. b.i.d.
9. Renagel 800 mg three times a day.

DISCHARGE PLAN:
1. The patient will be discharged home today.
2. I will follow up on him in the clinic setting for further instructions on peritoneal dialysis and dialysis catheter care.
3. He will probably do well with 1.5 alternating with 2.5% to liter fill volumes, five exchanges a day.

2-3H:

SERVICE CODE(S): _____

ICD-9-CM DX CODE(S): _____

ICD-10-CM DX CODE(S): _____

CASE 2-4

Report Dr. Noonar's professional service.

2-4A VASCULAR LABORATORY REPORT-DUPLEX VENOUS EXAMINATION

LOCATION: Outpatient, Hospital

PATIENT: Rebecca Stone

ORDERING PHSYCIAN: Ronald Green, MD

PHYSICIAN: James Noonar, MD

INDICATION: Edema, right extremities, right ankle fracture, rule out pulmonary embolism

The patient is a 65-year-old female with an ankle fracture. Since this has occurred, the patient has developed edema and this is done to rule out pulmonary embolism.

Both legs were interrogated at the common femoral, superficial femoral, popliteal, and saphenous levels. The right leg could only be examined down to the knee. The left leg was examined below the knee as well. We examined for spontaneous flow, phasicity, augmentation, and compressibility. There is no evidence of thrombus.

CONCLUSION: This study is "negative," but the leg was not interrogated at the lower right leg, which would be the most concerned area. If the physician wishes, bandages could be removed and the technologist brought back for that.

There was no evidence of thrombophlebitis, but the study was not complete.

2-4A:

SERVICE CODE(S): _____

ICD-9-CM DX CODE(S): _____

ICD-10-CM DX CODE(S): _____

CASE 2-5

Report the ultrasound professional service provided by Dr. Monson.

2-5A ULTRASOUND, LOWER EXTREMITIES

LOCATION: Outpatient, Hospital

PATIENT: Daniel Adams

REQUESTING PHYSICIAN: Alma Naraquist, MD

PHYSICIAN: Morton Monson, MD

EXAMINATION OF: Ultrasound of both lower extremities

CLINICAL SYMPTOMS: Leg pain

ULTRASOUND OF BOTH LOWER EXTREMITIES: FINDINGS: Ultrasound examination of the deep venous system of the lower extremities shows a deep venous thrombosis of the superficial femoral vein of the right leg. Bilateral posterior tibial, greater saphenous, femoral and popliteal veins are patent with no evidence of thrombus seen there.

2-5A:

SERVICE CODE(S): _____

ICD-9-CM DX CODE(S): _____

ICD-10-CM DX CODE(S): _____

CASE 2-6

2-6A PHOTODYNAMIC THERAPY

LOCATION: Outpatient, Clinic

Dr. Barton provided Tim Johnson with four photodynamic therapy exposures over the course of several weeks as a treatment for several premalignant lesions on the skin of his back. Report the four sessions.

2-6A:

SERVICE CODE(S): _____

ICD-9-CM DX CODE(S): _____

ICD-10-CM DX CODE(S): _____

CASE 2-7

The following is a full-length hand therapy evaluation for which you are to report Mary Barneswell's service. This is not a consultation but a physical therapy evaluation.

2-7A PHYSICAL THERAPY EVALUATION

The following is an initial physical therapy evaluation for which you are to report Mary Barneswell's service.

LOCATION: Outpatient, Clinic

PATIENT: Michelle Jones

REFERRING PHYSICIAN: Ronald Green, MD

PROVIDER: Mary Barneswell, RPT

DIAGNOSIS: Right lymphedema, right breast cancer stage IV, pulmonary metastasis.

SUBJECTIVE: Michelle is a female patient seen in Hand Therapy on direct referral from Dr. Ronald Green with the above diagnosis. This is a patient that was diagnosed with breast cancer a year ago. She currently is undergoing active chemotherapy treatments. She had surgery a year ago and had no edema until the past month. She is also complaining of some shoulder discomfort in the right.

OBJECTIVE: The patient presents today with a right upper extremity that has some areas of red, blotchy skin with some slight increase in edema through the entire arm. Patient indicates that at times the red areas in her arm are fairly bright red and inflamed looking. She notes that the swelling is somewhat down today compared to other days.

Circumferential measurements taken today are as follows: On the right, the metacarpals are 20 cm, wrist 17.5 cm, 9 cm above the wrist 21.3 cm, 16 cm above the wrist 23.7 cm, elbow 27 cm, 12 cm above the elbow 33 cm, and axilla 35 cm. On the left, the metacarpals 18.5 cm, wrist 17 cm, 9 cm above the wrist 19.8 cm, 16 cm above the wrist 23 cm, elbow 25.2 cm, 12 cm above the elbow 30.2, and axilla 35 cm.

The patient has not had any hand or thumb swelling to speak of and fingers look comparable to the noninvolved left side. She has no numbness or tingling but does complain of some shoulder discomfort. Active range of motion in the right upper extremity is full with exception of end ranges of shoulder motion lacking 20 for flexion and extension.

DIRECT TREATMENT: The patient is seen today primarily for the fitting of a sleeve per physician's orders. Today we fitted her with an over-the-counter size VI Juzo sleeve. Fit was fairly good today. The patient was instructed to wear this sleeve during daytime activities and to remove it overnight. She is able to independently apply it. She was also sent with a tube of roll-on grip to utilize on her skin to help hold the sleeve in a good position on her arm. We then reviewed some gentle massage techniques focusing on moving the fluid up, out of the arm and towards the shoulder area. The patient was able to understand these and could complete these a couple times per day. We also reviewed some general lymphedema precautions as well as skin care.

ASSESSMENT: Lymphedema and arm swelling.

PLAN: This patient is not in need of direct ongoing care. I am hopeful that with the use of her over-the-counter sleeve her swelling will be well controlled. The patient's long-term goals are to achieve maintenance of decrease in the swelling in her arm and be able to use her arm unrestricted for all tasks. Short-term goals include pain free use of her arm for all activities including use of her crutch at home, no increase in swelling during the daytime with the use of the sleeve, continued assessment of the edema and the skin condition with progression to a more active massage program or bandaging if the need arises.

The patient was given a phone number and a card and instructed to phone us if things flare or if she is not doing well with the use of her sleeve.

2-7A:

SERVICE CODE(S): _____

ICD-9-CM DX CODE(S): _____

ICD-10-CM DX CODE(S): _____

2-7B PHYSICAL THERAPY EVALUATION

The following is an initial physical therapy evaluation for which you are to report Mary Barneswell's service.

LOCATION: Outpatient, Clinic

PATIENT: Donna Koelmer

PROVIDER: Mary Barneswell, RPT

DIAGNOSIS: Shoulder pain

HISTORY OF PRESENT ILLNESS: This is a 46-year-old female referred from Dr. Green for physical therapy evaluation and treatment. Specific diagnosis is right biceps tenodesis performed on 10/24/xx. Specific recommendations are for shoulder range of motion with no biceps strengthening until 6 weeks post-op. The patient is to be seen three times per week for 4 to 6 weeks.

SUBJECTIVE: The patient notes the surgery was performed on 10/24/xx with success. At the current time, the patient notes that she is not in any tremendous pain unless she actively uses the right shoulder. The patient notes that she has returned to work but is on light duty and performs absolutely no lifting with the involved extremity. The patient denies any cervical involvement or radiation of pain or any numbness or tingling. The patient simply isolates the pain directly to the shoulder region. The patient's goal is to encourage her strength and abolish her pain.

OBJECTIVE: Active range of motion of the right shoulder is noted to be 95 of flexion, and 80 of abduction. Passive range of motion is noted to be 150 of flexion, 140 of abduction, external rotation is 80, internal rotation to 60. Extension was not assessed. Strength was not assessed. Cervical range of motion was within normal limits and pain free. Elbow range of motion and wrist range of motion was within normal limits and pain free.

Physical therapy treatment at this time consisted of passive range of motion treatment, active assistive range of motion treatment, pulley times 15 minutes into scaption. As well, the patient was instructed in finger walking up the wall into flexion and abduction as tolerated.

ASSESSMENT: Biceps tenodesis. The patient tolerated treatment well. She does have some decreased range of motion and some pain involved. At this time we will work on range of motion until 6 weeks post-op until the time we will begin strengthening. Physical therapy goals will be (1) The patient will have within normal limits range of motion in 3 weeks time. (2) The patient will have good strength throughout the shoulder in 4 weeks time. Long-Term Goal to be accomplished in 1 to 2 months will be within normal limits range of motion and strength to allow the patient to return to work without restrictions.

PLAN: Initiate physical therapy on 3 x per week basis.

2-7B:

SERVICE CODE(S): _____

ICD-9-CM DX CODE(S): _____

ICD-10-CM DX CODE(S): _____

2-7C PHYSICAL THERAPY EVALUATION

The following is a physical therapy re-evaluation for which you are to report Mary Barneswell's service.

LOCATION: Outpatient, Clinic

PATIENT: Scott Freeman

PROVIDER: Mary Barneswell, RPT

DIAGNOSIS: Right knee mosaicplasty on 2/20/xx, ongoing knee pain.

SUBJECTIVE: The patient describes numerous surgeries on his knees as well as a surgery on his shoulder. He states that he has presently not been working. He has a goal of returning to his normal work and life activities with reduced pain.

OBJECTIVE: The patient is ambulatory independently with bilateral Lofstrand crutches. The instructions are to continue with his crutches for 2 to 3 more weeks and to progress weight bearing as tolerated with bilateral support. EXERCISE INSTRUCTION: The patient demonstrated early fatigue with activity. He has been performing active range of motion of the ankle and knee. He was now instructed to initiate stationary bicycling. He also was instructed in quadriceps and hamstring setting exercise as well as leg lifts for hip flexion and hip abduction.

ASSESSMENT: The patient did demonstrate an ability to perform the above exercises independently in the clinical setting. He did begin with a five repetition level due to early fatigue. He was instructed to progress up to 20 repetitions if able on a four times daily basis. Physical therapy goals are to assist the patient postoperatively to slowly regain strength and functional use. Fifteen minutes of isokinetic therapeutic exercise was provided to help the patient increase the range of motion in his knee.

PLAN: The patient has a recheck appointment with this therapist in 1 month for reassessment and progression as per mosaicplasty protocol.

2-7C:

SERVICE CODE(S): _____

ICD-9-CM DX CODE(S): _____

ICD-10-CM DX CODE(S): _____

CHAPTER 3

Radiology

CASE 3-1

Make sure to check
evolve
learning system
**for the latest
content updates**

In the following case, Dr. Monson has been requested by Dr. Sanchez to interpret the x-ray of the patient's chest to ensure that the previously placed line was correctly placed.

3-1A RADIOLOGY REPORT, LINE PLACEMENT

LOCATION: Outpatient, Hospital

PATIENT: Julie Franklin

PHYSICIAN: Gary Sanchez, MD

RADIOLOGIST: Morton Monson, MD

EXAMINATION OF: Chest

CLINICAL SYMPTOMS: Cardiovascular shock

CHEST, SINGLE VIEW: FINDINGS: Portable AP view submitted of the chest. Comparison is made with a chest radiograph from the previous day at 5 PM. There is again endotracheal tube, tip at the junction of the mid to distal trachea. There is again Swan Ganz catheter. That is unchanged. There is again nasogastric tube, distal portion beyond the margins of the film. There are multiple superimposed cardiac leads. Cardiac silhouette again appears enlarged. There again appears to be some

congestive change along the pulmonary vasculature. There is increased hazy opacity right lower lung field, probably relating to pleural effusion. There is also now retro-cardiac opacity and associated pleural effusion on the left is not excluded.

3-1A:

SERVICE CODE(S): _____

ICD-9-CM DX CODE(S): _____

ICD-10-CM DX CODE(S): _____

CASE 3-2

Report Dr. Monson's professional service.

3-2A RADIOLOGY REPORT, CHEST

LOCATION: Outpatient, Hospital

PATIENT: Jessie Murphy

PHYSICIAN: Ronald Green, MD

RADIOLOGIST: Morton Monson, MD

EXAMINATION OF: Chest

CLINICAL SYMPTOMS: Arteriosclerotic heart disease

TWO-VIEW CHEST: Frontal and lateral views submitted of the chest dated May 10. Comparison study is portable chest from 3/29. The patient's arms are not fully raised on the lateral view with overlying bony and soft tissue density. Cardiac silhouette is within normal limits and not significantly changed. No evidence of acute congestive heart failure or focal infiltrate. No pleural effusions. There is some scattered degenerative spurring seen, dorsal spine.

IMPRESSION: No evidence of acute infiltrate or acute congestive heart failure.

3-2A:

SERVICE CODE(S): _____

ICD-9-CM DX CODE(S): _____

ICD-10-CM DX CODE(S): _____

CASE 3-3

Report the global service for this x-ray that was performed at the clinic where Dr. Monson supervised the technician and then interpreted the results and wrote a report of the findings.

3-3A RADIOLOGY REPORT, KNEE

LOCATION: Outpatient, Clinic

PATIENT: Phillip Moris

PHYSICIAN: Leslie Alanda, MD

RADIOLOGIST: Morton Monson, MD

EXAMINATION OF: One view, right knee

CLINICAL SYMPTOMS: Knee pain

SINGLE VIEW, RIGHT KNEE: There appears to be slight narrowing of the medial compartment of the knee joint space. There are minimal degenerative changes of the distal femur and proximal tibia. No fractures or other bony abnormalities are seen.

3-3A:

SERVICE CODE(S): _____

ICD-9-CM DX CODE(S): _____

ICD-10-CM DX CODE(S): _____

CASE 3-4

This patient had a peritoneal dialysis catheter placed for chronic renal failure. Report the professional component of the x-ray that follows.

3-4A KUB

LOCATION: Outpatient, Hospital

PATIENT: Robin Lunn

PHYSICIAN: Ronald Green, MD

RADIOLOGIST: Edward Riddle, MD

EXAMINATION OF: KUB, abdominal view

CLINICAL SYMPTOMS: Complication, peritoneal dialysis catheter

KUB, No prior film. Definite dilated loops of bowel to suggest obstruction are not seen on this examination. The left upper abdomen is not included on the examination. Unusual density overlies the right lower abdomen and upper pelvis. That may be either on or in the patient. The usual appearance of a peritoneal dialysis catheter is not definitely seen on the current examination. There is prominent vascular calcification.

IMPRESSION: This was done to check placement of the patient's peritoneal dialysis catheter. It appears that the placement is not in the correct position, as it cannot be seen.

3-4A:

SERVICE CODE(S): _____

ICD-9-CM DX CODE(S): _____

ICD-10-CM DX CODE(S): _____

CASE 3-5

Report the radiologist's service for the following CT scan.

3-5A CT SCAN, BRAIN

LOCATION: Outpatient, Hospital

PATIENT: Kelly Priest

PHYSICIAN: Ronald Green, MD

RADIOLOGIST: Morton Monson, MD

EXAMINATION OF: Brain CT

CLINICAL SYMPTOMS: Mental status change

COMPUTED TOMOGRAPHIC EXAMINATION OF THE BRAIN was performed as an emergency procedure without contrast material. The patient has a tremor. It was necessary for the technologist to hold the patient's head. There is movement artifact on multiple images.

Atrophic changes and ventricular size agree with the age of the patient. No specific area of abnormal increased or decreased intensity within brain parenchyma. No intracranial hemorrhage or mass. No indication of raised intracranial pressure.

IMPRESSION: Considering the advanced age of the patient, I believe this is an unremarkable CT examination of the brain performed as described above. Movement artifact necessitating manual holding of the patient's head.

3-5A:

SERVICE CODE(S): _____

ICD-9-CM DX CODE(S): _____

ICD-10-CM DX CODE(S): _____

CASE 3-6

Report Dr. Hart's service.

3-6A CT SCAN, SINUSES

LOCATION: Outpatient, Hospital

PATIENT: Mark Fonn

PHYSICIAN: Ronald Green, MD

RADIOLOGIST: Phillip Hart, MD

EXAMINATION OF: CT of sinuses

CLINICAL SYMPTOMS: Seizures, blackouts

COMPUTED TOMOGRAPHIC EXAMINATION OF THE PARANASAL SINUSES was performed utilizing axial and coronal images computed for high resolution bone algorithm. Axial images were also computed for soft tissue algorithm. Axial images were also computed for soft tissue algorithm. The patient had MRI examination earlier today that showed an unusual abnormality of the left hemisphere of the brain. There was also abnormal soft tissue within the right maxillary sinus, thought to most probably represent inflammatory tissue. The present examination is to examine for possible osseous erosion.

The right maxillary sinus is almost filled with abnormal soft tissue density. This extends into the drainage pathway of the sinus. There is deviation of the inferior turbinates laterally, partially effacing the middle meatus. This may contribute to poor drainage of the sinus.

3-6A:

SERVICE CODE(S): _____

ICD-9-CM DX CODE(S): _____

ICD-10-CM DX CODE(S): _____

CASE 3-7

The patient in this case has had previous colon surgery due to colon cancer. Dr. Monson, the clinic physician, provides the professional service for the CT scan that was performed at the hospital outpatient department.

3-7A CT SCAN, ABDOMEN AND PELVIS

LOCATION: Outpatient, Hospital

PATIENT: Steve Hart

PHYSICIAN: Ronald Green, MD

RADIOLOGIST: Morton Monson, MD

EXAMINATION OF: CT scan of abdomen and pelvis

CLINICAL SYMPTOMS: Pelvic abscess, previous colon surgery

CT SCAN OF THE ABDOMEN WITHOUT IV CONTRAST: Axial images obtained with oral contrast only, previously given. Compared to 4/13. Atelectatic changes are noted in both lung bases, more pronounced on the left. Underlying left basilar pneumonia could not be excluded. Small left pleural effusion is seen and stable in size from prior study, if not minimally smaller. Previous laminectomy changes of the lumbar spine are present regarding these organs. Gallbladder is distended, a new finding. No layering sludge or gallstones are appreciated, however. No bile duct dilatation is seen. No free air is present. No ascites is noted, either. Bowel is less distended on the current study than seen on prior exam.

CT SCAN OF THE PELVIS WITHOUT IV CONTRAST: Axial images obtained with oral contrast only. Compared to 4/13. Ostomy site is again noted. Findings of pelvic abscesses are again seen with residual wall thickening around the abscesses noted. These have not significantly changed in size. The smaller, more superficial pocket seen on the left now demonstrates a small amount of air within it. Again noted is presacral soft tissue thickening, which may be inflammatory given the abscesses. Surgical changes are noted here within the pelvis. Tumor cannot be completely excluded.

IMPRESSION:
1. Bibasilar atelectatic changes, more pronounced on the left.
2. Minimal change in left pleural effusion.
3. Gallbladder distention with no radiopaque stones or biliary duct dilation seen.
4. Residual abscess collections noted in the pelvis with minimal change since 4/13.
5. Continued presacral soft tissue thickening. Inflammatory versus tumor.

3-7A:

SERVICE CODE(S): _____

ICD-9-CM DX CODE(S): _____

ICD-10-CM DX CODE(S): _____

CASE 3-8

Report Dr. Monson's service.

3-8A CT SCAN, CHEST, ABDOMEN, AND PELVIS

LOCATION: Outpatient, Hospital

PATIENT: Amy Larson

PHYSICIAN: Gregory Dawson, MD

RADIOLOGIST: Morton Monson, MD

EXAMINATION OF: CT of chest, abdomen, and pelvis

CLINICAL SYMPTOMS: Shortness of breath, nodule of lung, and level one trauma due to motor vehicle collision.

CT OF CHEST, ABDOMEN AND PELVIS: Technique: CT of the chest, abdomen, and pelvis was performed with oral and IV contrast material. No previous CTs for comparison.

FINDINGS: Chest: Small lymph nodes are noted within both axillae, but none are pathologically sized. However, there is lymphadenopathy within the mediastinum with nodes seen within the pretracheal, precarinal, paratracheal, and prevascular regions. The largest node is seen in the right paratracheal region and has a diameter of approximately 1.3 cm in short axis diameter. There are other nodules of approximately 1 cm in size. Bilateral pleural effusions are noted with presumed compressive atelectasis. There is some opacification in the left hilar region with air bronchograms seen within it, which could be due to atelectasis, although other etiology is possible. Aortic atherosclerotic change with mural thrombus is noted. There is some focal opacity seen, especially in the right lung with air bronchograms within it. Again, this is presumed to be due to some atelectasis. Posterolaterally within the left lung base there is also a pleural based opacity, again of uncertain significance. Multiple other right lung pleural based opacities are noted. This could be loculated pleural fluid collection, although other etiology including a nodule is not even excluded in this scenario. The adrenal glands are within limits as to size. The kidneys are small. A lesion within the spleen is not entirely excluded in this setting. Increased mural thrombus is noted within the aorta at the take-off of the celiac and SMA. On the lung window, there is diffuse increase in the density of the lungs, which are seen within lungs, which are fully expanded. Again seen are the numerous bilateral pleural based opacities as described previously. Nodular density seen is consistent with a subcentimeter calcified granuloma.

Abdomen and pelvis: Mild diffuse fatty infiltration of the liver with no focal hepatic or splenic lesions. Right pneumothorax. There are several lower right rib fractures. NG tube with tip in the proximal stomach. Negative adrenal glands, kidneys, gallbladder. Mild diffuse atrophy of the pancreas. Aortoiliac calcification. The abdominal aorta is of normal caliber. Foley catheter is within the bladder. No free air, free fluid or adenopathy within the abdomen or pelvis. No fractures are seen involving the spine or pelvis.

3-8A:

SERVICE CODE(S): _____

ICD-9-CM DX CODE(S): _____

ICD-10-CM DX CODE(S): _____

CASE 3-9

Report Dr. Monson's service.

3-9A CT SCAN, ABDOMEN AND PELVIS

LOCATION: Outpatient, Hospital

PATIENT: Fran Webster

PHYSICIAN: Larry Friendly, MD

RADIOLOGIST: Morton Monson, MD

EXAMINATION OF: CT of abdomen and pelvis

CLINICAL SYMPTOMS: Sepsis

CT OF ABDOMEN AND PELVIS TECHNIQUE: The patient was scanned from the dome of the diaphragm through the symphysis pubis. Oral contrast was administered. No intravenous contrast was administered due to elevated renal function tests.

FINDINGS: No prior CT examination is available for comparison. Lack of intravenous contrast causes significant limitation and evaluation of the solid body organs. The oral contrast was administered, however, the majority of it remains within either the stomach or the proximal portion of the duodenum. The majority of the bowel is not opacified. That causes further limitation. As visualized, the liver, spleen, pancreas and adrenal glands appear grossly unremarkable. There is evidence of calcification involving the gallbladder wall. There is free fluid present within the upper and lower portions of the abdomen and pelvis. Some fluid is seen to surround the gallbladder as well. There is also abnormal stranding present and fluid present within the retroperitoneum. This includes the pararenal and perirenal spaces. That also includes the presacral space. The etiology of all of this fluid is indeterminate. There is apparent irregularity of the kidneys bilaterally, and definitive evaluation is difficult due to the adjacent stranding and fluid. Obvious gross adenopathy is not seen; however, visualization is limited. There are noted to be several tiny gas collections associated with the left colon. These appear to extend outside the colonic wall. This may relate only to diverticula associated with the colon, however, we cannot exclude the possibility of tiny areas of extraluminal gas. Close clinical correlation is suggested. Bilateral pleural effusions are present. There is dense consolidation present within both lung bases which may relate to either atelectasis or infiltrate. Indeterminate pulmonary nodule is seen within the anterior aspect of the right lung base. There is body wall edema present.

IMPRESSION:
1. Prominent amount of fluid is identified within both the abdomen and pelvis. Some of this is felt to be within the peritoneum. There is a prominent amount of fluid seen in the retroperitoneum, as well. This includes stranding and fluid adjacent to both kidneys. Abnormal fluid is also seen in the presacral space. Etiology of all of this fluid is indeterminate. Possibility of infectious etiology cannot be excluded.
2. Calcification of the gallbladder wall. There is pericholecystic fluid. Whether this relates to the gallbladder disease or is merely a part of adjacent fluid cannot be determined.
3. There are several small areas of gas collection adjacent to the left side of the colon. This may relate only to gas in diverticula; however, I cannot exclude the possibility of small amounts of free intraperitoneal air. Close clinical correlation is suggested.

4. Bilateral pleural effusions with bibasilar pulmonary opacities.

5. Indeterminate pulmonary nodule within the right lung base. Follow-up for that finding in 3 months is recommended.

3-9A:

SERVICE CODE(S): _____

ICD-9-CM DX CODE(S): _____

ICD-10-CM DX CODE(S): _____

CASE 3-10

Report Dr. Monson's service.

3-10A CT SCAN, BRAIN

LOCATION: Inpatient, Hospital

PATIENT: Marcus Weber

PHYSICIAN: Timothy Pleasant, MD

RADIOLOGIST: Morton Monson, MD

EXAMINATION OF: CT of the brain

CLINICAL SYMPTOMS: Weakness and memory loss

COMPUTED TOMOGRAPHIC EXAMINATION OF THE BRAIN was performed without contrast material, and there are no previous films for comparison.

FINDINGS: Mild prominence of ventricles and subarachnoid spaces due to mild atrophy. There are multiple mature lacunar type infarctions in the basal ganglia bilaterally. There are areas of diminished density within the frontal lobe white matter bilaterally consistent with small vessel ischemic changes. There is ipsilateral dilation of the left frontal horn due to asymmetric volume loss. There is no acute intracranial hemorrhage. There is no mass effect or midline shift. There is no evidence of recent dominant cortical-based infarction. No posterior fossa mass or hemorrhage. Bony calvaria and the skull are unremarkable.

CONCLUSION:
1. Multiple mature-appearing lacunar infarctions in the basal ganglia bilaterally with small vessel ischemic changes in the frontal lobes and associated volume loss as described.
2. There is no acute hemorrhage or mass effect.

3-10A:

SERVICE CODE(S): _____

ICD-9-CM DX CODE(S): _____

ICD-10-CM DX CODE(S): _____

CASE 3-11

Report Dr. Monson's service.

3-11A ULTRASOUND, ABDOMEN

LOCATION: Outpatient, Hospital

PATIENT: Delores Flats

PHYSICIAN: Larry Friendly, MD

RADIOLOGIST: Morton Monson, MD

EXAMINATION OF: Abdomen ultrasound

CLINICAL SYMPTOMS: Nausea and vomiting; abdominal pain. Rule out cholelithiasis.

ABDOMINAL ULTRASOUND: FINDINGS: The liver is normal in size and echo texture with no focal masses. Large shadowing stone in the gallbladder lumen with gallbladder wall thickening and pericholecystic fluid. No bile duct dilatation. Survey view of the right kidney shows mild to moderate amount of free fluid in the right lower quadrant. The appendix itself is not identified.

3-11A:

SERVICE CODE(S): _____

ICD-9-CM DX CODE(S): _____

ICD-10-CM DX CODE(S): _____

CASE 3-12

Report Dr. Riddle's service.

3-12A ULTRASOUND, GALLBLADDER

LOCATION: Outpatient, Hospital

PATIENT: Adam Kuda

PHYSICIAN: Ronald Green, MD

RADIOLOGIST: Edward Riddle, MD

EXAMINATION OF: Gallbladder ultrasound

CLINICAL SYMPTOMS: Right upper quadrant abdominal pain

GALLBLADDER ULTRASOUND: FINDINGS: This is a limited ultrasound to the right upper quadrant. The gallbladder contains several small echogenic foci in the posterior aspect of the fundus, which do not appear to move but which do produce a small amount of shadowing. No gallbladder wall thickening, pericholecystic fluid, intra- or extrahepatic ductal dilation is identified with the common bile duct measuring 3 mm. Gallbladder is distended at 9 cm.

IMPRESSION:
1. Distended gallbladder.
2. Small echogenic nonmobile foci in the fundus of the gallbladder. Differential considerations include adherent stones, polyps, or thrombus.

3-12A:

SERVICE CODE(S): _____

ICD-9-CM DX CODE(S): _____

ICD-10-CM DX CODE(S): _____

CASE 3-13

Report Dr. Monson's service.

3-13A ULTRASOUND, RENAL

LOCATION: Outpatient, Hospital

PATIENT: Derrick Smith

PHYSICIAN: Ronald Green, MD

RADIOLOGIST: Morton Monson, MD

EXAMINATION OF: Renal ultrasound

CLINICAL SYMPTOMS: Anuria

RENAL ULTRASOUND: The right kidney measures 12.9 × 6.4 × 5.3 cm. The left measures 11.8 × 5.0 × 6.5 cm. There is no evidence for hydronephrosis within either of the kidneys. Focal density is seen within the midportion of the right kidney, which may relate only to a prominent column of Bertin; however, those do appear slightly different from the adjacent parenchyma and cannot exclude the possibility of mass in this area. Correlation with renal CT is recommended. There is a large cyst associated with the lower pole of the right kidney measuring 8.1 × 8.0 × 5.2 cm. Within the left kidney, there are two echogenic shadowing foci. One is within the upper pole measuring 4 mm and, in the lower pole, the second is seen measuring 3 mm to 4 mm. Both of these are compatible with small left renal calculi. Urinary bladder demonstrates an unremarkable sonographic appearance well distended. It demonstrates an approximately 66 cc post-void residual.

IMPRESSION:
1. Density noted within the midportion of the right kidney, which may relate only to a prominent column of Bertin; however, the possibility of underlying mass cannot be excluded. Renal CT is recommended.
2. Large lower pole cyst involving the right kidney.
3. At least two left renal calculi are identified.
4. Post-void residual, as given.

3-13A:

SERVICE CODE(S): _____

ICD-9-CM DX CODE(S): _____

ICD-10-CM DX CODE(S): _____

CASE 3-14

Note the thoracentesis procedure report is not included in this case. Report only Dr. Monson's professional service. For the facility, report the facility portion of the ultrasound.

3-14A ULTRASOUND, LEFT LOWER HEMITHORAX—MARKING

LOCATION: Outpatient, Hospital

PATIENT: Samuel Lloyd

PHYSICIAN: Gregory Dawson, MD

RADIOLOGIST: Morton Monson, MD

ULTRASOUND OF THE LEFT LOWER HEMITHORAX:

HISTORY: Left pleural effusion marking the thoracentesis. Ultrasound guidance provided to Dr. Dawson. See his report for thoracentesis procedure.

FINDINGS: Limited ultrasound of the left lower hemithorax to mark for thoracentesis left-sided pleural effusion, which measures approximately 3.9 cm to the middle of the pocket of pleural fluid.

3-14A:

SERVICE CODE(S): _____

ICD-9-CM DX CODE(S): _____

ICD-10-CM DX CODE(S): _____

CASE 3-15

Assign the code for Dr. Monson's professional component of a ventilation-perfusion scan of the lungs.

3-15A VENTILATION-PERFUSION LUNG SCAN

LOCATION: Outpatient, Hospital

PATIENT: Ella Gerald

PHYSICIAN: Ronald Green, MD

RADIOLOGIST: Morton Monson, MD

EXAMINATION OF: Ventilation-perfusion scan of lungs

CLINICAL SYMPTOMS: Chest pain, arm weakness

VENTILATION-PERFUSION SCAN OF LUNGS: DOSE: The patient received 2.0 millicuries of technetium-99m DTPA via aerosol and 6.0 millicuries of technetium-99m MAA IV.

FINDINGS: There appears to be an area of ventilation-perfusion mismatch in the region of the lingula. That demonstrates decreased perfusion and better ventilation. There is matched decreased ventilation and perfusion to the apices. There is some inhomogeneity regarding the left lung base with matched areas involving the left lung base. On chest radiograph, there is some mild patchy opacity along the left heart border. Findings are intermediate to indeterminate for pulmonary embolism. Obvious additional segmental ventilation-perfusion mismatches are not seen.

IMPRESSION:
1. There again appears to be ventilation-perfusion mismatch seen anteriorly in the region of the lingual with better ventilation in this area compared with perfusion. There is some mild hazy opacity in this area on chest x-ray. Findings are intermediate to indeterminate for pulmonary embolus. Similar finding noted previously.
2. No definite additional segmental ventilation-perfusion mismatches are seen. There are matched areas, left lung base and apical regions bilaterally.

3-15A:

SERVICE CODE(S): _____

ICD-9-CM DX CODE(S): _____

ICD-10-CM DX CODE(S): _____

CHAPTER 4

Pathology and Laboratory

CASE 4-1

4-1A THERAPEUTIC DRUG ASSAYS

Code the following drug assays that can be located in the Therapeutic Drug Assays subsection of the CPT manual (80150-80299):

Make sure to check
evolve
learning system
**for the latest
content updates**

CPT Code	Drug	Used to Treat
1 _____	Doxepin	Depressive disorders, anxiety
2 _____	Amikacin	Serious infection, meningitis
3 _____	Primidone	Seizures
4 _____	Lidocaine	Anti-arrhythmia resulting from MI
5 _____	Gold	Malaria (an anti-infective)
6 _____	Salicylate	Inflammation, pain (aspirin)
7 _____	Valproic acid	Seizures, migraines
8 _____	Gentamicin	Conjunctivitis, corneal ulcers

CASE 4-2

Fill in the hemogram code of each of the counts indicated on the Hematology section of the form as follows:

I _____	Bleeding time
2 _____	Prothrombin time
3 _____	Clotting factor (XI)
4 _____	Thrombin time; titer
5 _____	Hematocrit
6 _____	Hemoglobin, fetal differential lysis
7 _____	Platelet count, auto
8 _____	Reticulocyte count, manual
9 _____	Sedimentation rate, nonautomated
10 _____	WBC, manual differential
I I _____	CBC, with auto diff Hgb, Hct, RBC, WBC, Platelet
12 _____	Bone marrow, smear interpretation

The following laboratory tests were conducted on February 1. Assign CPT codes to the tests:

Laboratory Test	02/01	Rate	Normal
13 Coombs' test*			
Direct _____	N		Negative
14 Coombs' test*			
Indirect, qual _____	P	P	Negative
15 Hematocrit			
Male _____	31	L	40-54 ml/dl
16 Hematocrit			
Newborn _____	55	H	49-54 ml/dl
17 Hemoglobin			
Female_____	15.0	WNL	12.0-16.0 g/dl
18 Hemoglobin, fetal _____			
chemical _____ qual	2	H	<1.0% of total
19 Hemoglobin A2 quan _____			
(electrophoresis)	3	WNL	1.5-3.0% of T
20 Hemoglobin, plasma _____	5.0	WNL	0-5.0 mg/dl
21 Methemoglobin _____ qual			
_____ quan	90	WNL	30-130 mg/dl

22 Sedimentation rate (ESR)
   Wintrobe, Male non-automated _____
   automated _____   6   H   0-5 mm/hr

23 Alkaline phosphatase, leukocyte _____   66   WNL   14-100

24 Leukocytes, differential cell count,
   manual _____

   Myelocytes   4   H   0%
   Band neutrophils   3   WNL   3%-5%
   Segmented neutrophils   62   WNL   54%-62%
   Lymphocytes   27   WNL   23%-33%
   Monocytes   4   WNL   3%-7%
   Eosinophils   6   N   1%-3%
   Basophils   3   WNL   0%-1%

25 Platelets/automated _____   250,000   WNL   150,000-
                                                              350,000/mm^3

26 Reticulocytes/manual _____   36,000   WNL   25,000-75,000/
                                                              mm^3 (0.5%-15%
                                                              of erythrocytes)

CASE 4-3

4-3A IMMUNOHEMATOLOGY

Enter the CPT codes for the following immunohematology tests:

1 _____   Cold agglutinin; titer
2 _____   Growth hormone, human, antibody
3 _____   Tuberculosis, intradermal
4 _____   Syphilis test; quantitative

CASE 4-4

4-4A BODY FLUID

Enter the CPT codes for the following body fluid tests:

1 _____ Protein, serum, total

2 _____ Glucose

3 _____ Semen Analysis, Complete

4 _____ Cell Count w/Diff

CASE 4-5

4-5A TRANSFUSION MEDICINE

1. Delores, a laboratory technician, performs splitting of blood products, 1 unit.

SERVICE CODE(S) _____

2. Jessica, a laboratory technician, performs screening of RBC antibodies, serum technique.

SERVICE CODE(S) _____

CASE 4-6

4-6A ANATOMIC PATHOLOGY

1. Forensic examination is performed on a white female, approximate age 25, who sustained multiple gunshot wounds.

SERVICE CODE(S) _____

2. An autopsy is performed on a 53-year-old male who appears to have died from liver disease. Gross and microscopic to liver only.

SERVICE CODE(S) _____

CASE 4-7

4-7A CYTOPATHOLOGY AND CYTOGENIC STUDIES

1. A laboratory technician performs screening by automated system of a cervical smear, under physician supervision.

SERVICE CODE(S) _____

2. An amniotic fluid sample is received in the laboratory for a suspected non-neoplastic disorder. A tissue culture chromosome analysis was performed.

SERVICE CODE(S) _____

CASE 4-8

4-8A OTHER PROCEDURES

1. Dr. Friendly performs a gastric intubation and aspiration, single specimen, diagnostic for chemical analysis.

SERVICE CODE(S) _____

2. Dr. Friendly performs a gastric intubation and aspiration that includes gastric stimulations lasting 2 hours.

SERVICE CODE(S): _____

CHAPTER 5

Integumentary System

CASE 5-1

Make sure to check
evolve
learning system
**for the latest
content updates**

5-1A OPERATIVE REPORT, DEBRIDEMENT

LOCATION: Inpatient, Hospital

PATIENT: Arnie Holmes

PREOPERATIVE DIAGNOSIS: Right heel ulcer

POSTOPERATIVE DIAGNOSIS: Right heel ulcer with *Staphylococcus aureus* infection

SURGEON: Gary Sanchez, MD

PROCEDURE PERFORMED: Debridement of right heel ulcer down to the bone

INDICATIONS FOR THIS PROCEDURE: Mr. Holmes is a 58-year-old male who has a large heel ulcer, measuring at least 7 cm × 3.5 cm in a curvilinear ovoid shape. This needs to be sharply debrided. There is a lot of necrotic tissue here. We need to see how deep this goes. We also need to obtain cultures. We need to determine for sure if he also has osteo. If he does have other ongoing infection (this is reportable), this will require antibiotic therapy. Cultures will be obtained of the deep tissues as well as the bone. The procedure and the risks were all discussed with the patient and his wife preoperatively. They understand, and their questions were answered. I also met with them in the preop holding room, and they had no new questions.

PROCEDURE: The more proximal aspect of this wound on the plantar aspect of the heel went deep basically down to the bone. This was all sharply debrided back. We cleared some of the tissue overlying the bones there. The tissues were basically all necrotic down to there. We sent this off as a specimen. The remainder of the heel ulcer was not as deep. We sharply debrided the eschar off of it. We sharply debrided all of the edges of the wound. The tissues appeared to be viable there. I am somewhat concerned about how much deeper tissue of the foot and surrounding areas are necrotic. We appear to have some area of viability there. Hemostasis was achieved. We washed it out with a liter of antibiotic solution of Bacitracin and Kanamycin using an Ortholav system. The wound was packed open with wet-to-dry dressings. The patient tolerated the procedure well.

Pathology Report Later Indicated: *Staphylococcus aureus*

5-1A:

SERVICE CODE(S): _____

ICD-9-CM DX CODE(S): _____

ICD-10-CM DX CODE(S): _____

CASE 5-2

5-2A OPERATIVE REPORT, LESIONS

LOCATION: Outpatient, Clinic

PATIENT: James Lee

SURGEON: Gary Sanchez, MD

PREOPERATIVE DIAGNOSIS: Mole, back

POSTOPERATIVE DIAGNOSIS: Benign lesion, back

SUBJECTIVE: James is here today for a mole on his back that has been growing quite fast over the past several months. He has had it for quite a while.

OBJECTIVE: On examination today, this is a well-appearing 48-year-old male who is in no distress. His blood pressure is 140/84. His weight is 185. Focal examination of the mole measuring 1 cm on his back reveals a raised, fleshy nevus connected with a stalk. It is nonpigmented.

ASSESSMENT: Nevus on back, likely benign.

PLAN: I gave the patient reassurance. I numbed his back using sterile technique and 1% Lidocaine. The lesion was snipped off with sterile scissors. The base was cauterized, and the lesion was sent to pathology for review. The patient tolerated the procedure well. Again, he was given reassurance, as I do not think this was any type of malignancy.

Pathology Report Later Indicated: See Report 5-2B

5-2A:

SERVICE CODE(S): _____

ICD-9-CM DX CODE(S): _____

ICD-10-CM DX CODE(S): _____

5-2B PATHOLOGY REPORT

LOCATION: Outpatient, Clinic

PATIENT: James Lee

SURGEON: Gary Sanchez, MD

PATHOLOGIST: Grey Lonewolf, MD

CLINICAL HISTORY: 1 cm mole, back

SPECIMEN RECEIVED: Mole removed from back

GROSS DESCRIPTION: The specimen is labeled with the patient's name and "specimen taken from back" and consists of a 1 cm diameter ovoid polypoid piece of skin.

MICROSCOPIC DESCRIPTION: Section shows polypoid skin with hyperkeratosis. The dermis shows expansion with fat cells.

DIAGNOSIS: Mole, back, excision: Soft fibroma, benign.

5-2B:

SERVICE CODE(S): _____

ICD-9-CM DX CODE(S): _____

ICD-10-CM DX CODE(S): _____

CASE 5-3

5-3A OPERATIVE REPORT, LIPOMA

LOCATION: Outpatient, Hospital

PATIENT: Patty Olson

SURGEON: Gary Sanchez, MD

PREOPERATIVE DIAGNOSIS: 10 cm lipoma, right flank

POSTOPERATIVE DIAGNOSIS: 10 cm lipoma, right flank

PROCEDURE PERFORMED: Excision of 10 cm right flank lipoma

INDICATIONS: Patty Olson is a very pleasant, 37-year-old female who presented with a large lipoma of her right flank. She wants to have this resected. The patient understands the surgery and the risks of bleeding, infection, and postoperative fluid collections, and she wished to proceed.

PROCEDURE: The patient was brought to the operating room, given IV sedation, and then prepped and draped with Betadine solution. The area was then anesthetized with a total of 40 cc of 0.5% Sensorcaine with epinephrine solution. A skin incision was made with a #15 blade, and the lipoma was resected sharply. Bleeding was controlled with the electrocautery, the skin was closed with subcuticular 4-0 undyed Vicryl. Steri-Strips and a sterile bandage were applied. The patient tolerated the procedure well and was discharged home.

Pathology Report Later Indicated: Benign lipoma

5-3A:

SERVICE CODE(S): _____

ICD-9-CM DX CODE(S): _____

ICD-10-CM DX CODE(S): _____

CASE 5-4

5-4A OPERATIVE REPORT, EPITHELIOMA

LOCATION: Outpatient, Hospital

PATIENT: Julie Harwood

SURGEON: Gary Sanchez, MD

PREOPERATIVE DIAGNOSIS: Cyst, forehead

POSTOPERATIVE DIAGNOSIS: Calcifying epithelioma of Malherbe, forehead, middle aspect

SURGICAL FINDINGS: A 0.9-cm-diameter nonruptured calcifying epithelioma of Malherbe

SURGICAL PROCEDURE: Excision of calcifying epithelioma of Malherbe

ANESTHESIA: General endotracheal anesthesia plus 1 cc of 1% Xylocaine with 1:100,000 epinephrine

DESCRIPTION OF PROCEDURE: The patient's forehead was prepped with Betadine scrub and solution and draped in a routine sterile fashion. I injected 1 cc of 1% Xylocaine with 1:100,000 epinephrine around it and waited 5 minutes. I made an incision in the forehead and entered the capsule of the epithelioma. I was then able to dissect the capsule out completely along with the contents of the sac. There were no contents of the sac or sac left with the wound. I closed the wound with suture of 5-0 Prolene. Surgicel and an antibiotic ointment were applied. The patient tolerated the procedure well and left the operating room in good condition.

Pathology Report Later Indicated: Benign epithelioma of Malherbe, forehead, middle

5-4A:

SERVICE CODE(S) _____

ICD-9-CM DX CODE(S): _____

ICD-10-CM DX CODE(S): _____

CASE 5-5

5-5A OPERATIVE REPORT, WIDE EXCISION, MELANOMA

LOCATION: Outpatient, Hospital

PATIENT: Roger Adams

SURGEON: Gary Sanchez, MD

PREOPERATIVE DIAGNOSIS: Malignant melanoma, mid-chest (1 cm)

POSTOPERATIVE DIAGNOSIS: Malignant melanoma, mid-chest (1 cm)

PROCEDURE PERFORMED: Wide excision of malignant melanoma, mid-chest

PROCEDURE: The mid-chest was prepped, draped, and cleaned with Betadine solution. A margin of 2 cm laterally and medially around the lesion site was taken. The incision was carried down to the muscle fascia, which was included in the specimen. Bleeding was controlled by electrocautery, and we closed the defect with a running subcuticular 4-0 undyed Vicryl using layered closure. Steri-Strips and a sterile bandage were applied. The patient tolerated the procedure well.

Pathology Report Later Indicated: Malignant melanoma

5-5A:

SERVICE CODE(S): _____

ICD-9-CM DX CODE(S): _____

ICD-10-CM DX CODE(S): _____

CASE 5-6

5-6A OPERATIVE REPORT, WIDE EXCISION, MALIGNANT MELANOMA

LOCATION: Outpatient, Hospital

PATIENT: Jane Love

SURGEON: Gary Sanchez, MD

PREOPERATIVE DIAGNOSIS: Large lipoma of the lower back

POSTOPERATIVE DIAGNOSIS: Malignant melanoma, lower back

PROCEDURE PERFORMED: Excision of large mass of the lower back, which measured 9 cm × 12 cm

ANESTHESIA: General anesthesia

INDICATION: The patient has a mass in the lower back. This is becoming quite bothersome to her. We discussed treatment options of observation versus surgical excision. She wishes to have this excised. We discussed the procedure as well as the risk involved. She understands and wishes to proceed.

PROCEDURE: The patient was brought to the operating room and placed in the supine position on the operating table. After receiving general anesthetic, she was placed in a prone position. She was prepped and draped in sterile fashion. The area of the mass was identified and marked out. This was an ovoid lesion measuring 9 × 12 cm. This was basically between the iliac crest and lower abdomen. An incision line down the central aspect of this in a transverse fashion was infiltrated with 0.5% Marcaine. After waiting a couple of minutes, an incision was made. Dissection was carried down into the subcutaneous tissues. We then sharply circumferentially dissected out a large lipomatous mass. This was quite large. This was sent to pathology and came back as malignant melanoma. To minimize scarring, we did not go all the way to the end with our skin incision; however, we were able to retract this up and dissect out the lipomatous mass from under it. This was taken out all the way down to the fascia. This was then removed in total. There did not appear to be any masses there. Hemostasis was achieved. This left a 12.5 cm open wound and the subcutaneous tissues were closed with layered sutures of 3-0 Vicryl. The skin was closed with 4-0 Vicryl in running subcuticular fashion. Steri-Strips and sterile dressings, multiple Fluffs and ABDs, and then an Ace wrap were applied. The Ace wrap went around a few times across the lower abdomen and pelvic region as well as across the iliac structures to help provide pressure to the area and to decrease the chance of developing seromas or hematomas. The patient tolerated the procedure well and went to the recovery room in stable condition.

I met with the patient's mother postoperatively and discussed the diagnosis. Discharge instructions were discussed with the patient and her mother. I discussed a referral to oncology for further treatment. Their questions were answered.

Pathology Report Later Indicated: Malignant melanoma

5-6A:

SERVICE CODE(S): _____

ICD-9-CM DX CODE(S): _____

ICD-10-CM DX CODE(S): _____

CASE 5-7

While riding a four-wheeler, Brad Nelson fell off and hit his face on the ground. He sustained a laceration to the eyebrow area.

5-7A OPERATIVE REPORT, LACERATION

LOCATION: Outpatient, Hospital Emergency Department

PATIENT: Brad Nelson

SURGEON: Paul Sutton, MD

PREOPERATIVE DIAGNOSIS: Complex eyebrow laceration, 2.8 cm.

POSTOPERATIVE DIAGNOSIS: Complex eyebrow laceration, 2.8 cm.

PROCEDURE PERFORMED: Cleaning and suturing of laceration.

ANESTHESIA: 1% Lidocaine with epinephrine.

INDICATIONS FOR PROCEDURE: The patient is a 12-year-old male who fell off a four-wheeler while driving it. The patient sustained a complex eyebrow laceration, and he is now undergoing repair.

PROCEDURE: The area was anesthetized with 1% Lidocaine with epinephrine. We then irrigated the area thoroughly. The wound was then scrubbed with Betadine. The entire skin area was prepped with the same Betadine solution. Sterile dressings were placed around the wound. The wound was then closed in 2 layers, the first layer with interrupted 4-0 Vicryl suture. The skin was then closed with 5-0 interrupted nylon suture in the area of the eyebrow. The rest of the incision in both directions was closed with interrupted 6-0 nylon suture. This was a complex laceration. The wound was then covered with Bacitracin. The patient was then discharged home with a prescription for Keflex. He has had a recent tetanus shot, so this will not be necessary. He is instructed to follow up in 1 week to have the sutures removed.

5-7A:

SERVICE CODE(S): _____

ICD-9-CM DX CODE(S): _____

ICD-10-CM DX CODE(S): _____

CASE 5-8

5-8A OPERATIVE REPORT, EXCISION HISTIOCYTIC TUMOR

LOCATION: Outpatient, Hospital

PATIENT: Jill Dorgen

SURGEON: Gary Sanchez, MD

PREOPERATIVE DIAGNOSIS: Histiocytic tumor of the left shoulder

POSTOPERATIVE DIAGNOSIS: Same

PROCEDURES PERFORMED: Excision of plexiform fibrous histiocytic tumor (4.1 cm) of the left shoulder and evacuation of hematoma.

ANESTHESIA: General endotracheal with approximately 20 cc of tumescent solution prepared by adding to 1 L of Ringer's lactate, 25 cc 2% Xylocaine, 1 cc of 1:100,000 epinephrine, and 3 cc of 8.4 sodium bicarbonate.

ESTIMATED BLOOD LOSS: Negligible

SURGICAL FINDINGS: There was a 40-cc hematoma beginning to organize in the area of the left shoulder in the subcutaneous space.

DESCRIPTION OF PROCEDURE: The patient was intubated. The area of the left shoulder was prepped with Betadine scrub and solution and draped in a routine sterile fashion. An incision was made 2 cm and carried down to the fascia of the muscle where a hematoma was entered. The skin portion of the lesion was removed, and the fascia and a portion of the muscle were removed secondarily. The lesion measured 2.5 cm at the widest point. Bleeding was electrocoagulated, and a no. 7 Jackson-Pratt drain was inserted in the depth of the wound. The wound was closed with interrupted 0 Monocryl for the deep fascia layer and subcuticular 4-0 Monocryl using a few vertical mattress sutures of 3-0 Monocryl. Steri-Strips and Kerlix fluffs plus Elastoplast were applied. The patient tolerated the procedure well and left the operating room in good condition.

Pathology Report Later Indicated: Benign lesion

5-8A:

SERVICE CODE(S): _____

ICD-9-CM DX CODE(S): _____

ICD-10-CM DX CODE(S): _____

CASE 5-9

5-9A OPERATIVE REPORT, SCAR REVISION, DERMABRASION

LOCATION: Outpatient, Hospital

PATIENT: Trudy Brown

SURGEON: Gary Sanchez, MD

PREOPERATIVE DIAGNOSIS: Widened keloid scar of the neck

POSTOPERATIVE DIAGNOSIS: Same

PROCEDURES PERFORMED:
1. Dermabrasion
2. Scar revision

ANESTHESIA: General endotracheal with approximately 7 cc of 1% Xylocaine and 1:100,000 epinephrine

ESTIMATED BLOOD LOSS: Less than 25 cc

COMPLICATIONS: None

SPONGE AND NEEDLE COUNT: Correct

INDICATION: This patient has a widened scar with large suture marks as a result of resection of a dermatofibrosarcoma protuberans about 1 year ago.

SURGICAL FINDINGS: A 20-cm-long unsightly scar of the neck with suture marks and widening of the scar.

DESCRIPTION OF PROCEDURE: The patient's neck was prepped with Betadine scrub and solution and draped in a routine sterile fashion. The scar was injected with 7 cc of 1% Xylocaine and 1:100,000 epinephrine and dermabraded. It was excised to include parts of the suture marks. This was excised down to fat, but some residual scarring remained. This was left in to help provide support and blood supply. I closed the wound with subcuticular 3-0 Monocryl and interrupted twists of 5-0 Prolene. The dressing consisted of thymol iodide powder and 4 × 4s. The patient tolerated the procedure well and left the area in good condition.

Pathology Report Later Indicated: Benign keloid tissue

5-9A:

SERVICE CODE(S) _____

ICD-9-CM DX CODE(S): _____

ICD-10-CM DX CODE(S): _____

CASE 5-10

5-10A OPERATIVE REPORT, SCAR REVISION

LOCATION: Outpatient, Hospital

PATIENT: Kerry Grant

SURGEON: Gary Sanchez, MD

PREOPERATIVE DIAGNOSIS: Scar of the left cheek and foreign body granuloma of the left cheek.

POSTOPERATIVE DIAGNOSIS: Scar of the left cheek and foreign body granuloma of the left cheek.

SURGICAL FINDINGS: There is about a 2-cm transverse scar located on the left upper cheek, and beneath this there was extensive foreign body reaction extending beneath the muscle. There was extensive involvement of the subcutaneous tissue and the tissue extending all the way down to the cheekbone.

PROCEDURES PERFORMED:
1. A 2 cm complex scar revision, left cheek
2. Excision of extensive (2.5 cm) foreign body granuloma of the cheek involving the muscle.

ANESTHESIA: General endotracheal with approximately 2 cc of 1% Xylocaine with 1:100,000 epinephrine.

ESTIMATED BLOOD LOSS: Negligible

COMPLICATIONS: None

SPONGE AND NEEDLE COUNT: Correct

DESCRIPTION OF PROCEDURE: The patient's face was prepped with Betadine scrub and solution and draped in a routine sterile fashion. The scar was dermabraded, and then excised. In the subcutaneous tissue, I came down on a foreign body granulomatous reaction that contained what appeared to be a mixture in the previous foreign body. I excised this on top of the musculature. It appeared that this had been injected underneath the muscles. This chronic inflammatory and granulomatous process was involved over about 2.5 × 2.5-cm area of the cheek. After removal of this, considerable dead space remained, and I cauterized the bleeding. I reapproximated the muscle with 5-0 Monocryl, put subcuticular 5-0 Monocryl to close the dead space partially, but needed to use horizontal mattress sutures of 6-0 Prolene to complete closure of the dead space in the subcutaneous area. I then better apposed the skin edges with interrupted 7-0 Prolene using a combination of twists and plain sutures. I applied surgical and antibiotic ointment. A portion of the specimen was submitted for frozen section and showed foreign body granulomatous reaction, which in fact had multiple sites of what appeared to be the previous injected glue surrounded by an intense foreign-body reaction. The patient tolerated the procedure well and left the operating room in good condition.

Pathology Report Later Indicated: Benign granuloma

5-10A:

SERVICE CODE(S): _____

ICD-9-CM DX CODE(S): _____

ICD-10-CM DX CODE(S): _____

CASE 5-11

5-11A OPERATIVE REPORT, WIDE EXCISION, BASAL CELL CARCINOMA

LOCATION: Outpatient, Hospital

PATIENT: Karen Rhodes

SURGEON: Gary Sanchez, MD

PREOPERATIVE DIAGNOSIS: Left leg lateral lesion

POSTOPERATIVE DIAGNOSIS: Basal cell carcinoma, left calf

SURGICAL FINDINGS: A 1×1 cm lesion, morphologically resembling a basal cell carcinoma

PROCEDURE PERFORMED: Excision of the left leg basal cell carcinoma

ANESTHESIA: General endotracheal; 30 mL of Marcaine was infiltrated into the wound prior to making the incision.

DESCRIPTION OF PROCEDURE: The patient was brought to the operating room, and the left leg was dressed. An elliptical incision taking a 0.5 cm margin was made around the previous basal cell carcinoma, and dissection was carried down to subcutaneous tissue. After this, hemostasis was obtained with electrocautery and the wound was closed with mattress sutures of 4-0 nylon. This was sterilely dressed. The patient tolerated the procedure well and was returned to the recovery room in good condition. Sponge and needle counts were correct.

Pathology Report Later Indicated: See Report 5-11B

5-11A:

SERVICE CODE(S): _____

ICD-9-CM DX CODE(S): _____

ICD-10-CM DX CODE(S): _____

5-11B PATHOLOGY REPORT

LOCATION: Outpatient, Hospital

PATIENT: Karen Rhodes

SURGEON: Gary Sanchez, MD

PATHOLOGIST: Grey Lonewolf, MD

CLINICAL HISTORY: Left leg lateral lesion

SPECIMENT RECEIVED: Lesion, left leg

GROSS DESCRIPTION: The specimen is labeled with the patient's name and "left leg lesion," which consists of a tan-white ellipse of skin and subcutaneous tissue, $1.5 \times 1 \times 0.8$ cm. The specimen was bisected and processed in toto in 1 cassette labeled A.

MICROSCOPIC DESCRIPTION: Sections of skin showing basal cell carcinoma.

DIAGNOSIS: Left calf lesion, excision: Skin showing basal cell carcinoma.

5-11B:

SERVICE CODE(S): _____

ICD-9-CM DX CODE(S): _____

ICD-10-CM DX CODE(S): _____

CASE 5-12

The procedure that Dr. Sanchez is performing involves deeper tissue than what is reported with the free skin graft codes. In this case, the repair involves the muscle and skin. Both procedures are reported separately.

5-12A OPERATIVE REPORT, MUSCLE FLAP

LOCATION: Inpatient, Hospital

PATIENT: Jane Miller

SURGEON: Gary Sanchez, MD

PREOPERATIVE DIAGNOSIS: Right lower extremity open wound

POSTOPERATIVE DIAGNOSIS: Open wound, right lower extremity, with exposed tibia and exposed plate

PROCEDURES PERFORMED: 1. Soleus muscle flap. 2. Split-thickness skin graft 3.0 × 3.0 cm from the right thigh to the right lower extremity.

ANESTHESIA: General endotracheal

ESTIMATED BLOOD LOSS: 60 cc

DRAINS: 1 no. 1 Jackson-Pratt

SURGICAL FINDINGS: There was an open wound extending from the lower third of the tibia up into the middle third of the right leg with an exposed plate, but tissue loss of the lower third of the right leg was evident.

PROCEDURE: An incision was made 3.0 cm medial to the tibial border. I developed a bilobed flap and identified the separation of the soleus muscle and the gastrocnemius medial head following incision of the deep fascia. The soleus muscle was freed distally as far as possible and then cut distally at the Achilles tendon insertion. The bilobed flap was formed covering the area of soft-tissue loss by using bolsters that were tied in place with 0 Prolene. With the open area covered, I then closed the remainder of the area, closing the donor area also with 0 Prolene. I put Nitro paste along the edges where there was some skin blanching and put a no. 1 Jackson-Pratt drain in the distal end of the wound, bringing it out through a separate stab wound incision. A spit-thickness skin graft about 3.0 × 3.0 cm was taken from the right thigh, meshed with a mesher, and applied to the defect with 2-0 Prolene, sutures, and staples. We dressed the wound with Xeroform, Kerlix fluffs, Kerlix roll, Kling, and a Sof-Rol, and then the orthopedic technician applied a cast. The donor site was dressed with scarlet red and an ABD pad. The patient tolerated the procedure well and left the area in good condition.

5-12A:

SERVICE CODE(S): _____

ICD-9-CM DX CODE(S): _____

ICD-10-CM DX CODE(S): _____

CASE 5-13

5-13A OPERATIVE REPORT, ABDOMINOPLASTY

LOCATION: Inpatient, Hospital

PATIENT: Cindy Kohl

SURGEON: Gary Sanchez, MD

PREOPERATIVE DIAGNOSIS: Abdominal deformity secondary to weight loss (redundant [key term for locating the diagnosis code] abdominal skin, upper and lower abdomen)

POSTOPERATIVE DIAGNOSIS: Abdominal deformity secondary to weight loss (redundant [key term for locating the diagnosis code] abdominal skin, upper and lower abdomen)

PROCEDURE PERFORMED: Circumferential abdominoplasty with removal of 2,395 grams posteriorly and 1,365 grams anteriorly.

ANESTHESIA: General endotracheal

ESTIMATED BLOOD LOSS: 250 cc

FLUIDS: 5 liters of Ringer's lactate

URINARY OUTPUT: 1400 cc

SPONGE AND NEEDLE COUNTS: Correct.

PROCEDURE: The patient was intubated and placed in the supine position. The abdomen was prepped with Betadine scrub and solution and draped in routine sterile fashion, and the lower incision was continued anteriorly onto the abdomen outlining an ellipse that extended to about the level of the umbilicus, which we made an incision around and dissected down to the abdominal wall. I undermined completely the area up to the umbilicus, but, above the umbilicus, I tried to restrict undermining only to the lateral extent of the rectus abdominis muscle. After limited undermining, I noted that there was a small hernia in the fascia superiorly. I dealt with this by imbrication of the rectus sheath with interrupted 2-0 Ethibond sutures. This was carried from about the xiphoid down to the umbilicus and then below from the umbilicus to the symphysis pubis. Undermining was then carried out to allow the skin to be pulled down, and I raised the mons pubis by about 4 cm, suturing it to the center of the previous umbilical site. I then closed the right side quite easily with deep sutures of 3-0 Monocryl, but on the left side there was some difficulty in closing the deep wound. I used deep 2-0 Ethibond sutures and interrupted 3-0 Monocryl subcuticularly for the dermal closure. The skin was closed with running 4-0 Prolene anteriorly. Prior to the skin closure, I had sutured a nonlatex catheter to the umbilicus and, prior to the completion of closure, inserted four #10 flat Jackson-Pratt drains, bringing them out through separate stab wound incisions. After the closure, I made an incision in the old scar that was on the abdomen and identified the umbilicus, which I sutured to the skin using subdermal 3-0 Monocryl and interrupted 3-0 and 4-0 Prolene for the skin at the level of the iliac crest. The patient tolerated the procedure well and left the operating room in good condition. Estimated blood loss was 250 cc. There were no other complications.

Code only the abdominoplasty.

5-13A:

SERVICE CODE(S): _____

ICD-9-CM DX CODE(S): _____

ICD-10-CM DX CODE(S): _____

CASE 5-14

5-14A OPERATIVE REPORT, DEBRIDEMENT

LOCATION: Inpatient, Hospital

PATIENT: Lori Nielsen

SURGEON: Gary Sanchez, MD

PREOPERATIVE DIAGNOSIS: Right foot, nonhealing ulcer

POSTOPERATIVE DIAGNOSIS: Right foot, nonhealing ulcer

PROCEDURE PERFORMED: Incision and debridement of the right nonhealing ulcer

INDICATIONS: Mrs. Nielsen is a 45-year-old female who is post kidney transplant and now has a nonhealing ulcer of her right foot. She has been followed in the Wound Clinic for this. She now has increasing cellulitis, erythema, and a pustule on the top of her foot. She was brought to the Operating Room for cultures and debridement of her foot.

PROCEDURE: The patient was given sedation and prepped and draped with Betadine solution with the right foot being prepped and draped free. Skin and subcutaneous tissue were debrided sharply and then I opened the area over the top of the foot and debrided skin and subcutaneous tissues sharply down to bleeding viable tissue. I irrigated the wound with saline. I packed it with saline-soaked gauze. Kerlix and Ace wrap were applied. The patient tolerated the procedure well and was taken back to the floor in stable condition.

5-14A:

SERVICE CODE(S): _____

ICD-9-CM DX CODE(S): _____

ICD-10-CM DX CODE(S): _____

CASE 5-15

5-15A OPERATIVE REPORT, BREAST MASS

LOCATION: Outpatient, Hospital

PATIENT: Elizabeth Jones

SURGEON: Gary Sanchez, MD

PREOPERATIVE DIAGNOSIS: Right breast mass

POSTOPERATIVE DIAGNOSIS: Infiltrating ductal carcinoma, right breast

PROCEDURE PERFORMED: Excisional biopsy, right breast mass

HISTORY: This patient has a very highly suspicious mass of her right breast. Tru-Cut biopsies were negative. I chose not to believe this. It was elected to do an open excisional biopsy.

OPERATIVE NOTE: With the patient under general anesthesia, she was prepped and draped in the supine fashion. I made an incision in the upper-outer section of her right breast and went right down to the mass. It was hard as a rock. It was hard to actually get a hold of. I could not even dissect it off with Metz. I ended up using a knife. I could get above the mass superiorly and medially and laterally, but the mass was going inferiorly quite significantly and it was sitting right underneath the nipple. I had to use a knife to cuff it off at this area knowing that I probably was leaving tumor if this was indeed cancer. I ended up using two knives because they got dull so fast being this was such a hard mass. Frozen section came back positive for infiltrating ductal carcinoma, which appears to be high grade. I will have to wait and see the exact size of it. I obtained excellent hemostasis with cautery. I then brought the subcutaneous tissue together with Vicryl, and the skin was closed with subcuticular 3-0 Prolene stitch. Steri-Strips, gauze, and tape were applied. The patient tolerated the procedure well and went to the recovery room in good condition.

Pathology Report Later Indicated: See Report 5-15B

5-15A:

SERVICE CODE(S): _____

ICD-9-CM DX CODE(S): _____

ICD-10-CM DX CODE(S): _____

5-15B PATHOLOGY REPORT

LOCATION: Outpatient, Hospital

PATIENT: Elizabeth Jones

SURGEON: Gary Sanchez, MD

PATHOLOGIST: Grey Lonewolf, MD

CLINICAL HISTORY: Right breast mass

SPECIMEN RECEIVED: Right breast biopsy

GROSS DESCRIPTION: The specimen is labeled with the patient's name and "right breast biopsy" and consists of a biopsy of white-tan lobulated tissue with adipose, 5.7 × 3.6 × 2.2 cm. Surgical margins are inked black. Cut sections show a white-tan, firm, lobulated, glistening lesion, 4.5 × 2.9 × 1.8 cm. The lesion shows solid white-tan tissue throughout. Representative sections are submitted in 5 cassettes.

MICROSCOPIC DESCRIPTION: Sections of breast showing an infiltrating neoplasm consisting of nests of cells infiltrating the desmoplastic stroma. Cells are enlarged and have increased nuclear cytoplasmic ratio. Surgical margins were not examined.

DIAGNOSIS: Infiltrating ductal carcinoma, right breast.

5-15B:

SERVICE CODE(S): _____

ICD-9-CM DX CODE(S): _____

ICD-10-CM DX CODE(S): _____

CASE 5-16

Rosemary Ely had breast cancer and in this operative report, Dr. Sanchez performed a segmental mastectomy that removed a portion of her breast. Additionally, the surgeon dissected some axillary lymph nodes.

5-16A OPERATIVE REPORT, SEGMENTAL MASTECTOMY WITH EXCISION OF AXILLARY LYMPH NODES

LOCATION: Outpatient, Hospital

PATIENT: Rosemary Ely

SURGEON: Gary Sanchez, MD

PREOPERATIVE DIAGNOSIS: 0.8 cm cancer, left breast

POSTOPERATIVE DIAGNOSIS: Same

PROCEDURE PERFORMED: Left segmental mastectomy and axillary node dissection

ANESTHESIA: General

PROCEDURE: The patient was given a general anesthetic. I did an ultrasound, which showed the node in the axilla was 2.16 cm. The cavity itself was 3.22 cm with a depth from skin to the top of the cavity of 0.52 cm. Prints were made and placed on the chart. I then proceeded with free-draping her left arm, and she was prepped and draped in this position. I started with the axilla. I made an incision in the axilla and went down through clavipectoral fascia. I identified this large lymph node and it looked quite terrible. I sent it for frozen section, and it came back signet cell variation, which concerned the pathologist. He felt that there may be a GI component rather than the breast; however, I had a copy of the pathology report showing that this small cancer had signet cell variation, so it is likely from the breast. The oncologist was in the room, and we felt that we should explore the upper GI tract afterwards just to be sure. The oncologist will organize that for us.

I then completed the axillary dissection. I identified the thoracodorsal vessel and nerves, long thoracic nerve, intercostals brachial nerve, and the axillary vein. We made sure there were no palpable nodes left. We stripped right from the axillary vein all the way down. I used clips and ties during this dissection. I then did the segmental mastectomy. I developed the superior flap and then the inferior flap. I then removed the segmental mastectomy going from lateral to medial. I sent it out for frozen section margins. The pathologist felt that our margins were clear. I then put a Hemovac drain in with one limb in the axilla and one limb on the chest wall. I sutured the drains in and then brought the subcutaneous tissue together with Vicryl. Staples were placed in the skin. Telfa, Toppers, and gauze were applied. The patient tolerated the procedure well and went to the recovery room in good condition.

Pathology Report: See 5-16B

5-16A:

SERVICE CODE(S): _____

ICD-9-CM DX CODE(S): _____

ICD-10-CM DX CODE(S): _____

5-16B PATHOLOGY REPORT

LOCATION: Outpatient, Hospital

PATIENT: Rosemary Ely

SURGEON: Gary Sanchez, MD

PATHOLOGIST: Grey Lonewolf, MD

CLINICAL HISTORY: Infiltrating ductal carcinoma

SPECIMEN RECEIVED:

> A) Lymph node, left with FS
>
> B) Left breast mass with FS
>
> C) Lymph nodes, left axilla

GROSS DESCRIPTION: The specimens were received in 3 containers:

A. In the container labeled "lymph node left," there was an encapsulated lymph node measuring 2.3 × 1.6 × 1.1 cm. The cut surface demonstrates a uniform solid tan-yellow appearance. The frozen section is submitted as AFS1. The remainder of the tissue is submitted as A2 to A3.

INTRAOPERATIVE FROZEN SECTION DIAGNOSIS: Lymph node, left axilla: Malignant, metastatic adenocarcinoma, signet ring type.

B. In the container labeled "segmental resection left breast mass," there was a fragment of fibrofatty breast tissue measuring 10.5 × 5.5 × 5 cm in greatest dimension. An ellipse of skin measuring 10 × 3 × 0.3 cm is present on the ventral surface. The superior and medial margins were identified. The specimen is step-sectioned and demonstrates abundant yellow adipose stroma. A biopsy cavity measuring 3 × 2.5 × 4 cm is present near the skin surface. The wall is granular and tan-gray. No gross tumor is evident. The specimen is step-sectioned, and multiple representative portions are submitted as B1 to B36.

INTRAOPERATIVE GROSS DIAGNOSIS: Left breast, excision biopsy: Grossly benign, await permanent sections.

C. In the container labeled "lymph nodes, left axilla," there are multiple fragments of adipose tissue totaling 5.5 × 4 × 2.5 cm as an aggregate mass. Lymph nodes are dissected and average 0.3 to 0.8 cm in greatest dimension. Multiple lymph nodes are submitted as C1 to C10.

MICROSCOPIC DESCRIPTION:

A. The left axillary lymph node is replaced over significant portion by a metastatic tumor consisting of nests of pleomorphic mucin-containing cells. The distended cytoplasm creates a signet ring appearance. The nuclei are pleomorphic and eccentrically placed in many of the cells.

B. The left breast excisional biopsy demonstrates extensive fat necrosis and focal fibrosis with granulation tissue. There is no evidence of residual tumor. The majority of the breast stroma is adipose tissue and slender strands of fibrous supporting stroma containing small numbers of atrophic ducts and lobules. The accompanying skin shows an intact epidermis showing normal morphology.

C. 2 of 9 lymph nodes of the left axilla exhibit foci of metastases. The metastatic sites show a morphology as previously described on the left axillary lymph node.

DIAGNOSIS:

A. Lymph node, axilla, excision:

   Adenocarcinoma, metastatic, mucinous, consistent with breast carcinoma.

B. Left breast, excisional biopsy:

Biopsy cavity showing fibrosis, fat necrosis, and chronic inflammation. Lipomatous breast tissue with no evidence of residual tumor.

C. Lymph nodes, left axilla

Metastatic adenocarcinoma, mucin-containing, consistent with breast carcinoma in 2 of 9 lymph nodes.

COMMENT: The above-described specimen demonstrates metastatic adenocarcinoma in a total of 3 out of 10 axillary lymph nodes.

5-16B:

SERVICE CODE(S): _____

ICD-9-CM DX CODE(S): _____

ICD-10-CM DX CODE(S): _____

CASE 5-17

Susan Hall has been admitted to the hospital for a bilateral breast reduction (mammoplasty or mammaplasty). Report the services provided to her by Dr. Erickson, the clinic's plastic surgeon.

5-17A OPERATIVE REPORT, MAMMOPLASTY

LOCATION: Inpatient, Hospital

PATIENT: Susan Hall

SURGEON: Mark Erickson, MD

PREOPERATIVE DIAGNOSIS:
1. Bilateral mammary hypertrophy.
2. Bilateral mammary ptosis.

POSTOPERATIVE DIAGNOSIS:
1. Bilateral mammary hypertrophy.
2. Bilateral mammary ptosis.

PROCEDURE PERFORMED: Bilateral reduction mammoplasty using inferior pedicle technique.
1. 800 grams resected from the right side.
2. 900 grams from the left side.

ANESTHESIA: General endotracheal

ESTIMATED BLOOD LOSS: 125 cc

DRAINS: None

SPONGE AND NEEDLE COUNT: Correct

COMPLICATIONS: None

SURGICAL FINDINGS: The breasts were predominantly glandular, with about 75% very firm fibrous glandular tissue interspersed with 25% fat.

INDICATIONS: The patient has interscapular back pain and neck pain, which she has had for several years. This has become progressively severe and is not relieved by the usual measures. It is felt that the back pain is caused by her large and pendulous breasts with regard to her body habitus.

DESCRIPTION OF PROCEDURE: In accordance with the preoperatively marked new nipple site, we marked out an inferior pedicle breast pattern, and instilled about 75 cc of tumescent solution into the right side of the breast. Tumescent solution was prepared with 25 cc of 2% Xylocaine and 1 cc of 1:1,000 epinephrine plus 3 cc of 8.4% sodium bicarbonate added to 1,000 cc Ringer's lactate. After installation of solution at the junctional points and along the suture lines, the vertical stalk was de-epithelialized leaving about 1.5 cm of de-epithelialized stalk above the areola. The new areolar site and the areolar size were planned using the 45 mm cookie cutter marker as a guide. The 3, 6, 9, and 12 o'clock positions were marked on the new areolar window and on the areola itself. The vertical stalk having been de-epithelialized, deep dissection was started at the 12 o'clock position and came toward the 3 o'clock position between the upper end of the vertical limb and the medial flap. At the caudal edge of the medial flap, we began to bevel away from the vertical limb, and connected this with an incision in the inframammary area at the level of the pectoralis major fascia. The incision on the caudal edge of the medial flap was beveled in such a way as to leave about 2 cm of thickness on the flap, and the incision between the upper part of the vertical limb and the medial flap was not carried down deeply into the tissue, leaving some glandular tissue connected with the central stalk. After resection of the medial triangle, deep dissection then started at the 12 o'clock position and came toward the 9 o'clock position between the upper end of the vertical limb and the lateral flap, but not going deeply into the space between the lateral flap and the vertical limb. In other words, we left some glandular tissue attached to the central stalk. We then connected this with an incision at the inframammary level down to the pectoralis major fascia, and began our dissection on the caudal edge of the lateral flap leaving about 1.5 cm of thickness of the lateral flap. The superior triangle was then resected, but we attempted to leave this area also with much of the vertical stalk, which carried the nipple areola, and after resection of approximately 800 grams of tissue on the right side, we detached the dermis inferiorly at the vertical stalk, and inset the lateral and medial flaps with a subcuticular 3-0 Monocryl suture. We then used subcuticular 3-0 Monocryl to secure key points on the areolar window to the vertical and inframammary limbs. We used skin staples to better appose the skin edge. Final weight on the right was about 800 grams. On the left side, we once again made our junctional incisions and instilled about 125 cc of tumescent solution at these sites along the suture line. De-epithelialization of the vertical stalk was carried out. We then began our initial dissection at the 12 o'clock position and came toward the 9 o'clock position coming between the upper end of the vertical stalk and the medial flap. We began to bevel away from the vertical limb at the caudal edge of the medial flap, and connected this with an incision at the inframammary area at the level of the pectoralis major fascia. We also beveled underneath the medial flap in such a manner as to leave about 2 cm of thickness on the leading edge, but attempted to maintain continuity between the deep tissue of the medial flap and the central vertical limb. On the lateral side, deep dissection started at the 12 o'clock position and came toward the 3 o'clock position between the upper end of the vertical limb and the lateral flap, once again trying to maintain continuity of the deep tissue of the lateral flap with the vertical limb, and beveling away from the vertical limb starting at the caudal edge and to the lateral flap. After connecting this with an incision on the caudal edge of the lateral flap, we also included the Tail of Spence in the dissection. On the right side, we had also included the Tail of Spence in our lateral dissection. After resection of the lateral triangle, the dermis was detached at the vertical limb inferiorly, and we in-set the lateral and medial flaps at the midpoint, the vertical limb with a horizontal half mattress suture of 0 Prolene, in-setting the new areolar size at the new window with subcuticular 3-0 Monocryl, and using 3-0 Monocryl for the vertical limb. Subcuticular 3-0 Monocryl was also used for the inframammary limb, and skin staples were used to better appose the skin edges. Dressings consisted of Xeroform, Kerlix fluffs, a support bra, and an external Ace bandage. Estimated blood loss was 125 cc. The patient tolerated the procedure well and left the area in good condition.

5-17A:

SERVICE CODE(S): _____

ICD-9-CM DX CODE(S): _____

ICD-10-CM DX CODE(S): _____

CASE 5-18

5-18A OPERATIVE REPORT, INSERTION OF TISSUE EXPANDER

LOCATION: Inpatient, Hospital

PATIENT: Janet Kehl

SURGEON: Gary Sanchez, MD

PREOPERATIVE DIAGNOSIS: Giant congenital pigmented nevus, left forearm

POSTOPERATIVE DIAGNOSIS: Giant congenital pigmented nevus, left forearm

FINDINGS: An 80 × 80 mm diameter giant congenital nevus of the left forearm.

PROCEDURE PERFORMED: Insertion of a 175 mL volume tissue expander measuring approximately 6 × 5 cm at its maximal dimensions.

ANESTHESIA: 5 mL 1% Xylocaine and 1:100,000 epinephrine, plus general endotracheal

DESCRIPTION OF PROCEDURE: The patient's left arm was prepped with Betadine scrubbing solution and draped in the routine sterile fashion. I injected 1% Xylocaine and 1:100,000 epinephrine distally, and made an incision adjacent to the distal portion of the giant congenital nevus in the forearm, dissecting down to the muscle fascia where I created a pocket to accommodate the expander. It was necessary to come up some on the pigmented lesion to undermine it to get the expander in, and because of the proximity of the radius in this area and the lower end of the humerus, and the necessity to make a large pocket, I did not insert the second tissue expander above this. It was felt that if necessary, a flap could be created superiorly and would produce less surgical trauma in this area. The wound was closed with interrupted horizontal mattress sutures of 3-0 Prolene, and Nitropaste was applied to the suture line. Xeroform, Kerlix fluffs, Kerlix roll, Kling, Sof-Roll, and a long arm fiberglass cast were then applied. Estimated blood loss was negligible. The patient tolerated the procedure well and left the operating room in good condition.

5-18A:

SERVICE CODE(S): _____

ICD-9-CM DX CODE(S): _____

ICD-10-CM DX CODE(S): _____

CHAPTER 6

Cardiovascular System

CASE 6-1

Code the following CABG. Be certain to identify the type of graft(s) (veins and/or arteries), location, and how many grafts were used to complete the procedure.

6-1A CORONARY ARTERY BYPASS

LOCATION: Inpatient, Hospital

PATIENT: Michael Phelps

SURGEON: David Barton, MD

PREOPERATIVE DIAGNOSIS: Atherosclerotic heart disease

POSTOPERATIVE DIAGNOSIS: Same

PROCEDURE PERFORMED: Coronary artery bypass graft from the left internal mammary artery to left anterior descending bypass and sequential saphenous vein bypass grafts from the aorta to the first and then to the third obtuse marginal branches of the left circumflex.

ANESTHESIA: General

INDICATIONS: This 57-year-old male patient with progressive angina was noted on cardiac catheterization to have distal left main disease as well as high-grade proximal dominant left circumflex disease.

FINDINGS AT SURGERY: Revealed a greater saphenous vein conduit, which was 3.5 mm in diameter, was of good quality, and was used in reverse fashion. The left internal mammary artery was a 1 mm diameter vessel and was of good quality with excellent flow. The left anterior descending artery was 2 mm in diameter and was of good quality. The first and third obtuse marginal branches were both 2 mm in diameter and were of good quality. All grafts were probed and patent prior to closure.

DESCRIPTION OF PROCEDURE: The patient was brought to the operating room and placed in the supine position. Under general intubation anesthesia, the anterior chest, abdomen, and legs were prepped and draped in the usual manner. A segment of greater saphenous vein was harvested from the right leg using the endoscope. A segment of greater saphenous vein was harvested from the left thigh using the endoscope and prepared for grafting. The sternum was opened in the usual fashion, and the left internal mammary artery was taken down and prepared for grafting. The pericardium was incised sharply, and a pericardial well was created. The patient was systemically heparinized and placed on single right atrial to aortic cardiopulmonary bypass with a pump in the main pulmonary artery for cardiac decompression. The patient was cooled to 26 degrees, and upon fibrillation the aortic cross-clamp was applied and potassium-rich cold crystalline cardioplegic solution was administered through the aortic root with satisfactory cardiac arrest. Subsequent doses were given via the coronary sinus in a retrograde fashion. The end of the greater saphenous vein was anastomosed to the aorta and then the first obtuse marginal branch. The end of the other greater saphenous vein was then anastomosed to the third obtuse marginal branch with 7-0 Prolene. The left internal mammary artery was then brought down to the midportion of the left anterior descending artery and then anastomosed with 8-0 continuous Prolene. The aortic cross-clamp was removed after 56 minutes with spontaneous cardioversion to normal sinus rhythm. The patient was then warmed to 37 degrees esophageal temperature and weaned from cardiopulmonary bypass without difficulty after 78 minutes. The patient was decannulated, protamine was given, and hemostasis obtained. Temporary pacer wires were placed in the right atrium and right ventricle. The chest was drained with two Argyle chest tubes and closed in layers in the usual fashion. The leg was closed similarly. Sterile compression dressings were applied, and the patient returned to the surgical intensive care unit in satisfactory condition. Sponge count and needle count was correct $\times$ 2.

6-1A:

SERVICE CODE(S): _____

ICD-9-CM DX CODE(S): _____

ICD-10-CM DX CODE(S): _____

CASE 6-2

The patient presented to Dr. Elhart with complaints of chest pain and SVT. A 2-D Doppler and color-flow Doppler was performed at the local hospital in the outpatient department, and Dr. Elhart monitored the echocardiography. You are reporting the service before the test results are known.

6-2A ECHOCARDIOGRAM

LOCATION: Hospital Outpatient

PATIENT: Emily Watts

PHYSICIAN: Marvin Elhart, MD

STUDY: The study is a transthoracic 2-D and color-flow Doppler echocardiography

INDICATION: Chest pain and SVT

M-MODE MEASUREMENTS:
1. Left atrium is 3.9, aortic root 2.3.
2. RV dimension 1.7.
3. LV diastole 5.
4. LV systole 2.6.
5. Fraction shortening 0.46.
6. Interventricular septum 0.7.
7. Posterior wall thickness 0.7.

DOPPLER:
1. Mild mitral regurgitation.
2. Mild to moderate tricuspid regurgitation.
3. RV systolic pressure 73 mmHg.

2-D FINDINGS:
1. Left ventricle is normal in size with good LV systolic function noted.
2. Normal left atrium, right atrium, and right ventricle.
3. No pericardial effusion seen.
4. Aortic root is normal in size with normal aortic valve.
5. The mitral valve is structurally normal with mild mitral regurgitation.
6. Mild tricuspid regurgitation.

CONCLUSION:
1. Normal LV size with preserved LV systolic function.
2. No significant aortic or mitral valve disease.
3. No dilation of the chambers noted.

6-2A:

SERVICE CODE(S): _____

ICD-9-CM DX CODE(S): _____

ICD-10-CM DX CODE(S): _____

CASE 6-3

6-3A ADENOSINE CARDIOLITE STRESS TEST

The stress test was conducted at the cardiology laboratory at the local hospital with the clinic physician supervising the test and interpreting the results.

LOCATION: Hospital Outpatient

PATIENT: Matt Arman

PHYSICIAN: Marvin Elhart, MD

INDICATIONS: The patient is status post heart catheterization and stent placement × 3 and now has recurring chest pain.

IDENTIFICATION: 61-year-old male, 5′ 8″, 210 pounds.

The patient underwent stress test according to Bruce protocol with Myoview injection.

HEMODYNAMIC RESPONSE: Heart rate at rest was 68 and at peak exercise was 132. Blood pressure at rest was 138/78 and at peak was 168/78.

During the stress test, the patient had no chest pain. The test was stopped due to fatigue. At baseline, the patient had a normal sinus rhythm with no ST segment changes. At peak exercise, the patient had no ST segment changes noted.

The patient exercised for a total of 10 minutes, achieving 11.3 METS.

CONCLUSION:
1. Excellent exercise tolerance.
2. Good hemodynamic response to exercise.
3. This EKG stress test is not suggestive for significant obstructive disease. No chest pain clinically. The Myoview part of the stress test will be reported separately.

6-3A:

SERVICE CODE(S): _____

ICD-9-CM DX CODE(S): _____

ICD-10-CM DX CODE(S): _____

6-3B RADIOLOGY REPORT, PERFUSION SCAN

LOCATION: Hospital Outpatient

PATIENT: Matt Arman

PHYSICIAN: Marvin Elhart, MD

EXAMINATION OF: Treadmill stress test and rest myocardial perfusion scan with ejection fraction.

INDICATIONS: Chest pain

STRESS TEST WITH EJECTION FRACTION: TECHNIQUE: Yesterday 29.6 mCi of technetium 99 m tetrofosmin IV administered for the stress portion of the study. The patient was stressed using the Bruce protocol. The patient exercised about 10 minutes and had a predicted maximum heart rate of only 83%. Ideally, it should be 85% or more. Then the following day, 30.7 mCi of technetium 99 m tetrofosmin IV was administered for the resting portion of the study. The LVEF is 60%.

IMPRESSION:
1. Possible minimal fixed defect involving the anteroseptal region.
2. Possible small fixed defect involving the posterior wall.
3. No reversible defects.
4. Hypokinesia involving the septum.

6-3B:

SERVICE CODE(S): _____

ICD-9-CM DX CODE(S): _____

ICD-10-CM DX CODE(S): _____

6-3C ECHO DOPPLER REPORT

LOCATION: Hospital Outpatient

PATIENT: Matt Arman

PHYSICIAN: Marvin Elhart, MD

INDICATION STUDY: Chest pain

M-MODE MEASUREMENT:
1. Left atrium is 4.5.
2. Aortic root is 3.9.
3. RV dimension is 1.8.
4. LV Diastole is 5.5.
5. LV systole is 4.0.
6. Fraction shortening is 0.27.
7. Interventricular septum is 1.
8. Posterior wall thickness is 0.9.

DOPPLER:
1. Mild mitral regurgitation.
2. Trace tricuspid regurgitation.
3. RV systolic pressure of 40 mmHg.

2-D FINDINGS:
1. Normal LV size with mildly reduced LV systolic function.
2. Probable dilated left atrium.
3. Normal RV and normal right ventricle and right atrium.
4. The mitral valve is suggestive of possible fibrocalcific with no stenosis with mild mitral regurgitation.
5. Possible trace tricuspid regurgitation.
6. There is no aortic stenosis.

IMPRESSION:*

1. This study is technically limited due to poor echo window. The LV displays normal size with mildly reduced LV systolic function and some segmental wall motion abnormalities noted suggestive of coronary artery disease.
2. Possible fibrocalcific change of the aortic and mitral valve with mild mitral regurgitation.
3. There is probable moderate pulmonary hypertension.

---

*The information in the Impression section was obtained from the color-flow mapping Doppler for identification of blood flow.

6-3C:

SERVICE CODE(S): _____

ICD-9-CM DX CODE(S): _____

ICD-10-CM DX CODE(S): _____

CASE 6-4

The patient presents to the hospital outpatient department for an echocardiography. Code the physician and facility portions of the service that was provided in the cardiology laboratory of the hospital.

6-4A ECHO DOPPLER REPORT

LOCATION: Hospital Outpatient

PATIENT: Allison Gunderson

PRIMARY CARE PHYSICIAN: Alanda Naraquist, MD

CARDIOLOGIST: James Noonar, MD

INDICATION: Congestive heart failure

A 2-D echocardiographic study with color-flow interrogation, spectral Doppler, and M-mode measurements was performed.

2-D AND M-MODE MEASUREMENTS:
1. Aortic root 3.8 cm.
2. Aortic valve excursion not measured.
3. Left atrium 5.2 cm.
4. Right ventricle not measured.
5. Left ventricle end-diastole 4.7 cm.
6. Left ventricle end-systole 4.2 cm.
7. Fractional shortening 0.10.
8. Ejection fraction 23%.
9. Interventricular septum 1.1 cm.
10. Left ventricular posterior wall 1.1 cm.

DOPPLER MEASUREMENTS:
1. Aortic valve peak velocity 3.19 m/sec.
2. Aortic valve peak gradient 41 mmHg.
3. Aortic valve mean gradient 30 mmHg.
4. Aortic valve area 0.82 cm #2 by continuity equation.
5. Severe aortic stenosis by continuity equation.
6. Trace mitral regurgitation.
7. Trace tricuspid regurgitation.

2-D ECHOCARDIOGRAPHIC REPORT:
1. Technically adequate study.
2. Normal left ventricular cavitary dimensions, end-diastole and end-systole. Mild left ventricular concentric hypertrophy. Moderate LV systolic dysfunction. Dyskinetic LV wall motion consistent with atrial fibrillation.
3. Mildly dilated aortic root.
4. Severely calcified, thickened, fibrotic aortic valve with markedly restricted opening and markedly reduced leaflet excursion. Severe aortic stenosis by continuity equation with aortic valve area of 0.82 cm #2, aortic valve peak velocity 3.2 m/s, peak gradient 41 mmHg, and mean gradient 30 mmHg. Fibrocalcific disease of the aortic valve root and annulus.
5. Mildly thickened, calcified mitral valve leaflets with good opening and adequate excursion. Mitral annular calcification. Normal subvalvular chorda tendineae

apparatus. No prolapse, flail, redundancy, or myxomatous changes of mitral valve leaflets.

6. Dilated left atrial cavitary dimensions.

7. Top normal right-sided chamber dimensions and function. Normal morphologic appearance of the tricuspid valve.

8. Trace mitral insufficiency. Trace tricuspid insufficiency.

9. No significant pericardial effusion, intracardiac mass, or thrombus. No intracavitary spontaneous echo contrast. No valvular vegetations or left ventricular apical mural thrombus detected. Intact interatrial and interventricular septum. No PFO by color-flow Doppler.

IMPRESSION: Normal LV cavitary dimensions. Mild concentric left ventricular hypertrophy. Moderate LV systolic dysfunction. Left ventricular dyskinesis secondary to conductive arrhythmia, atrial fibrillation. Ejection fraction 23%. Moderate global hypokinesis with dyskinetic wall motion secondary to atrial fibrillation. Mildly dilated aortic root. Highly calcified, thickened, restricted aortic valve leaflet opening and markedly diminished leaflet excursion. Severe aortic valvular stenosis with aortic valve area of 0.82 cm #2 by continuity equation, aortic valve peak velocity 3.2 m/s, peak gradient 41 mmHg, mean gradient 30 mmHg. Trace MR. Trace tricuspid insufficiency. Mitral annular calcification. Left atrial enlargement. (The preceding findings are indicative of congestive heart failure.)

6-4A:

SERVICE CODE(S): _____

ICD-9-CM DX CODE(S): _____

ICD-10-CM DX CODE(S): _____

CASE 6-5
6-5A EMERGENCY AND OUTPATIENT RECORD
6-5B RADIOLOGY REPORT, CHEST
6-5C HOSPITAL ADMISSION
6-5D CARDIOLOGY CONSULTATION
6-5E OPERATIVE REPORT, HEART CATHETERIZATION
6-5F PTCA/STENTING REPORT

CASE 6-5

The following reports are for a 65-year-old white male patient who is seen in the emergency department of the local hospital. The patient was first seen in the emergency department, by the physician on staff. The emergency department physician then turned the case over to the patient's primary doctor, Dr. Alanda. Dr. Alanda then consults a cardiology physician, Dr. Elhart. The patient then goes on to have a heart catheterization and stent procedure. Report each service that was provided to the patient.

6-5A EMERGENCY AND OUTPATIENT RECORD

LOCATION: Hospital Outpatient

PATIENT: Harold Smith

PHYSICIAN: Paul Sutton, MD

SUBJECTIVE: A 65-year-old male who presents with the chief complaint of back and chest pain. He was awakened 15 hours ago at 2:30 AM with sharp interscapular pain, which he rated as 7 out of 10. It has been a steady discomfort since then. It has been accompanied by substernal pressurelike discomfort, which is much milder in intensity. The pain is also accompanied by some shortness of breath, but no sweating. None of his pain is pleuritic in nature. No dizziness or headaches.

The patient has a history of coronary artery disease. He was admitted for an angiogram 4 months ago and had an angioplasty and stent. He states that his chest pain is somewhat reminiscent of the chest pain he had prior to the angioplasty. He also states he has a history of pancreatitis and that this pain is somewhat similar to that as well.

Past medical history and social history are noted on the patient's history sheet.

REVIEW OF SYSTEMS: Complete and negative except for the above.

OBJECTIVE: This is an alert 65-year-old male who appears to be in moderate discomfort. Temperature is 37.3° C. Pulse 96. Respirations 17. Blood pressure 143/85. Oxygen saturation 97%. HEENT: Conjunctivae and lids normal. Tympanic membranes are normal. Mouth is well hydrated. Pharynx is normal. Neck is supple without lymphadenopathy. No thyromegaly. Respirations are easy. Lungs are clear to auscultation. Heart has a regular rate and rhythm. No murmurs or extra heart sounds heard. Chest wall is without deformities and no localizing tenderness. On abdominal exam, his bowel sounds were normal. No hepatosplenomegaly. No pulsatile mass. No ventral hernia. Extremities negative. Skin: No rash. No nodules felt.

ASSESSMENT: Chest pain.

PLAN: EKG was done and compared to previous EKG and no acute changes are noted. Subsequent to this, he was started on nitroglycerin drip and we ordered CT scan of the chest to rule out aortic dissection. This came back negative. In the meantime, lab work came back with a normal troponin and a normal lipase. Nitroglycerin drip had no effect on his discomfort. He was given morphine which gave him partial symptomatic relief. The case was discussed with Dr. Alanda, and patient will be admitted for further workup and treatment.

6-5A:

SERVICE CODE(S): _____

ICD-9-CM DX CODE(S): _____

ICD-10-CM DX CODE(S): _____

6-5B RADIOLOGY REPORT, CHEST

LOCATION: Hospital Outpatient

PATIENT: Harold Smith

PHYSICIAN: Paul Sutton, MD

RADIOLOGIST: Morton Monson, MD

EXAMINATION: Chest

CLINICAL SYMPTOMS: Chest pain, single view

ONE-VIEW CHEST: FINDINGS: This examination is compared to the prior examination dated February 13. The heart size and pulmonary vascular markings appear within normal limits. Definite acute focal infiltrates are not seen within the lungs. No pleural effusions are seen.

6-5B:

SERVICE CODE(S): _____

ICD-9-CM DX CODE(S): _____

ICD-10-CM DX CODE(S): _____

6-5C HOSPITAL ADMISSION

LOCATION: Hospital Inpatient

PATIENT: Harold Smith

PHYSICAIN: Leslie Alanda, MD

REASON FOR ADMISSION: Chest pain with history of MI

HISTORY OF PRESENT ILLNESS: The patient is a 65-year-old male with multiple medical problems, including atherosclerotic heart disease. He comes into the emergency room this evening with complaints of chest pain, which has been fairly steady starting at about 3 AM. He describes it as across his chest, but also between his shoulder blades. He feels that it is deep. It is somewhat similar in nature to prior episodes of chest pain he has had, including 4 months ago when he came in with an acute MI and had cardiac catheterization with two angioplasties. The pain does not radiate into the arms or jaw. No associated diaphoresis, nausea, or dyspnea. The patient gets short of breath at times due to chronic obstructive pulmonary disease.

PAST MEDICAL HISTORY:
1. Atherosclerotic heart disease, as above. The patient recently had angioplasty ×2 in February. He did have an acute MI.
2. Chronic obstructive pulmonary disease.
3. Hypertension.
4. Gastroesophageal reflux disease.
5. History of alcohol dependence/abuse. The patient has been sober for approximately 7 months. He has in the past had alcohol withdrawal seizures and DTs.
6. Brain surgery in December 2003 for removal of meningioma, which was benign.
7. Severe left leg burn many years ago requiring skin grafts.
8. Depression.
9. History of sexual dysfunction.
10. Past history of fractures, including ribs and right foot.

PAST SURGERIES:
1. Skin grafting, left leg.
2. Cataract surgery, left eye.
3. Brain surgery for removal of meningioma.

CURRENT MEDICATIONS: It should be noted that the patient does not take his medications on a regular basis. Part of this is due to the cost of medications.
1. Ambien 5 mg p.o. at h.s. p.r.n.
2. Celebrex 200 mg p.o. daily.
3. Combivent inhaler 2 puffs q.i.d.
4. Darvocet-N 100, 1 to 2 daily p.r.n. The patient usually takes these at night.
5. Dilantin 100 mg p.o. t.i.d.
6. Lexapro 10 mg p.o. daily.
7. Lipitor 10 mg p.o. daily.
8. Nexium 40 mg p.o. daily.
9. Toprol XL 100 mg daily.
10. Norvasc 5 mg p.o. daily.
11. Viagra 50 mg p.r.n.

ALLERGIES: None

FAMILY HISTORY: Father and sister died of cancer. Mother had history of diabetes.

SOCIAL HISTORY: The patient is single and lives alone. He says that he has not had any alcohol for the past 7 months. He does smoke less than 1 pack a day of cigarettes.

REVIEW OF SYSTEMS: No recent illness. He denies fever, chills, or night sweats. HEENT: His hearing and vision are generally good. He has had cataract surgery, left eye. CARDIO-VASCULAR/PULMONARY: As above. GI: The patient reported to the ER physician that he had pancreatitis in the past. Appetite had generally been good. He feels hungry now. GU: Negative. MUSCULOSKELETAL: He has a history of back pain and says this is why he takes Darvocet. DERMATOLOGIC: Negative. HEMATOLOGIC: Negative. ENDO-CRINE: Negative. NEUROLOGIC: History of meningioma. PSYCHIATRIC: History of depression and chronic alcohol dependence and past history of abuse.

PHYSICAL EXAMINATION: VITAL SIGNS: Blood pressure 143/85, pulse 96, respirations 17, temperature 37.3° C, O_2 sat 97% on room air. On exam, the patient is a middle-aged male who is in no acute distress. He is able to answer questions without any difficulty and does not appear uncomfortable. The patient is alert and oriented, although he appears to have some trouble with memory as he did not remember why he had his brain surgery just 6 months ago. EYES: Pupils are reactive. There is scleral injection bilaterally. EARS: TMs are normal. THROAT: No lesions or erythema. NECK: Supple. No adenopathy. LUNGS: Clear to auscultation. HEART: Regular rate and rhythm. No murmurs. ABDOMEN: Bowel sounds are positive. Soft and nontender. No masses. BACK: Very mild tenderness on palpation between scapulae. EXTREMITIES: No edema.

LABORATORY: Laboratory actually looks good. CBC and basic metabolic panel are normal. Cardiac enzymes are normal, magnesium is normal at 1.5, lipase is normal at 276. Liver functions are also normal. He does have a blood alcohol level pending. PTT, PT/INR are normal.

EKG: EKG shows normal sinus rhythm, rate is 92. There are no acute changes.

CHEST X-RAY: Chest x-ray shows clear lung fields. No evidence of failure.

ASSESSMENT:
1. Chest/interscapular pain in patient with significant atherosclerotic heart disease, status post recent angioplasty ×2 in February. He continues to smoke.
2. Chronic obstructive pulmonary disease.
3. Hypertension.
4. Gastroesophageal reflux disease.
5. History of alcohol dependence/abuse.
6. History of depression.
7. History of brain surgery for removal of meningioma.

PLAN: The patient is being admitted to 5th floor, telemetry. Serial cardiac enzymes have been ordered. The patient is already on IV nitroglycerin and had been given a few doses of morphine, without cardiac pain; however, on his prior admit, his symptoms were also atypical and at that time he had an acute MI. We may also try Toradol. He had been on Nexium, and we will substitute Protonix. He will be given Dilantin, Toprol XL, and aspirin. He will also be on Heparin. Cardiology will also be consulted.

6-5C:

SERVICE CODE(S): _____

ICD-9-CM DX CODE(S): _____

ICD-10-CM DX CODE(S): _____

6-5D CARDIOLOGY CONSULTATION

LOCATION: Hospital Inpatient

PATIENT: Harold Smith

PHYSICIAN: Marvin Elhart, MD

REFERRING PHYSICIAN: Leslie Alanda, MD

REASON FOR CONSULTATION: Chest pain with history of MI

HISTORY: This is a 65-year-old white male who has undergone a stent of his right coronary artery that had been uneventful, and angioplasty of the circumflex. He was doing well up until recently. In the last 2 days, he started having chest pressure and shoulder pain that had been responsive to sublingual nitroglycerin. In the emergency room, he had recurrence of the chest pain and he was given nitroglycerin with resolution of the chest pressure and he was admitted with chest pain to rule out MI.

The patient had been doing well after his stent placement and, unfortunately, he still smokes. He has not been compliant with medications, and his symptoms have recurred in the last 2 to 3 days.

MEDICATIONS: He is on aspirin. There is no listing of Plavix, but he has Plavix, according to him. He is also on Lipitor and Lopressor.

PAST MEDICAL HISTORY:
1. Coronary artery disease.
2. Chronic smoker.

REVIEW OF SYSTEMS:

CARDIOVASCULAR SYSTEM: He has chest pressure the last 2 days.

RESPIRATORY SYSTEM: He has a cough from his smoking.

ABDOMINAL SYSTEM: No complaints.

RENAL SYSTEM: No complaints.

GI SYSTEM: No complaints.

ENDROCRINE SYSTEM: He has hyperlipidemia.

GU SYSTEM: No complaints.

VASCULAR SYSTEM: No claudication.

CENTRAL NERVOUS SYSTEM: No complaints.

PHYSICAL EXAMINATION: The patient is alert and oriented and in no distress. Blood pressure is 130/80, heart rate 72, breathing 16 per minute. Normocephalic. NECK: Supple. No carotid bruit, no jugular venous distention. CARDIAC: S1, S2. No murmur, no gallop. LUNGS: Clear. ABDOMEN: Soft. Bowel sounds present, no masses. 2+ distal pulses. No pedal edema. No calf tenderness. NEURO: Grossly intact.

EKG shows sinus rhythm. No acute ST segment changes.

IMPRESSION:
1. Chest pain.
2. Atherosclerotic heart disease.
3. Status post stent to the right coronary artery.

PLAN: Due to the recurrence of the patient's symptoms and with cardiac enzymes not revealing anything at this point, I am recommending that he undergo cardiac catheterization.

This has been discussed with the patient, understanding the risks and benefits, and the possibility of requiring revascularization of one of his coronary arteries, or even bypass surgery, and he is willing to undergo the test.

The patient has been well hydrated overnight. He will receive 600 mg of Plavix, considering the doubt I have that he was taking his Plavix, to have him well prepped for the procedures.

Thank you, Dr. Alanda, for consulting me on this patient.

6-5D:

SERVICE CODE(S): _____

ICD-9-CM DX CODE(S): _____

ICD-10-CM DX CODE(S): _____

6-5E OPERATIVE REPORT, HEART CATHETERIZATION

LOCATION: Hospital Inpatient

PATIENT: Harold Smith

SURGEON: Marvin Elhart, MD

PROCEDURES PERFORMED: Left-sided heart catheterization, selective coronary angiogram, left ventriculography.

INDICATION: Chest pain and atherosclerotic heart disease

HEMODYNAMICS: Aortic pressure 100/58. LV 100/5. There is a 4 mm gradient across the aortic valve.

VENTRICULOGRAM: LV shows normal LV size. Small apical area of hypokinesis, but overall good function. Ejection fraction of 53%.

CORONARY ANGIOGRAM:

RIGHT CORONARY ARTERY: The right coronary artery is a moderate-size vessel. The RCA has in its midportion a stent that had good TIMI 3 flow in it.

After the crux of the heart, the RCA branches to give rise to the posterior descending artery that has at its origin, 50% stenosis and posterior artery branch that has diffuse disease thereafter.

LEFT MAIN CORONARY ARTERY: The left main artery is normal.

LEFT ANTERIOR DESCENDING ARTERY: The left anterior descending artery is tortuous, but through its course, the LAD has no severe disease.

The LAD gives rise in its proximal third to a first diagonal that has no significant disease.

CIRCUMFLEX ARTERY: The circumflex artery is a large system. Early on, it branches to give rise to a large marginal. It has a plaque extending from its origin all the way down to its proximal third. It is very eccentric and ragged, and question of dissection is seen within the circumflex system itself.

The second part of the circumflex, the distal circumflex, is a small vessel that has luminal disease and stenosis of 30% to 40%.

IMPRESSION & CONCLUSION:
1. Preserved systolic function.
2. Patent stent of the right coronary artery with some disease in the ostium of the posterior descending artery that may be 50% obstructive.
3. There is significant plaque involving the large part of the circumflex with questionable dissection within it. This appears to be the artery responsible for the patient's symptoms.

RECOMMENDATIONS: Percutaneous revascularization of the circumflex artery.

6-5E:

SERVICE CODE(S): _____

ICD-9-CM DX CODE(S): _____

ICD-10-CM DX CODE(S): _____

6-5F PTCA/STENTING REPORT

Use appropriate HCPCS modifiers to indicate stenting locations.

LOCATION: Hospital Inpatient

PATIENT: Harold Smith

SURGEON: Marvin Elhart, MD

PROCEDURE: Percutaneous transluminal angioplasty/stenting of the left circumflex artery.

PROCEDURE NOTE: A mach 10.5 guide was used. Thereafter, the patient received intravenous heparin. He was pretreated with Plavix. BMW was advanced into the circumflex. Thereafter, a 2.75 × 32 Taxus stent was advanced and deployed up to 16 atmospheres with good angiographic result and no residual stenosis of the circumflex.

IMPRESSION & CONCLUSION: Successful primary stent of the circumflex with a 2.75 × 32 Taxus drug eluting stent with good angiographic result.

6-5F:

SERVICE CODE(S): _____

ICD-9-CM DX CODE(S): _____

ICD-10-CM DX CODE(S): _____

CASE 6-6
6-6A HOSPITAL ADMISSION
6-6B CARDIOLOGY CONSULTATION
6-6C RADIOLOGY REPORT, CHEST
6-6D CARDIAC CATHETERIZATION REPORT
6-6E ANGIOPLASTY/STENT REPORT

CASE 6-6

6-6A HOSPITAL ADMISSION

Mr. Logan comes into the emergency room complaining of chest pain. He has an established diagnosis of ASHD. He is admitted to the hospital by his family physician, Dr. Alanda, and then cardiology is called in to consult him.

LOCATION: Inpatient, Hospital

PATIENT: Matthew Logan

PHYSICIAN: Leslie Alanda, MD

REASON OF ADMISSION: Chest pain with atherosclerotic heart disease

HISTORY OF PRESENT ILLNESS: The patient is a 45-year-old male with known atherosclerotic heart disease. He presents to the emergency room complaining of intermittent chest pain over the last 24 hours. He reports that the chest pain comes on with exertion, lasts 5 minutes or less, and then resolves. It is similar in nature to prior episodes of chest pain. At times, the pain radiates into his neck. He also has had associated shortness of breath at times. His last episode of pain occurred at about noon. He says that it was brought on after he got upset about something with his daughter. No nausea or diaphoresis. Even though he initially reported that the pain has been intermittent over the last 24 hours, he has actually had episodes prior to this, and sometimes they have awakened him at night.

PAST MEDICAL HISTORY:
1. Atherosclerotic heart disease. The patient has undergone a cardiac catheterization with angioplasty.
2. Diabetes mellitus, type 2.
3. Hypertension.
4. Peptic ulcer disease.
5. Dyslipidemia.

PAST SURGICAL HISTORY: None

CURRENT MEDICATIONS:
1. Lipitor 20 mg daily.
2. Glucotrol 10 mg daily.
3. Glucophage 500 mg b.i.d.
4. Aspirin 325 mg daily.
5. He had also been on Toprol XL, but it sounds as though he stopped this on his own.

ALLERGIES: None

FAMILY HISTORY: Mother and sister have diabetes mellitus, type 2. No known heart disease.

SOCIAL HISTORY: The patient is married. He is employed as a construction worker. He continues to smoke about 10 cigarettes per day. Occasional alcohol use.

REVIEW OF SYSTEMS: Complete review of systems performed, all are negative.

PHYSICAL EXAMINATION: VITAL SIGNS: Blood pressure 219/99 on admit, pulse initially 126, respirations 14, temperature 36.6°C, O_2 sat 98% on room air. On exam, the patient is an adult male who is currently comfortable, in no acute distress. He is pain free. EYES: Pupils are reactive. EARS: TMs are normal. THROAT: No lesions or erythema. NECK: Supple. No adenopathy. LUNGS: Clear to auscultation. HEART: Regular rate and rhythm. No murmurs. ABDOMEN: Slightly protuberant. Bowel sounds are positive. Abdomen is soft and nontender. No masses. EXTREMITIES: No edema.

LABORATORY: CBC, including platelet count, is normal. The patient apparently has history of thrombocytopenia, according to old chart notes. Basic metabolic shows a BUN of 26, creatinine 1.2, sodium slightly low at 132, bicarb 21.1, glucose elevated at 490, calcium 8.1. Cardiac enzymes are normal, including troponin of less than 0.04. PT, INR, and PTT are normal.

EKG: EKG shows sinus tachycardia, rate is 101; there are Q waves inferiorly; no acute changes.

CHEST X-RAY: Chest x-ray does not show any obvious infiltrate or evidence of failure. The patient does apparently have history of a lung nodule, which apparently was stable on CT last year.

ASSESSMENT:
1. Chest pain in a patient with known atherosclerotic heart disease.
2. Diabetes mellitus, type 2, poor control.
3. Hypertension.
4. Dyslipidemia.
5. History of peptic ulcer disease.

PLAN: The patient is admitted to 5th Floor, Telemetry, for further evaluation and treatment. IV heparin, nitroglycerin. Restart metoprolol; he was given metoprolol in the emergency room. Serial cardiac enzymes and Cardiology consult. This diabetes is not under good control. He will do frequent Accu-Cheks and give insulin as needed. His Glucophage will be on hold while in the hospital; continue Glucotrol.

6-6A:

SERVICE CODE(S): _____

ICD-9-CM DX CODE(S): _____

ICD-10-CM DX CODE(S): _____

6-6B CARDIOLOGY CONSULTATION

LOCATION: Inpatient, Hospital

PATIENT: Matthew Logan

ATTENDING PHYSICIAN: Leslie Alanda, MD

CONSULTANT: James Noonar, MD

REASON OF CONSULTATION: Chest pain

HISTORY IS AS FOLLOWS: A 46-year-old, diabetic, Hispanic male, known to have atherosclerotic heart disease. He is status post stent 2 years ago, had been doing well up until the last 2 to 3 days. He started complaining of chest pressure and left shoulder pain for which he had not taken nitroglycerin, which brought him to the emergency room. In the emergency room, he received nitroglycerin with resolution of his pressure. The patient had been physically quite active. Since his stent was placed, he has had no complaints similar to the ones he was complaining about yesterday.

He denies light-headedness, dizziness, syncope, or near-syncope. He denies paroxysmal nocturnal dyspnea, orthopnea, or pedal edema.

MEDICATIONS: He is on aspirin, Statin, and his antidiabetic regimen.

REVIEW OF SYSTEMS: MUSCULOSKELETAL: No complaints.

CARDIOVASCULAR system: Chest pain recently, has been increasing in intensity.

RESPIRATORY system: No complaints.

VASCULAR system: Has no claudication.

GASTROINTESTINAL system: No complaints.

URNIARY system: No complaints.

NERVOUS system: No complaints.

BREAST system: No complaints.

ENDOCRINE: Has hyperlipidemia and diabetes mellitus.

PHYSICAL EXAMINATION: The patient is alert, oriented, and in no distress. Blood pressure is 130/80, HEART rate 72, breathing 16 × per minute. HEAD: Normocephalic. NECK: Supple. No carotid bruits, no jugular venous distention. CARDIAC exam: S1, S2; no murmur, no gallop. LUNGS are clear. ABDOMEN is soft. Bowel sounds are positive. NEURO exam is grossly intact. Distally has no pedal edema, 2+ pulse.

EKG: Shows sinus rhythm with no ST-T segment changes noted. There was some ST depression noted that appeared to be nonspecific.

IMPRESSION: Patient is known to have atherosclerotic heart disease and type 2 diabetes mellitus. He is status post stent and is now admitted with crescendo chest pain, responsive to nitroglycerin, suggestive of coronary artery disease.

He had no evidence of myocardial infarctions or myocardial injury. Considering his risk factor and his prior history of heart disease and his prior stenting, I am recommending that he undergo cardiac catheterization to assess anatomy and need for revascularization.

The patient understands his alternatives. He understands also that there is the possibility of requiring angioplasty, stent, or even bypass surgery.

The patient is agreeable to undergo the test. He had been hydrated overnight, he is started on the IV Heparin. I am going to preload him with 600 mg of Plavix in case we need to stent him. He will be preset.

Thank you, Dr. Alanda, for consulting me on this patient, I will inform you of the results after testing.

6-6B:

SERVICE CODE(S): _____

ICD-9-CM DX CODE(S): _____

ICD-10-CM DX CODE(S): _____

6-6C RADIOLOGY REPORT, CHEST

LOCATION: Inpatient, Hospital

PATIENT: Matthew Logan

ATTENDING PHYSICIAN: Leslie Alanda, MD

RADIOLOGIST: Morton Monson, MD

EXAMINATION OF: Chest, single view

CLINICAL SYMPTOMS: Chest pain

CHEST, SINGLE VIEW: COMPARISON: Comparison is made to a previous examination 2 years ago.

FINDINGS: The heart size and pulmonary vascular markings appear within normal limits. No focal infiltrates are seen within the lungs. No pleural effusions are seen. Correlate clinically the need for additional or follow-up imaging.

6-6C:

SERVICE CODE(S): _____

ICD-9-CM DX CODE(S): _____

ICD-10-CM DX CODE(S): _____

6-6D CARDIAC CATHETERIZATION REPORT

LOCATION: Inpatient, Hospital

PATIENT: Matthew Logan

ATTENDING PHYSICIAN: Leslie Alanda, MD

SURGEON: James Noonar, MD

PROCEDURES PERFORMED: Right and left coronary angiogram, LV-gram left heart.

INDICATION: Unstable angina

HEMODYANAMICS:
1. Aortic pressure is 142/74.
2. LV pressure is 142/20 with no gradient on pullback.

VENTRICULOGRAM: Ventriculogram showed normal LV size. There is an inferior wall hypokinesis with an ejection fraction of 55%.

CORONARY ANGIOGRAM:

RIGHT CORONARY ARTERY: The right coronary artery is totally occluded in its proximal third. There is a large stent deployed from the proximal right coronary artery all the way close to the distal third that has in-stent restenosis with total occlusion and with TIMI-0 flow, and preobstructive collateral from the conus branch filling and the distal right coronary artery.

LEFT MAIN CORONARY ARTERY: The left main is normal.

LEFT ANTERIOR DESCENDING ARTERY: The left anterior descending artery has in its proximal third plaque that appears to be eccentric and severely obstructive. The left anterior descending artery thereafter has no significant disease. It gives rise in the mid-portion to a small diagonal that has no significant obstruction.

CIRCUMFLEX ARTERY: The circumflex artery as rises from the left main is trifurcate. The first marginal is diffusely diseased and in its midportion has a 50% to 70% stenosis. Thereafter, the circumflex bifurcates there to give two branches, the first of which is small in size and has a 50% stenosis in its proximal third, and the second marginal has a stent placed in it with severe in-stent restenosis.

IMPRESSION/CONCLUSION:
1. Preserved systolic function with inferior wall severe hypokinesis (decreased mobility).

2. Total closure of the right coronary artery with this in-stent restenosis of a very long stent placed in the proximal right coronary artery with very obstructive collateral filling from the conus branch to the distal right coronary artery that appears to be small.
3. Disease in the proximal left anterior descending artery.
4. In-stent restenosis of the second marginal and diffuse disease in the small marginal.

RECOMMENDATIONS: At this point, my recommendation is to percutaneously revascularize the left anterior descending artery as well as the in-stent restenosis of the circumflex.

The right coronary artery is currently totally occluded with preobstructive collateral filling the right coronary artery. (Restenosis of the stent is a complication of a cardiac implant NEC.)

6-6D:

SERVICE CODE(S): _____

ICD-9-CM DX CODE(S): _____

ICD-10-CM DX CODE(S): _____

6-6E ANGIOPLASTY/STENT REPORT

LOCATION: Inpatient, Hospital

PATIENT: Matthew Logan

ATTENDING PHYSICIAN: Leslie Alanda, MD

SURGEON: James Noonar, MD

INDICATION: ASHD

PROCEDURES PERFORMED: Stenting of the LAD and angioplasty of the second marginal

ANGIOPLASTY AND STENT OF THE LEFT ANTERIOR DESCENDING ARTERY: Mach 2.5 guide was used. The patient received intravenous heparin. He was preloaded with Plavix. A BMW was advanced to the LAD. Thereafter a 3.0×15 balloon was dilated into the LAD. Thereafter, a 3.0×24 Taxus stent was deployed at 15 atmospheres with good angiographic result and no residual stenosis.

ANGIOPLASTY OF IN-STENT RESTENOSIS OF THE SECOND MARGINAL OF THE LEFT CORONARY ARTERY: The BMW wire was advanced to the circumflex, and the stent was dilated with 2.5×20 Quantum Maverick balloon with good angiographic result and no residual stenosis. Distal to the stent, there was a lesion that has a remainder of 20% to 30%, and I was not willing to stent the small vessel that is going to be prone to restenosis like it had done previously.

6-6E:

SERVICE CODE(S): _____

ICD-9-CM DX CODE(S): _____

ICD-10-CM DX CODE(S): _____

CASE 6-7

6-7A TRANSESOPHAGEAL ECHOCARDIOGRAM REPORT

LOCATION: Outpatient, Hospital

PATIENT: Tom White

SURGEON: David Barton, MD

RADIOLOGY: Morton Monson, MD

PROCEDURE: Transesophageal echocardiogram

INDICATIONS: Evaluation of the aortic valve considering the stenosis that was not well-documented angiographically.

PROCEDURE: The patient received 2 mg of Versed, and a transesophageal probe was advanced to the lower part of the esophagus. We had good visualization of the heart. The mitral valve was thickened with slight prolapse, but there was no significant regurgitation noted. The LV displayed normal size and normal function. The aortic root is normal in size. The aortic valve is calcified with diffuse cusp excursions with still adequate opening. Valve area was variable in different incidents varying from 1 to even above 2.

CONCLUSION: This transesophageal echo shows aortic valve disease but does not appear to be severe. It appeared to be moderately stenotic, and considering the angiography and the hemodynamics, this patient does not need valve surgery yet.

6-7A:

SERVICE CODE(S): _____

ICD-9-CM DX CODE(S): _____

ICD-10-CM DX CODE(S): _____

CASE 6-8

6-8A OPERATIVE REPORT, ARTERIOVENOUS FISTULA

LOCATION: Outpatient, Hospital

PATIENT: Andrea Love

SURGEON: George Orbitz, MD

PREOPERATIVE DIAGNOSIS:
1. Steal syndrome, left hand.
2. Ischemic/necrotic ulcer of the left fifth digit.
3. End-stage renal disease.

POSTOPERATIVE DIAGNOSIS:
1. Steal syndrome, left hand.
2. Ischemic/necrotic ulcer of the left fifth digit.
3. End-stage renal disease.

PROCEDURE PERFORMED: Takedown of left arteriovenous fistula.

ANESTHESIA: IV Sedation

INDICATION: Andrea is a 55-year-old female who has end-stage renal disease and is on hemodialysis. She has had a fistula placed in her left arm. This is coming off either the radial, ulnar, or brachial artery and going to the cephalic vein. This is not functioning any longer. The remainder of the cephalic vein and venous system is not dilated. However, it is functional as you can feel that there is a good thrill present. Some of this is going into a deeper venous system. However, in the interim she has developed ischemic pain in her left hand. Also, she has a wound on the tip of her left fifth digit that is not healing. She had accidentally cut it with a knife a while ago. It is not healing and slowly getting worse. She currently is being dialyzed through a port system. She has even had problems with this and has had to undergo revision for this. She is not using the AVF in her arm as this is not functional as far as being able to do dialysis. She also underwent Doppler studies of it this morning. With the graft open, she has no flow out to fingertips. With the fistula occluded by handheld pressure, her pressures are running up to the 30s.

We discussed the procedure of a takedown of this fistula. We discussed the risk of bleeding, infection, and nerve injury and the significance of this. We also met with her in the Holding area again this morning preoperatively. She had no new questions. She understands and wishes to proceed with takedown of the left arm arteriovenous fistula.

PROCEDURE: The patient was brought to the operating room and placed in the supine position. After receiving IV sedation, she was prepped and draped in a sterile fashion. A transverse incision line 1 fingerbreadth below the antecubital fossa was marked out and infiltrated with 0.5% Marcaine. This was on the left arm. After waiting a couple of minutes, an incision was made. Dissection was carried down through the subcutaneous tissues. The venous limb of the arteriovenous fistula was identified. This was dissected out and controlled with vessel loops. We dissected out a segment so we would be able to transect this and ligate it. We then identified the artery. We did not dissect this out completely or circumferentially. We dissected out to identify where it was to be sure that we had two separate vascular structures, and what we were going to be dividing was the venous limb and not the arterial limb. We checked Doppler flow in the hand and in the fingertips when we occluded the graft. We could then get flow in the digital arteries, as well as greatly augment the Doppler signal in the palmar arch and even in the radial and ulnar vessels. When we occluded the artery, we lost signals in the hand. Therefore, we identified for sure our fistula. Again, by taking this down we were going to increase the flow into the hand and especially into the fingertips. We then oversewed each end with a 5-0 Prolene in a 2-layer running fashion. We checked pulses at the end of the procedure. We had nice Doppler on the radial and ulnar, the palmar arch, and each digital arteries of the left hand; there was good capillary refill. The wound was irrigated, and subcutaneous tissues were closed with interrupted sutures of 3-0 Vicryl after ensuring that hemostasis was present. This skin was closed with 4-0 Vicryl running in subcuticular fashion. Dermabond was applied as the dressing. The patient went to the recovery room in stable condition.

6-8A:

SERVICE CODE(S): _____

ICD-9-CM DX CODE(S): _____

ICD-10-CM DX CODE(S): _____

CASE 6-9

6-9A OPERATIVE REPORT, ABDOMINAL AORTIC ANEURYSM

LOCATION: Hospital Inpatient

PATIENT: Tim Webster

SURGEON: Gary Sanchez, MD

PREOPERATIVE DIAGNOSIS: 8 cm abdominal aortic aneurysm

POSTOPERATIVE DIAGNOSIS: 8 cm abdominal aortic aneurysm

OPERATIVE PROCEDURE: Repair of an abdominal aortic aneurysm with an 18 × 9 bifurcated Dacron graft

ANESTHESIA: General

INDICATIONS FOR SURGERY: The patient is a 62-year-old male who was experiencing abdominal pain. A CT scan of the abdomen was ordered, and the aneurysm was found. Patient is now in for repair of this.

DESCRIPTION OF OPERATION: The patient received Ancef 1 gram intravenously preoperatively. He was prepped and draped in the usual manner. A midline abdominal incision was made, and the abdomen was entered. The large 8 cm abdominal aortic aneurysm was found. It had not ruptured and was still intact. The aorta was dissected free from the surrounding tissues, and the bowel was retracted laterally. The neck of the aneurysm was dissected free from the surrounding tissues, allowing for a clamp to be placed across the aorta at this level. The patient then received 5,000 units of heparin. After the heparin took effect, the aorta was cross-clamped. The aorta was then opened, and 2 lumbars just below the aortic clamp were found; these were oversewn with 2-0 Tevdek sutures. Next, an 18 × 9 bifurcated Dacron graft was then cut to length and sutured end-to-end to the aorta using a running 3-0 Prolene suture. A clamp was placed on the graft, and the clamp on the aorta was released. This was a good, tight anastomosis. The distal iliac artery openings were then oversewn. The right and left limbs were then tunneled into each groin area. An end-to-side anastomosis was then done on each femoral artery. Just prior to completion of the left femoral anastomosis, the clamp on the aortic graft was released to allow flow to go through the left limb of the graft. After we completed this, the anastomosis was completed on the left side and blood was allowed to flow in the left femoral artery. The right anastomosis was completed, and then blood was allowed to flow into the artery. Hemostasis was checked. The abdominal incision was then inspected. There was a small bleeder off the left renal vein, and this was controlled with a small clip. The operative area was irrigated. The aneurysm was then oversewn over the graft using a running 2-0 Vicryl suture. The bowel was then returned to the abdomen. The abdominal incision was then closed using a running #1 looped PDS suture. Subcutaneous tissue was thoroughly irrigated, and the skin was closed with skin clips. The patient tolerated the operation and returned to the intensive care unit in stable condition. Estimated blood loss was 750 cc. Urine output was 1645 cc. Fluids given were saline 8900 cc, albumin 1000 cc, Hespan 1000 cc, RBCs 613 cc, and Cell Saver 1694 cc.

6-9A:

SERVICE CODE(S): _____

ICD-9-CM DX CODE(S): _____

ICD-10-CM DX CODE(S): _____

6-9B PATHOLOGY REPORT

LOCATION: Hospital Inpatient

PATIENT: Tim Webster

SURGEON: Gary Sanchez, MD

PATHOLOGIST: Grey Lonewolf, MD

CLINICAL HISTORY: Abdominal aortic aneurysm

SPECIMEN RECEIVED: 8 cm abdominal aortic plaque and clot

GROSS DESCRIPTION: The specimen is labeled with the patient's name and "abdominal aortic plaque and clot," which contains multiple pink-tan laminated fibrin thrombus fragments up to 8 cm in greatest diameter. Mixed in are fragments of dark red blood clots. A few tan-yellow plaque segments up to 3 cm in greatest dimension were also seen, with sections representing 6 cassettes.

MICROSCOPIC DIAGNOSIS: Severe atherosclerosis and plaque with fibrin thrombus and blood consistent with abdominal aortic aneurysm.

6-9B:

SERVICE CODE(S): _____

ICD-9-CM DX CODE(S): _____

ICD-10-CM DX CODE(S): _____

CHAPTER 7

Digestive System, Hemic/Lymphatic System, and Mediastinum/ Diaphragm

CASE 7-1

7-1A OPERATIVE REPORT, ANAL FISSURE

LOCATION: Hospital Inpatient

PATIENT: Annabelle Antman

SURGEON: Larry P. Friendly, MD

PREOPERATIVE DIAGNOSIS: Anal fissure

POSTOPERATIVE DIAGNOSIS: Anal fissure

OPERATIVE PROCEDURE:
1. Sphincterotomy with fissurectomy
2. Pallipectomy with excision of one sentinel tag

ANESTHESIA: Spinal

INDICATIONS: Annabelle is a pleasant 44-year-old female who is post three quadrant hemorrhoidectomy for severe external hemorrhoids. She has an anal fissure as well as sentinel tag and that is quite tender. She presents today for elective sphincterotomy, excision of the sentinel tag, understands the surgery and the risks of bleeding and infection, possible damage to the sphincter muscles, and wishes to proceed.

DESCRIPTION OF PROCEDURE: The patient was brought to the operating room, given spinal anesthesia and placed in a jackknife position. We could see the enlarged hemorrhoid/sentinel tag at the 10 o'clock position and the fissure right at the base of this. Anoscope was placed and we placed a Kelly clamp behind the hypertrophied scarred band of muscle and divided the muscle. We then excised the sentinel tag and fissure then closed the defect with interrupted 3-0 chromic sutures and running locked 3-0 chromic. There were no other internal hemorrhoids and there were no other fissures. We infiltrated the area with a total of 30 cc of 0.5%. Sensorcaine with epinephrine solution, placed four gauze dressings in the area that we will remove in 30 minutes, and she was taken to recovery in stable condition.

7-1A:

SERVICE CODE(S): _____

ICD-9-CM DX CODE(S): _____

ICD-10-CM DX CODE(S): _____

If an abscess is simply lanced and drained, report the services with an incision code (46020-46083).

CASE 7-2

7-2A OPERATIVE REPORT, PERIRECTAL FISTULECTOMY

In this case a fistula is removed with no mention of an abscess.

LOCATION: Inpatient, Hospital

PATIENT: Franklin Berg

SURGEON: Larry Friendly, MD

PREOPERATIVE DIAGNOSIS: Perirectal fistula

POSTOPERATIVE DIAGNOSIS: Perirectal fistula

PROCEDURE PERFORMED: Excision of a subcutaneous perirectal fistula.

ANESTHESIA: General anesthesia

INDICATION FOR SURGERY: Mr. Berg is a 64-year-old male who has developed a perirectal fistula. The patient is admitted for repair.

PROCEDURE: The patient was prepped and draped in the usual manner. He was given a general anesthetic. An incision was used to excise the perirectal fistula in its entirety. The specimen was sent to pathology. Hemostasis was obtained using Bovie cautery. The incision was then irrigated and injected with 0.5% Marcaine with epinephrine; 22 cc was used. A dressing was then applied. The patient tolerated the operation and returned to recovery in stable condition.

7-2A:

SERVICE CODE(S): _____

ICD-9-CM DX CODE(S): _____

ICD-10-CM DX CODE(S): _____

CASE 7-3

Use the correct approach and code to the fullest extent of the procedure.
The endoscopic procedure uses an existing orifice (opening), a laparoscopic procedure uses a small incision, and an open procedure uses a larger incision.

7-3A OPERATIVE REPORT, DIALYSIS CATHETER

LOCATION: Hospital Inpatient

PATIENT: Betty Peters

SURGEON: Gary Sanchez, MD

PREOPERATIVE DIAGNOSIS: End-stage renal disease; hemodialysis catheter malfunctioning

POSTOPERATIVE DIAGNOSIS: End-stage renal disease

PROCEDURE PERFORMED: Placement of a temporary dialysis catheter

INDICATION: This is an 89-year-old female with chronic renal failure. It was found that her hemodialysis catheter had poor blood flow rates, and it was decided to place a temporary dialysis catheter until a new permanent one could be placed.

PROCEDURE: The area was prepped in the usual fashion. I could not advance the wire through the blue port of the catheter. There was no flow initially. The flow did improve. I was able, afterwards, to get a wire to go through without difficulty. I placed an 11.5 French, 13.5 cm temporary dialysis catheter over the guidewire, after removing the old one, using the Seldinger technique without difficulty. Both ports had good blood return after the wire was taken out. Both ports were flushed with saline. The catheter was secured to the skin. The patient tolerated the procedure well without immediate complications.

7-3A:

SERVICE CODE(S): _____

ICD-9-CM DX CODE(S): _____

ICD-10-CM DX CODE(S): _____

CASE 7-4

CASE 7-4A OPERATIVE REPORT, COLON POLYPECTOMY

Report the services for the following case. When reporting the diagnosis for the operative procedure, reference the pathology report located in 7-4B.

LOCATION: Outpatient, Hospital

PATIENT: Jeffrey Henrys

SURGEON: Larry Friendly, MD

SCOPE USED: Pentax video colonoscope

MEDICATION GIVEN: Fentanyl 100 mcg IV; Versed 2 mg IV

PREOPERATIVE DIAGNOSIS: Polyp found on flexible sigmoidoscopy

POSTOPERATIVE DIAGNOSIS:
1. Two small 2-mm polyps in the descending sigmoid colon.
2. An 8-mm semipedunculated rectal polyp, snare removed.

PROCEDURE PERFORMED: Colonoscopy with polypectomy

INDICATION: This is a 65-year-old white male referred for colonoscopy. The patient had a screening flexible sigmoidoscopy. He is asymptomatic and was found to have a small colon polyp at 22 cm and a 4-mm polyp in the rectum.

FINDINGS: The Pentax video colonoscope was inserted easily to the cecum. The ileocecal valve was identified. The appendiceal orifice was seen. Careful inspection in the cecum, ascending colon, hepatic flexure, transverse colon, splenic flexure, and descending colon revealed no erythema, ulceration, exudates, friability, or other mucosal abnormalities. The distal descending sigmoid revealed two small polyps 2 mm or less in size. These were hot biopsied off. The rectum, however, did reveal an 8-mm semipedunculated polyp. This was snared piecemeal. The patient did have one medium to large size internal hemorrhoid, now bleeding. The patient tolerated the procedure well.

IMPRESSION:
1. Two diminutive polyps in the descending sigmoid colon, hot biopsied off.
2. An 8-mm semipedunculated polyp in the rectum, snared off.
3. A medium-sized internal hemorrhoid.

PLAN: As the polyps are adenomatous, which is what I suspect they are, the patient can return again in 5 years for surveillance.

Pathology Report Later Indicated: See Report 7-4B

7-4A:

SERVICE CODE(S): _____

ICD-9-CM DX CODE(S): _____

ICD-10-CM DX CODE(S): _____

7-4B PATHOLOGY REPORT

LOCATION: Outpatient, Hospital

PATIENT: Jeffrey Henrys

SURGEON: Larry Friendly, MD

PATHOLOGIST: Morton Monson, MD

CLINICAL HISTORY: Adenoma

TISSUE RECEIVED: Rectal polyp, sigmoid polyp

GROSS DESCRIPTION: The specimen is labeled with the patient's name and "rectal polyp" and consists of small polypoid yellow-tan tissue fragments, up to 6 mm. Also submitted is a 9 mm in diameter, soft, pink-tan lobulated polyp, labeled sigmoid polyp. This large polyp is serially sectioned. The fragments are filtered, and the specimen is submitted in 1 cassette.

MICROSCOPIC DESCRIPTION: Sections of polyp showed closely crowded and elongated tubular glands separated by a fibrovascular stroma. These glands show mild decreased goblet cell activity with cell crowding and slightly enlarged hyperchromatic nuclei with occasional mitoses.

DIAGNOSIS: Rectal polyp, endoscopic biopsies: Fragments of villous adenoma, benign.

7-4B:

SERVICE CODE(S): _____

ICD-9-CM DX CODE(S): _____

ICD-10-CM DX CODE(S): _____

CASE 7-5

7-5A OPERATIVE REPORT, SIGMOIDOSCOPY

LOCATION: Outpatient, Hospital

PATIENT: Charles Smith

SURGEON: Larry Friendly, MD

SCOPE USED: Pentax video sigmoidoscope

MEDICATIONS: None

PREOPERATIVE DIAGNOSIS: Rectal polyps

POSTOPERATIVE DIAGNOSIS: Sigmoid and rectal polyps

INDICATIONS: This is a 61-year-old male who presents for a sigmoidoscopy due to rectal polyps. Polyps were found, and now the patient is referred for further treatment of these. He is asymptomatic. There is no family history of colon cancer or polyps.

FINDINGS: The Pentax video sigmoidoscope was inserted easily; four polyps were seen on this examination scattered between the rectum and proximal sigmoid colon. The largest measured about 1.5 cm in diameter. The others were diminutive, about 4 or 5 mm in diameter. Biopsies were taken of two of these polyps.

DESCRIPTION OF PROCEDURE: Consent was obtained. The patient was prepared for a sigmoidoscopy. He was placed in the left lateral decubitus position and given no medication. A digital rectal examination was performed and was unremarkable. The lubricated Pentax video sigmoidoscope was guided digitally into the rectum and advanced to 70 cm; four polyps were seen to range from 4 to 10 mm in diameter between the sigmoid colon and the proximal rectum. Biopsies were taken of two of these. They appeared to be adenomas. There were no diverticula. The patient tolerated the procedure well and was discharged ambulatory.

PLAN: Polyp biopsies were reviewed. These appear to be adenomas, and the patient will be scheduled for colonoscopy for polypectomy.

Pathology Report Later Indicated: See Report 7-5B

7-5A:

SERVICE CODE(S): _____

ICD-9-CM DX CODE(S): _____

ICD-10-CM DX CODE(S): _____

7-5B PATHOLOGY REPORT

LOCATION: Outpatient, Hospital

PATIENT: Charles Smith

SURGEON: Larry Friendly, MD

PATHOLOGIST: Morton Monson, MD

CLINICAL HISTORY: Polyps

SPECIMEN RECEIVED: Colon polyp biopsy

GROSS DESCRIPTION: The specimen is labeled with the patient's name and "colon polyp" and consists of two frozen fragments of tan tissue measuring 0.1 to 0.4 cm in greatest dimension. The specimen is totally submitted.

MICROSCOPIC DESCRIPTION: The colon biopsy demonstrates a polyp showing adenomatous and villous epithelial features within the glandular and surface epithelium. The glands vary in size and configuration and are separated by an intact lamina propria. The cells are enlarged with elongated hyperchromatic nuclei. Pseudostratification and crowding are evident.

DIAGNOSIS: Colon biopsy, mucosal: tubulovillous adenoma.

7-5B:

SERVICE CODE(S): _____

ICD-9-CM DX CODE(S): _____

ICD-10-CM DX CODE(S): _____

CASE 7-6

7-6A OPERATIVE REPORT, COLONOSCOPY

LOCATION: Hospital Inpatient

PATIENT: Jessica Andrews

ATTENDING PHYSICIAN: Gordon Jayco, MD

SURGEON: Daniel Olanka, MD

PROCEDURE: Colonoscopy to rule out GI bleeding

PREOPERATIVE DIAGNOSIS: Anemia

POSTOPERATIVE DIAGNOSIS: Anemia

INDICATION: This is a 45-year-old white female referred by Dr. Jayco for a colonoscopy. The patient was found to have a hemoglobin of 11.6 with MCV of 78. She has had problems with anemia in the past, probably related to her gastric bypass performed 8 years ago. She had only been on iron three times per week. The patient also has a history of polyps. Her last colonoscopy 2 years ago was unremarkable. She was also anemic at that time and had an upper endoscopy. She was recommended to continue iron and vitamin C at that time.

PREOPERATIVE MEDICATIONS: Fentanyl 100 mcg IV; Versed 6 mg IV

FINDINGS: The Pentax video colonoscope was inserted without difficulty to the cecum. The ileocecal valve was identified. The appendiceal orifice was seen. Careful inspection in the cecum, ascending colon, hepatic flexure, transverse colon, splenic flexure, descending colon, sigmoid colon, and rectum revealed no erythema, ulceration, exudates, friability, or other mucosal abnormalities. The patient tolerated the procedure well.

IMPRESSION: Normal colonoscopy.

PLAN: We will do an upper endoscopy.

7-6A:

SERVICE CODE(S): _____

ICD-9-CM DX CODE(S): _____

ICD-10-CM DX CODE(S): _____

7-6B OPERATIVE REPORT, ESOPHAGOGASTRODUODENOSCOPY

LOCATION: Hospital Inpatient

PATIENT: Jessica Andrews

ATTENDING PHYSICIAN: Gordon Jayco, MD

SURGEON: Daniel Olanka, MD

OPERATIVE PROCEDURE: Esophagogastroduodenoscopy, EGD

PREOPERATIVE DIAGNOSIS: Anemia, rule out peptic ulcers

POSTOPERATIVE DIAGNOSIS: Gastric bypass with presumed gastrojejunostomy with Roux-en-Y. No ulcer. Biopsies obtained to rule out sprue.

INDICATION: This is a 45-year-old white female who had a colonoscopy to try to find cause for her anemia. The colonoscopy was negative so now patient is here for upper endoscopy. The patient was found to have a hemoglobin of 11.6 with MCV of 78. She has had problems with anemia in the past, probably related to her gastric bypass performed 8 years ago. She had only been on iron three times per week. She had an upper endoscope done about 2 years ago and that was negative. She was recommended to continue iron and vitamin C at that time.

FINDINGS: The Pentax video pediatric endoscope was passed without difficulty into the oropharynx. The gastroesophageal junction was seen at 39 cm. Inspection of the esophagus revealed no erythema, ulceration, exudates, friability, stricture, varices, or other mucosal abnormalities. There is a very short gastric remnant. The presumed gastrojejunostomy was entered a distance of about 20 cm. The mucosa was normal. Biopsies were obtained to rule out sprue. The patient tolerated the procedure well.

IMPRESSION: Normal presumed gastrojejunostomy with Roux-en-Y. No ulcer. Biopsies obtained of jejunum to rule out sprue.

PLAN: The patient's anemia is probably due to the gastric bypass. Microcytic anemia is probably due to the gastric bypass. I would recommend iron 325 mg per day and vitamin C 500 mg per day indefinitely.

Pathology Report Later Indicated: Ruled out sprue. All tissue benign.

7-6B:

SERVICE CODE(S): _____

ICD-9-CM DX CODE(S): _____

ICD-10-CM DX CODE(S): _____

7-6C KUB

A barium study is a contrast barium enema, also known as air-contrast barium enema, air-contrast study, or barium-contrast study of the colon.

LOCATION: Hospital Inpatient

PATIENT: Jessica Andrews

ATTENDING PHYSICIAN: Gordon Jayco, MD

RADIOLOGIST: Morton Monson, MD

EXAMINATION OF: KUB

CLINICAL SYMPTOMS: Diarrhea in a patient with anemia and past gastric bypass surgery.

KUB DONE PRIOR TO BARIUM STUDY: There is no prior study for comparison. No lesions are appreciated. Bypassed stomach is noted. Bowel gas pattern is above normal. Small distended bowel loops are seen. There is bowel gas from the stomach to the rectum. No enlargement of the liver or spleen. No significant calcification seen. Entirety of pelvis not imaged on film.

IMPRESSION:
1. History of gastric bypass surgery.
2. Above normal bowel gas pattern.
3. Anemia.

7-6C:

SERVICE CODE(S): _____

ICD-9-CM DX CODE(S): _____

ICD-10-CM DX CODE(S): _____

CASE 7-7

7-7A OPERATIVE REPORT, CHOLECYSTECTOMY

The patient in this case presents with biliary colic. The patient is electing to have her gallbladder removed.

LOCATION: Outpatient, Hospital

PATIENT: Annabelle Felt

PHYSICIAN: Larry Friendly, MD

PREOPERATIVE DIAGNOSIS: Biliary colic

POSTOPERATIVE DIAGNOSIS: Biliary colic

PROCEDURE PERFORMED: Laparoscopic cholecystectomy

ANESTHESIA: General

INDICATIONS: The patient is a 42-year-old female who presents with upper abdominal pain and is found to have biliary colic. She presents today with for elective laparoscopic cholecystectomy. She understands the risks and possible open cholecystectomy.

PROCEDURE: The patient was given a general anesthetic. She was prepped and draped in the head-up position. A curvilinear incision was made above the umbilicus and I worked my way down to the fascia, incised the fascia, and put in retaining Vicryl stitches. I carefully worked my way into the abdomen, put in Hasson, the gas, and a 30-degree scope. We put a 10 mm trocar below the xiphisternum, a 5-mm port below this, and a 5-mm port laterally to the right. We lifted up the gallbladder and dissected in the region of the triangle of Calot. I could very easily see cystic nodes, cystic artery, cystic duct, and common duct. I came around the cystic artery and divided it. I made sure I removed the gallbladder from the gallbladder bed for about 20% prior to clipping the cystic artery. As mentioned, I clipped the cystic artery, and then the triangle of Calot was completely opened. I dissected the gallbladder from the gallbladder bed for about 10% more and it was wide open. I then clipped the cystic duct and divided. I then removed the gallbladder from the gallbladder bed using combination of blunt dissection and cautery. Once we had the gallbladder removed we found we had no spill of bile and excellent hemostasis. I then put a camera in the upper 10 mm port and brought the gallbladder out through the umbilical port in an Endopouch. We then confirmed our excellent hemostasis. I removed the upper 10 mm trocar and closed it with the GraNee Needle System. I then again confirmed my excellent hemostasis and removed the rest of the trocars and closed the umbilical fascial defect with interrupted Vicryl stitches. Subcutaneous tissue was brought together with Vicryl stitches. All skin incisions were closed with 3-0 Prolene. Steri-Strips and Posits were applied. The patient tolerated this well and went to the recovery room in good condition.

7-7A:

SERVICE CODE(S): _____

ICD-9-CM DX CODE(S): _____

ICD-10-CM DX CODE(S): _____

CASE 7-8

7-8A OPERATIVE REPORT, CYSTECTOMY

LOCATION: Inpatient, Hospital

PATIENT: Amber Black

ATTENDING PHYSICIAN: Ronald Green, MD

SURGEON: Gary Sanchez, MD

PREOPERATIVE DIAGNOSIS: Left intra-abdominal lesion seen on CT scan

POSTOPERATIVE DIAGNOSIS: Left sigmoid colon cyst

PROCEDURE PERFORMED: Excision of an ascending colon area cyst

ANESTHESIA: General

INDICATION: This is a 33-year-old white female who had a CT scan of her abdomen due to abdominal pain. On CT a lesion was noted inside the patient's abdominal cavity. The patient is now being brought to the operating room for exploratory laparotomy with possible excision of the lesion.

PROCEDURE: The patient has previously undergone bowel prep the day before. She was prepped and draped in the usual manner. She received Mefoxin 3 g intravenously before surgery. The incision was made in the lower, middle part of the abdomen. The abdomen was entered and the lesion was found. It was a cyst located on the wall of the sigmoid colon. The cyst was carefully excised sharply and dissected free of the colon. This was then sent to pathology. Hemostasis was achieved using Bovie cautery. No other abnormalities were noted. The incision was then closed using a running #1 double-stranded suture. The subcutaneous tissues were irrigated and closed with a running 3-0 Vicryl suture. The skin was then closed with Steri-Strips. The patient tolerated the procedure well and went on to the recovery room in stable condition.

Pathology Report Later Indicated: Benign colon cyst

7-8A:

SERVICE CODE(S): _____

ICD-9-CM DX CODE(S): _____

ICD-10-CM DX CODE(S): _____

CASE 7-9

7-9A INITIAL HOSPITAL SERVICE

The patient, Stephen Moore, was brought to the hospital emergency room by air ambulance from Loganville. Stephen was involved in a motor vehicle rollover in which he was the driver. Dr. Paul Sutton treated the patient in the emergency department and then contacted Dr. Sanchez, the general surgeon on call, who admitted the patient to the hospital.

LOCATION: Inpatient, Hospital

PATIENT: Stephen Moore

ATTENDING PHYSICIAN: Gary Sanchez, MD

HISTORY: Mr. Moore is a 25-year-old young man who was involved in a motor vehicle rollover just outside of town. According to the paramedics who brought him down via air ambulance, the patient had arrested three times during the flight. The patient also was reported to be hypothermic with a temperature of 27° C. The patient is transported with bilateral chest tubes in place. He also has no neck collar in place but is on a backboard with the neck stabilized with straps. There is no family available. The paramedics have no other history at the present time, other than there is a possibility that after the rollover he was immersed in cold water for approximately 5 minutes, but this history is speculative at the present time.

ROS, PAST, FAMILY, SOCIAL HISTORY: Unable to obtain due to patient being unconscious.

PHYSICAL EXAM: The patient is hypotensive. His temperature is 27° C with a blood pressure of 60 systolic. He has a tense distended abdomen. His pupils are fixed and dilated. He has no other injuries.

ASSESSMENT:
1. Major intra-abdominal injuries.
2. Hypotension
3. Hypothermia.
4. Unconscious.

PLAN: He is going to be taken immediately to the operating room while we resuscitate him there in a more stable einviroment. X-ray had been asked previously to place a portable machine in the OR.

The patient is critically ill and is at high risk for mortality. The fixed dilated pupils are of concern, but control of his intra-abdominal bleeding and correction of the hypothermia are a priority.

7-9A:

SERVICE CODE(S): _____

ICD-9-CM DX CODE(S): _____

ICD-10-CM DX CODE(S): _____

7-9B OPERATIVE REPORT, LAPAROTOMY

LOCATION: Inpatient, Hospital

PATIENT: Stephen Moore

ATTENDING PHYSICIAN: Gary Sanchez, MD

SURGEON: Gary Sanchez, MD

PREOPERATIVE DIAGNOSIS: Massive thoracic and abdominal injuries.

POSTOPERATIVE DIAGNOSIS: Same.

PROCEDURE PERFORMED: Damage control laparotomy (This is reported as an exploration of the retroperitoneal area) with suture of a bleeding liver laceration.

This young man presented with a temperature of 27° C (indicates hypothermia) after being involved in a rollover accident. During the transport down he apparently had an arrest three times. The patient has a 60 systolic blood pressure at this stage. He had not had a collar placed during transport but was controlled on the backboard with his head stabilized. Immediately on arrival in the operating room a cervical collar was placed. The patient had already been intubated. He had bilateral chest tubes in place.

Once he was on the operating room table, an attempt was made to get chest x-ray, but radiology could not get a plate under the patient. With good function of the chest tubes and the patient's continued severe hypotension, it was elected to proceed with the laparotomy and proceed with further evaluation as the case progressed. As the abdomen was being prepped, anesthesia was giving him fluids and blood and trying to warm him up (further indicates hypothermia). All fluids were run in warmers, including the blood that was being infused. Immediately upon having the abdomen prepped and draped, a long midline incision was made; the patient was found to have approximately a liter and one-half of blood present within the abdomen. He was cold. He had an actively bleeding liver tear (this diagnosis provides the medical necessity for the liver repair) that was on the dorsum just lateral to the ligament teres. Several 0 chromic sutures were placed through this in figure-of-eight fashion and this stopped the bleeding. This was done after we had immediately packed both the left and right upper quadrants, as well as the pelvis. After being assured that his bleeding was controlled with the packing, anesthesia was continuously warming him and we used warm irrigation in the abdomen. The chest tubes were draining adequately. According to anesthesia, the patient still had fixed dilated pupils. By the end of the procedure the patient's temperature was up to about 30° C.

As the anesthesia was infusing the blood and fluids and the patient's blood pressure was now coming up we started looking at each of the quadrants. The patient is found to have a non-expanding hematoma involving the pelvis consistent with a pelvic fracture. This was repacked to make sure there was no active bleeding in this area but there was no active bleeding. The packs were removed from the left upper quadrant slowly. The spleen was then visualized and there was no active bleeding; this was repacked. The right side was then evaluated. Most of the blood was around the liver. The patient had a laceration at the dome of the liver just to the right of the ligamentum teres and this was oversewn as noted above. At this point, because of the patient's hypothermia and instability, the abdomen was re-packed. A Vac-Pac was quickly placed. The patient's pupils at this stage were still fixed and dilated. There was a question whether the fixed pupils were due to either a primary head injury with an intracranial bleed, or whether this was just a hypoxic related issue related to the original injury, and the 3 arrests during transport. The patient was taken immediately from the operating room to the CAT scanner with neurosurgeon available. CAT scan will be done immediately. If the patient does not have anything intracranial that needs to be fixed immediately, he will be taken to the intensive care unit where we will continue resuscitation with the warm fluids and blood as necessary. The patient is in critical condition. At the end of the procedure the patient's blood pressure was up in the 80s systolic.

7-9B:

SERVICE CODE(S): _____

ICD-9-CM DX CODE(S): _____

ICD-10-CM DX CODE(S): _____

7-9C DISCHARGE SUMMARY

Typically any E&M related to the surgery, including discharge summary, within the surgical global period are not billable by the surgeon. However, for the purpose of practice, assign the discharge summary code for this case.

LOCATION: Inpatient, Hospital

PATIENT: Stephen Moore

ATTENDING PHYSICIAN: Gary Sanchez, MD

DIAGNOSES:
1. Head injury with fixed dilated pupils due to rollover car accident.
2. Liver laceration.
3. Hypotension.
4. Hypothermia.
5. Cardiac arrest.

SUMMARY: The patient was admitted through the emergency department after being involved in a one-car rollover accident. Patient was an unrestrained driver. We took him immediately to surgery and there we found abdominal bleeding and liver laceration. His abdominal injuries were repaired, and patient was then taken for a CT of his head to try and find cause of his unconscious state and dilation and fixation of his pupils. When I got to the CT room the patient was not breathing. There was no chance for resuscitation, he just flat-lined immediately. There was nothing we could do for him and patient was pronounced dead at 2100 hours. His family was notified and pastoral services were called in.

7-9C:

SERVICE CODE(S): _____

ICD-9-CM DX CODE(S): _____

ICD-10-CM DX CODE(S): _____

CASE 7-10

7-10A OPERATIVE REPORT, APPENDECTOMY

LOCATION: Inpatient, Hospital

PATIENT: Rachel Wiggins

ATTENDING PHYSICIAN: Leslie Alanda, MD

PREOPERATIVE DIAGNOSIS: Acute appendicitis

POSTOPERATIVE DIAGNOSIS: Acute appendicitis

ANESTHESIA: General

INDICATIONS: Rachel is a 17-year-old female who has a history and exam consistent with acute appendicitis. Her diagnosis as well as the recommended procedure of an appendectomy was discussed with the patient as well as her parents. We discussed the other possible diagnoses that could be present. We discussed some of these are treated medically and some are treated operatively. I would recommend an appendectomy as this is quite suspicious that she indeed has appendicitis. We discussed potential problems with a perforated appendicitis. This is also possible that this has occurred even at this point. I discussed if her appendix appears to be grossly normal that we will still plan to remove her appendix at the time of the operation and then look for other causes of her abdominal pain. If something needs to be done surgically, we will go ahead and proceed with it even if it requires a larger incision or a completely different incision to manage this. We discussed the risk of bleeding and infection. We discussed injury to intestines, and other intra-abdominal structures. We discussed wound infections and abscesses that can occur. Her questions were answered. She understands and wishes to proceed with an appendectomy.

PROCEDURE: Rachel was then brought to the operating room and placed in a supine position on the table. After receiving a general anesthetic she was prepped and draped in a sterile fashion. Incision line was marked out in the right lower quadrant. This was just a little bit above McBurney's point. This was infiltrated with 0.5% Marcaine. We waited a couple of minutes. Incision was then made and carried down through Scarpa's down through the subcutaneous tissues down to the anterior fascia. The anterior fascia was sharply divided. Muscle-splitting incision was carried out down to the peritoneum. This was grasped in a three-step technique and the peritoneal cavity was entered sharply. The inflamed appendix was identified and brought out through the wound. This did appear to be grossly inflamed, especially the distal aspect of this. It appeared to be fairly early on. The mesoappendix was taken down between clamps, transected, and ligated with 3-0 Vicryl in continuity. The origin of this appendix was then crushed and clamped was moved just distal to this. No Vicryl was used to ligate the origin of the appendix. The appendix was then transected sharply and handed off the table as a specimen. The appendiceal stump was cauterized. A 3-0 silk pursestring suture was placed in the base of the cecum. This was used then to imbricate the appendiceal stump. We also used a Z-stitch of 3-0 silk over this to further "roll this in." Hemostasis was present. This was then returned to the peritoneal cavity. The right lower quadrant and the pelvis were irrigated out with warm normal saline. Clear returns were established. The posterior fascia and peritoneum was closed with a 0 Vicryl in a running fashion. The wound was irrigated out. 0 Vicryl was used to approximate the internal obliques in interrupted fashion. Wound was irrigated out. The anterior fascia was closed then with interrupted sutures of 0 Vicryl in a figure-of-eight fashion. The wound was irrigated out. Skin was closed with a 4-0 Vicryl in a subcuticular fashion. Steri-Strips and sterile dressings of Telfa and Tegaderm were applied. The patient tolerated the procedure well and went to the recovery room in stable condition.

Pathology Report Later Indicated: See Report 7-10B

7-10A:

SERVICE CODE(S): _____

ICD-9-CM DX CODE(S): _____

ICD-10-CM DX CODE(S): _____

7-10B PATHOLOGY REPORT

LOCATION: Inpatient, Hospital

PATIENT: Rachel Wiggins

ATTENDING PHYSICIAN: Leslie Alanda, MD

PATHOLOGIST: Grey Lonewolf, MD

CLINICAL HISTORY: Right lower quadrant abdominal pain

TISSUE RECEIVED: Appendix

GROSS DESCRIPTION: The specimen is labeled with the patient's name and "appendix," which is 5.5 × 0.8 × 0.4 cm. The serosal surface is tan with tan-white exudates. On sectioning, the wall is intact. The lumen contains tan-red soft material. Representative sections in 2 cassettes.

MICROSCOPIC DESCRIPTION: Sections of appendix show mucosal ulceration with interstitial hemorrhage. There are transmural neutrophilic infiltrates. There is serosal congestion and edema with fibrinous neutrophilic exudates extending into the attached fatty mesoappendix.

DIAGNOSIS: Acute suppurative appendicitis.

7-10B:

SERVICE CODE(S): _____

ICD-9-CM DX CODE(S): _____

ICD-10-CM DX CODE(S): _____

CASE 7-11

7-11A OPERATIVE REPORT, PLACEMENT OF GASTROSTOMY TUBE

This patient, Gene Rise, has been suffering from constipation for 2 months now. Patient was noted to have a small bowel obstruction. Patient is now in for placement of a gastrostomy tube.

LOCATION: Inpatient, Hospital

PATIENT: Gene Rise

SURGEON: Gary Sanchez, MD

PREOPERATIVE DIAGNOSIS: Small bowel obstruction

POSTOPERATIVE DIAGNOSIS: Small bowel obstruction

PROCEDURE PERFORMED: Placement of Moss gastrostomy tube, enterotomy

ANESTHESIA: General anesthesia

DESCRIPTION OF PROCEDURE: The patient was brought to the operating room and placed under general anesthesia. The patient was prepped and draped in the usual manner. The incision was made in the abdomen extending down the midline from just below the umbilicus. We then entered the abdominal cavity. There was marked dilatation of the small bowel. We identified a section of the small bowel that was around 5 or 8 inches from the ileocecal valve. This was stuck in the pelvis. The rest of the small bowel was volvulized around this forming an internal hernia and this is what caused the bowel obstruction. We were able to see a clear transition zone between the dilated bowel and the nondilated bowel. We performed an enterotomy, which revealed stool-like material within the bowel. This told us that this has been obstructed for a while. We were able to keep all of this outside the abdominal cavity. This enterotomy site was closed in layers with interrupted Vicryl being used on the inner layer and silk suture on the outer layer. After closure we irrigated the abdominal cavity and returned the bowel to the abdomen. A stab incision was then made in the anterior abdominal wall. We then placed a Moss gastrostomy tube through this incision and into the stomach. A balloon was inflated, and the distal portion of the tube was threaded through the pylorus into the duodenum. The stomach was then tacked up to the abdominal wall. The abdominal cavity was again irrigated with saline. We then closed the abdomen with running 0 loop nylon. We tacked the sutures around the umbilicus. We packed the wound with wet saline gauze. A sterile dressing was applied. The patient tolerated the procedure well and was taken to the recovery room in satisfactory condition.

7-11A:

SERVICE CODE(S): _____

ICD-9-CM DX CODE(S): _____

ICD-10-CM DX CODE(S): _____

CASE 7-12

7-12A SURGICAL CONSULTATION

LOCATION: Inpatient, Hospital

PATIENT: Rodney Asp

PRIMARY CARE PHYSICIAN: Gary Sanchez, MD

CONSULTANT: Ronald Green, MD

CHIEF COMPLAINT: Umbilical hernia

HISTORY OF PRESENT ILLNESS: The patient is a 46-year-old male who the previous week while doing some heavy lifting felt a tearing at the umbilical area. He was seen in the emergency room and evaluated and felt to have an umbilical hernia and is now referred for my evaluation.

PAST MEDICAL SURGERY: Unremarkable. He has had some nasal turbinate surgery in the past. He has no other medical or surgical problems.

SOCIAL HISTORY: He is employed working with heavy lifting.

MEDICATIONS: None

ALLERGIES: None

REVIEW OF SYSTEMS: There is no chest pain. No difficulty with breathing. No cough or sputum production. There have been no problems with his bowels. No nausea or vomiting. Urine is passing appropriately. The rest of the review of systems is unremarkable.

PHYSICAL EXAMINATION: The patient is well-developed in no acute distress. The head is normocephalic. Pupils are equal and reactive to light. The chest is clear to auscultation. The heart has a regular rhythm. No murmurs appreciated. The abdomen reveals a fingertip-size umbilical hernia at the upper end of the umbilicus. This does reduce although with some difficulty. There are no other abdominal masses. Good bowel sounds are heard. There are no inguinal hernias present.

IMPRESSION:
1. Umbilical hernia secondary to heavy lifting on the job.
2. General good health.

PLAN: The patient will have repair of the hernia using a small piece of mesh. We will schedule this in the morning.

7-12A:

SERVICE CODE(S): _____

ICD-9-CM DX CODE(S): _____

ICD-10-CM DX CODE(S): _____

7-12B OPERATIVE REPORT, UMBILICAL HERNIORRHAPHY

LOCATION: Inpatient, Hospital

PATIENT: Rodney Asp

SURGEON: Gary Sanchez, MD

PREOPERATIVE DIAGNOSIS: Umbilical hernia

POSTOPERATIVE DIAGNOSIS: Umbilical hernia

PROCEDURE PERFORMED: Umbilical hernia repair with mesh

ANESTHESIA: General anesthesia

OPERATIVE NOTE: With the patient under general anesthesia, the abdomen was prepped and draped in a sterile manner. A standard skin line incision just below the umbilicus was made with sharp dissection carried down to the fascia. The umbilicus was freed from the underlying hernia, which contained some fatty material. We did not enter the peritoneal sac at any time. We were able to free up the fascial edge all the way around using sharp dissection and electrocautery. We were then able to reduce the herniated fat through the fascial opening, and then we closed the fascial opening using interrupted 0 Vicryl. Once this was closed we did take a patch of Prolene mesh and placed it on top of our repair and tacked that around circumferentially with some additional 0 Vicryl. With this accomplished, hemostasis was in place. We then tacked the umbilicus back to the fascia using a 2-0 Vicryl and then closed the subcutaneous tissue using 3-0 chromic and skin using 4-0 Vicryl in a subcuticular manner. Steri-Strips were applied and we did place part of a cotton ball into the umbilicus for shape, and then a sterile dressing was applied. The patient tolerated the procedure well and was discharged from the recovery area in stable condition. At the end of the procedure all sponges and instruments are accounted for.

7-12B:

SERVICE CODE(S): _____

ICD-9-CM DX CODE(S): _____

ICD-10-CM DX CODE(S): _____

CASE 7-13

7-13A OPERATIVE REPORT, SPLENECTOMY

LOCATION: Inpatient, Hospital

PATIENT: Marie Hill

SURGEON: Gary Sanchez, MD

PREOPERATIVE DIAGNOSIS: Intra-abdominal bleeding; ruptured spleen

POSTOPERATIVE DIAGNOSIS: Intra-abdominal bleeding; ruptured spleen

PROCEDURE PERFORMED: Splenectomy, total

ANESTHESIA: General anesthesia

INDICATION: Patient is a 24-year-old female involved in a one-car accident when she lost control of her vehicle and went down a ditch and the vehicle rolled twice, landing in an upright position. Patient was only person in the vehicle and was restrained. Patient has been conscious since paramedics arrived. Tests revealed bleeding in the abdomen. The spleen was suspected.

PROCEDURE: The patient was brought emergently to the operating room and placed under general anesthesia. She was prepped and draped while in the supine position. A left-sided Kocher incision was made. We used the Omni retractor and were able to look way into the abdomen. All of the organs looked intact and clear. We then identified a lot of bleeding in the area of the spleen and a tear was noted. Under deeper inspection on the backside of the spleen a large tear was present and decision was made to remove it. We lifted up on the spleen and brought it through the wound. The major vessels were divided. The short gastric vessels were dealt with in the same way. The spleen was then removed in its entirety. The areas were doubly tied, and care was taken to ligate and suture all the major vessels. Bleeding was controlled. We then irrigated and suctioned out the abdominal cavity and closed the wound with #2 Vicryl stitches in a two-layer fashion. We then irrigated out the wound and put in some staples. Marcaine 1.25% was placed in the wound. Telfa, toppers, and gauze were applied. The patient came through the surgery well and went on to the recovery room in good condition.

7-13A:

SERVICE CODE(S): _____

ICD-9-CM DX CODE(S): _____

ICD-10-CM DX CODE(S): _____

CASE 7-14

7-14A BONE MARROW BIOPSY

LOCATION: Inpatient, Hospital

PATIENT: Julie Spy

SURGEON: Gary Sanchez, MD

PREOPERATIVE DIAGNOSIS: Pancytopenia

POSTOPERATIVE DIAGNOSIS: Pancytopenia

PROCEDURE PERFORMED: Bone marrow biopsy and bone marrow aspirate

PROCEDURE: The patient was sterilized and anesthetized by standard procedure. One bone marrow core biopsy was obtained from the right posterior crest with minimal discomfort. At the end of the procedure the patient was not having any discomfort. There were no obvious complications. I then obtained one bone marrow aspirate from the right posterior iliac crest with minimal discomfort. At the end of the procedure, the patient was in no obvious discomfort and there were no obvious complications.

7-14A:

SERVICE CODE(S): _____

ICD-9-CM DX CODE(S): _____

ICD-10-CM DX CODE(S): _____

Musculoskeletal System

CASE 8-1

Dr. Almaz applies a cranial halo to stabilize a C1-C2 fracture. This is the initial treatment of the injury.

8-1A OPERATIVE REPORT, APPLICATION OF HALO

LOCATION: Outpatient, Hospital

PATIENT: Josh Blake

SURGEON: Mohamad Almaz, MD

PREOPERATIVE DIAGNOSIS: Fracture of C1, C2

POSTOPERATIVE DIAGNOSIS: Fracture of C1, C2

PROCEDURE PERFORMED: Placement of a halo

INDICATION: Fracture occurred when the patient was involved in an unspecified motor vehicle collision. It is known that Mr. Blake was the driver of the vehicle.

PROCEDURE: The patient's head was prepped and draped in the usual manner. The head was shaved. The halo apparatus was applied with screws and four-points. Then the vest was applied. The patient was then discharged to the recovery room to have films taken in the recovery room.

8-1A:

SERVICE CODE(S): _____

ICD-9-CM DX CODE(S): _____

ICD-10-CM DX CODE(S): _____

CASE 8-2

8-2A OPERATIVE REPORT, PREAURICULAR AREA EXCISION

LOCATION: Outpatient, Hospital

PATIENT: Lionel First

SURGEON: Mohamad Almaz, MD

PREOPERATIVE DIAGNOSIS: Left ear lesion, preauricular area

POSTOPERATIVE DIAGNOSIS: Left ear lesion, preauricular area

PROCEDURE PERFORMED: Excision of the left ear lesion

HISTORY: Lionel is a 3-year-old seen in the office and diagnosed with the above condition. The decision was made in consultation with his family to take him to the operating room to undergo the above-named procedure.

PROCEDURE: The patient was admitted through the same-day surgery program and was taken to the operating room and administered anesthetic by inhalation. The skin behind the ear was prepped and draped in the usual manner. We then injected this with 1% Lidocaine with epinephrine. A #11 blade was used to incise an elliptical area of skin around this lesion. The curved iris scissors was used to dissect this off the underlying cartilage. The skin was then undermined slightly. The wound was closed with two interrupted 6-0 nylon sutures. The patient was then allowed to recover from the general anesthetic and was taken to the Post Anesthesia Care Unit in stable condition. Total length of the lesion was 1.1 cm.

Pathology Report Later Indicated: Benign lesion of skin

8-2A:

SERVICE CODE(S): _____

ICD-9-CM DX CODE(S): _____

ICD-10-CM DX CODE(S): _____

CASE 8-3

8-3A OPERATIVE REPORT, DISSECTION AND EXCISION

LOCATION: Outpatient, Hospital

PATIENT: Emily Jarr

SURGEON: Gary Sanchez, MD

PREOPERATIVE DIAGNOSIS: Umbilical granuloma

POSTOPERATIVE DIAGNOSIS: Umbilical granuloma

PROCEDURE PERFORMED: Excision of the umbilical granuloma

ANESTHESIA: General inhalational

INDICATIONS: Emily is 3 months old who has a draining umbilical granuloma. It has been present since birth. She presents today for excision. Parents understand the risks of bleeding, infection, drainage from the area, and wish to proceed.

PROCEDURE: The patient was brought to the operating room and given general inhalational anesthesia and prepped and draped with Betadine solution. The granuloma measuring 0.7 cm was grasped, was excised with electrocautery, and then the base was closed with a 3-0 chromic suture. I tried to probe the base but there was no internal opening. It was then dressed with a 2 × 2 gauze. The granuloma was sent to pathology. She tolerated this well and was taken to recovery in stable condition.

Pathology Report Later Indicated: See Report 8-3B

8-3A:

SERVICE CODE(S): _____

ICD-9-CM DX CODE(S): _____

ICD-10-CM DX CODE(S): _____

8-3B PATHOLOGY REPORT

LOCATION: Outpatient, Hospital

PATIENT: Emily Jarr

ATTENDING PHYSICIAN: Gary Sanchez, MD

PATHOLOGIST: Grey Lonewolf, MD

CLINICAL HISTORY: Umbilical granuloma

SPECIMEN RECEIVED: Umbilical polyp/cyst

GROSS DESCRIPTION: Received in a container labeled "umbilical polyp" is a polypoid tan-pink tissue fragment measuring 0.7 × 0.5 × 0.4 cm. The specimen is bisected and totally submitted.

MICROSCOPIC DESCRIPTION: The umbilical tissue consists of gastric antral mucosa showing dense infiltrates of mononuclear inflammatory cells and scattered neutrophils.

Focally the surface epithelium is absent and replaced with sheets of neutrophils. Foci of intestinal metaplasia are present within the surface epithelium.

DIAGNOSIS: Umbilical granuloma

8-3B:

SERVICE CODE(S): _____

ICD-9-CM DX CODE(S): _____

ICD-10-CM DX CODE(S): _____

CASE 8-4

8-4A OPERATIVE REPORT, COSTOVERTEBRAL TUMOR

LOCATION: Outpatient, Hospital

PATIENT: Casey Wild

PRIMARY CARE PHYSICIAN: Leslie Alanda, MD

SURGEON: Mohamad Almaz, MD

PREOPERATIVE DIAGNOSIS: Lipoma, right lumbar area

POSTOPERATIVE DIAGNOSIS: Lipoma, right lumbar area

PROCEDURE PERFORMED: Excision of lipoma, right lumbar area

ANESTHESIA: General endotracheal with 2 cc of 1% Xylocaine with 1:100,000 epinephrine.

SURGICAL FINDINGS: 3.5 cm diameter subcutaneous lesion sitting on the right latissimus dorsi muscle morphologically resembling a lipoma.

DESCRIPTION OF PROCEDURE: The patient was intubated and turned to a prone position. The lesion was prepped with Betadine scrub and solution and draped in a routine sterile fashion. I injected about 2 cc of 1% Xylocaine with 1:100,000 epinephrine over the site of the lesion and around it. I excised an ellipse of skin that I left attached to the lipoma and carried dissection down to the superficial muscular fascia from which I separated the lipoma. I cauterized the bleeding and closed the wound with subcutaneous 2-0 Monocryl to close the dead space and subcuticular 3-0 Monocryl. I used Steri-Strips to appose the skin edges, and used Kerlix fluffs and Elastoplast for the remainder of the dressing. The patient tolerated the procedure well and left the operating room in good condition.

Pathology Report Later Indicated: Lipoma

8-4A:

SERVICE CODE(S): _____

ICD-9-CM DX CODE(S): _____

ICD-10-CM DX CODE(S): _____

CASE 8-5

8-5A OPERATIVE REPORT, TUMOR EXCISION

LOCATION: Outpatient, Hospital

PATIENT: Alice Lyon

SURGEON: Mohamad Almaz, MD

PREOPERATIVE DIAGNOSIS: Neuroma (two, each 1.1 cm) right leg

POSTOPERATIVE DIAGNOSIS: Neuroma (two, each 1.1 cm) right leg

PROCEDURE PERFORMED: Excision of two 1.1 cm masses near the right tibial bone

ANESTHESIA: General endotracheal

ESTIMATED BLOOD LOSS: Negligible

SURGICAL FINDING: Two 1.1 cm masses of the right leg overlying the tibia within close proximity to each other.

DESCRIPTION OF PROCEDURE: Under satisfactory general endotracheal anesthesia, the patient's right leg was prepped with Betadine scrub and solution and draped in the routine sterile fashion. A tourniquet was applied. The leg was exsanguinated, and the tourniquet was inflated to 400 mm of pressure. An incision, in continuity, was made to encompass both of the lesions of the medial aspect of the right leg, and these were excised without difficulty. It did appear there was some scarred nerve tissue in the upper region. The wounds were then closed with interrupted 3-0 Prolene, and a dressing of Xeroform, Kerlix fluffs, Kerlix roll, Kling, and an Ace bandage from the toes to the knee were applied. The tourniquet was released, and circulation was intact in the leg following release of the tourniquet. The patient tolerated the procedure and left the area in good condition.

Pathology Report Later Indicated: Two 1.1 cm benign neoplasms of the connective tissue of leg

8-5A:

SERVICE CODE(S): _____

ICD-9-CM DX CODE(S): _____

ICD-10-CM DX CODE(S): _____

CASE 8-6

This report states that the reconstruction procedure was a repair with acromioplasty. An acromioplasty is the surgical removal of a portion of the acromion (the highest point on the shoulder) to relieve compression of the rotator cuff when the joint moves. The acromioplasty is bundled into the repair procedure and is not reported separately.

8-6A OPERATIVE REPORT, ROTATOR CUFF REPAIR

LOCATION: Outpatient, Hospital

PATIENT: Chad Allen

SURGEON: Mohamad Almaz, MD

PREOPERATIVE DIAGNOSIS: Right shoulder rotator cuff tear

POSTOPERATIVE DIAGNOSIS: Right shoulder rotator cuff tear

PROCEDURE PERFORMED: Open rotator cuff repair with grafting using tissue Mend

ANESTHESIA: General endotracheal

ESTIMATED BLOOD LOSS: Negligible

PROCEDURE: This is a 46-year-old male who has a retracted and complete rotator cuff tear of the right shoulder (traumatic rotator cuff tear) due to carrying something too heavy (E code for overexertion). He was brought to surgery. After an appropriate level of anesthesia was achieved, the right shoulder was prepped and draped in the usual manner. We made a stab wound 2 cm below the acromion. Sharp dissection was carried through the skin and blunt dissection was carried into the joint space. I identified a complete retracted rotator cuff tear. The biceps tendon was noted to be well attached. The capsule appeared to be well attached anteriorly. No significant orthosis was appreciated. We went ahead with an open repair. We made an incision from the coracoid and acromion about 11 cm long. Sharp dissection was carried to the skin and blunt dissection was carried down to the deltoid. We removed the deltoid from the anterior aspect of the acromion and also split it distally about 4 cm. Prior to dividing the coracoacromial ligament we determined that we could repair this but it felt to be tight. We went ahead and did our acromioplasty. We removed a triangle of bone 2 cm deep and 1 cm wide at the base. This gave us enough room to work and created enough space for the tendon. We were able to pull the tendon forward if we held the arm abducted. He had it split basically along the rotator cuff interval, then along the supraspinatus insertion all the way to the infraspinatus, and then up into the infraspinatus a little bit. We went ahead and used a burr to create a groove in the greater tuberosity sulcus. We then used mattress sutures to hold the end of the tendon down and we placed interrupted sutures again using Ethibond posteriorly at the infraspinatus and supraspinatus area, and anteriorly rather extensively along this supraspinatus and subscapularis tear. I did get the rotator cuff repaired but the tissue looked tight and a little questionable as it might re-tear, and it was felt that we should go ahead and reinforce this. This was done using TissueMend. This was held in place with interrupted Vicryl sutures. The patient's wound was closed in layers using drill holes in the acromion to re-approximate the deltoid.

The patient tolerated the procedure well, was placed in abduction wedge, and left the operating room in good condition.

8-6A:

SERVICE CODE(S): _____

ICD-9-CM DX CODE(S): _____

ICD-10-CM DX CODE(S): _____

CASE 8-7

This is the initial treatment of the injury. Both the tendon and nerve repairs are reported.

8-7A OPERATIVE REPORT, TENDON REPAIR

LOCATION: Outpatient, Hospital

PATIENT: Jeremy Anderson

ATTENDING PHYSICIAN: Mohamad Almaz, MD

SURGEON: Mohamad Almaz, MD

PREOPERATIVE DIAGNOSIS: Laceration right little finger with profundus and sublimes tendon involvement and ulnarward digital nerve involvement. Patient was cut on a glass window.

POSTOPERATIVE DIAGNOSIS: Laceration right little finger with profundus and sublimes tendon involvement and ulnarward digital nerve involvement.

PROCEDURE PERFORMED:
1. Repair of sublimes tendon in no man's land, right little finger.
2. Repair of profundus tendon in no man's land, right little finger.
3. Repair of ulnarward digital nerve, right little finger

ANESTHESIA: General

PROCEDURE: The patient was brought to the operating room and general anesthetic was induced. His right upper extremity was prepped with Betadine and draped in a sterile fashion. The limb was exsanguinated and a tourniquet inflated to 250 mmHg for 1 hour. There was a slightly oblique laceration at the level of the PIP joint flexor crease. We extended this proximally and distally in a Z-type fashion. Dissection was carried down to the flexor sheath. We protected the ulnarward neurovascular bundle. The radialward neurovascular had been lacerated. We identified both ends of the digital nerve. We then opened up the sheath between the A2 and A4 pulleys. We found the sublimes tendon was 90% lacerated. It was barely together on the radialward side and completely lacerated on the ulnarward side. Xeroform was applied and a compression hand bandage was applied with volar and interrupted 5-0 nylon sutures. We effected a repair with this with several interrupted 4-0 Tycron sutures. We next probed for the profundus tendon proximally and we found this the vincula intact. We pulled this out into the wound. We then hyperflexed the DIP joint, and the distal stump of the profundus came out from under the A4 pulley. We were able to place a 4-0 Tycron suture in modified Kessler fashion both in the distal tendon and then through the proximal portion of the tendon and then tied this. It coapted the tendon nicely. We added one additional locking core suture on the radialward side of the tendon with 4-0 Tycron suture. This was a four-strand repair. We then placed an epitenon suture of running 6-0 Prolene suture. The tendon was then pulled back out underneath the A4 pulley. We irrigated the wound with sterile saline and repaired the sheath where possible with 6-0 Prolene suture. We then effected a repair of the radialward digital nerve, suturing this with several interrupted sutures of 10-0 nylon suture. We then closed the skin with dorsal plaster splints immobilizing the middle, ring, and little fingers in slight wrist flexion, MP flexion, and IP extension. The tourniquet was released and good circulation returned to the hand. The patient tolerated the procedure well and went to the recovery room in excellent condition.

8-7A:

SERVICE CODE(S): _____

ICD-9-CM DX CODE(S): _____

ICD-10-CM DX CODE(S): _____

CASE 8-8

In Case 8-8A, code only the allograft.

8-8A OPERATIVE REPORT, FUSION WITH ALLOGRAFT

LOCATION: Outpatient, Hospital

PATIENT: Harvey Wilson

SURGEON: Mohamad Almaz, MD

PREOPERATIVE DIAGNOSIS: Displacement of cervical disc

POSTOPERATIVE DIAGNOSIS: Displacement of cervical disc

PROCEDURE PERFORMED: Cervical discectomy at C5-6 and C6-7 with osteofacetectomy, placement of allograft, and arthrodesis from C5 to C7. This case was monitored with sensory evoked potentials. (Do not report these evoked potentials.) There were no changes throughout the case.

HISTORY: The patient as been counseled regarding the inability to relieve his pain, the fact that the fusion may not take, the fact that he may have persistent pain and numbness, and he agrees to go ahead with surgery.

PROCEDURE: Under general anesthesia, the patient was placed in the cervical outrigger, and the patient's right neck was prepped and draped in the usual manner. An incision was made along the medial border of the sternocleidomastoid. The platysma was divided, then with sharp dissection we got onto the prevertebral fascia. The interspace at C5-6 was localized. I then scored it with cautery. I then put the Farley-Thompson retractor in, and we began the discectomy at C4-6 and then proceeded to C6-7. At C5-6, the extruded fragment was removed, and we got right down to the dura. We also removed the osteophytes. This was done with curettes and Kerrison rongeurs, 1 mm and 2 mm biting. I cleared out the disc space, and then I paid attention to the C6-7 interspace and the 7 at the C5-6 interspace. I then measured and counter-sunk the Allograft, and I think they were 6 and 7, the 6 at the C5-6-7 interspace and the 7 at the C5-6 interspace. I then measured and countersunk the Allograft, and these were placed in the interspace. We then picked a plate from the tray and measured a tray so that we could get screws in to C5 down to C7 and one into C6. This was done. Zephyr plating was placed. X-rays were done. The screws were checked out that they were in the vertebral bodies. Satisfied that they were, I then closed the wound in layers, utilizing 2-0 chromic on the platysma with 2-0 plain in the subcutaneous tissue and surgical staples on the skin. A dressing was applied. The patient was discharged to the recovery room.

Code the allograft and diagnosis only.

8-8A:

SERVICE CODE(S): _____

ICD-9-CM DX CODE(S): _____

ICD-10-CM DX CODE(S): _____

CASE 8-9

This is the initial treatment of the injury.

8-9A OPERATIVE REPORT, CLOSED REDUCTION

LOCATION: Outpatient, Hospital

PATIENT: Kelli Klarkor

SURGEON: Mohomad Almaz, MD

DIAGNOSIS: Displaced fractured base, left first metacarpal

PROCEDURE PERFORMED: Closed reduction of metacarpal fracture

INDICATION: Kelli is a 15-year-old girl who fell while roller blading. She has now fractured her left thumb and will need manipulation to put it back in place. I have recommended a closed reduction and thumb spica cast application. The mother agrees with this.

PROCEDURE: Under a satisfactory level of sedation the fracture was carefully manipulated and a well-padded and very well-molded fiberglass cast was placed over the base of the thumb. After this was applied, we applied repeat mini C-arm views and confirmed improvement in position of the fracture but still not in anatomic position. Where it is presently, if it heals it still will be completely functional. I reviewed this with the mother, and I have recommended that we cast this and re-manipulate it as the swelling goes down, and we will do this sometime next week.

8-9A:

SERVICE CODE(S): _____

ICD-9-CM DX CODE(S): _____

ICD-10-CM DX CODE(S): _____

CASE 8-10

8-10A ORTHOPEDIC CONSULTATION, SUPRACONDYLAR FRACTURE

LOCATION: Outpatient, Clinic

PATIENT: Ryan Sund

PRIMARY CARE PHYSICIAN: Maxamillian Conclave, MD

CONSULTATION: Mohamad Almaz, MD

CHIEF COMPLAINT: Left elbow, type 3, supracondylar humerus fracture.

HISTORY OF PRESENT ILLNESS: Ryan is a 7-year-old right-hand-dominant boy who at approximately 12:30 today was walking up the steps of a slide at the park, slipped, fell, and landed on his left elbow. The child was brought into the clinic and seen by his primary physician, Dr. Conclave, and I was then contacted by him to give my opinion on his arm injury. Dr. Conclave informed me that he was grossly neurovascularly intact. No other injuries. He did not strike his head. He denies significant paresthesias. He denies other complaints.

PAST MEDICAL HISTORY: He is otherwise healthy.

ALLERGIES: No known drug allergies.

MEDICATIONS: Denies.

SOCIAL HISTORY: He has one other sibling, otherwise healthy.

PHYSICAL EXAMINATION: Temperature 36.7° C. Vital signs are grossly stable except for he does demonstrate tachycardiac secondary to likely pain. Heart: S1 and S2 with tachycardia. Lungs: Clear to auscultation bilaterally. Left arm evaluation does demonstrate left elbow deformity with ecchymosis over the antecubital fossa region. The skin is closed. He is able to flex and extend his fingers, not 100% but approximately 75% as limited by pain. He is able to extend his wrist minimally as well as extend his fingers to command. I was able to have him make an OK sign as well as flex at the left thumb IP joint with his proximal phalanx stabilized. His radial and ulnar pulses were strong, 2+. His fingers were pink, warm, and with brisk refill. Sensation was somewhat difficult to tell but did appear grossly intact to light touch. No significant distal radius tenderness.

X-RAYS: X-rays reveal a posterior laterally displaced type 3 supracondylar humerus fracture. Again, significant displacement.

IMPRESSION: Left type 3 closed supracondylar humerus fracture.

PLAN: I had a long discussion with the parents regarding my findings. We discussed the risks, benefits, and alternatives to closed versus open reduction and pinning. We discussed the significant increased risk of nerve palsy as well as brachial artery injury. I also discussed the risk of anterior interosseous palsy as well as radial nerve palsy. We discussed the risk of nonunion, malunion, and cubital varus deformity. We discussed the postoperative course. We also discussed the risk of possible future need for osteotomy secondary to and potential future malalignment or malposition. On long discussion, they agree to proceed. This is being done on an urgent basis. He last ate at noon. I did make him a Class II, meaning surgery should proceed within the next hour. All questions answered. We will admit him to the pediatric floor postoperatively. Thank you, Dr. Conclave, for this consult. I will inform you of the results of surgery.

8-10A:

SERVICE CODE(S): _____

ICD-9-CM DX CODE(S): _____

ICD-10-CM DX CODE(S): _____

8-10B OPERATIVE REPORT, SUPRACONDYLAR FRACTURE

In Case 8-10B, code only the treatment of the fracture, not the Doppler or fluoro-scopic guidance.

LOCATION: Inpatient, Hospital

PATIENT: Ryan Sund

PRIMARY CARE PHYSICIAN: Maxamillian Conclave, MD

SURGEON: Mohamad Almaz, MD

PREOPERATIVE DIAGNOSIS: Left type II closed supracondylar humerus fracture, posterior lateral displace.

PROCEDURE PERFORMED: Closed reduction initially followed by open treatment of supracondylar fracture.

ANESTHESIA: General

PROCEDURE: Ryan was brought to the operating room. He was placed under general anesthesia. He was transferred to the operating room table. Prior to prepping and draping his left upper extremity, I was able to again obtain pulses. I did initially bring in the mini C-arm. A closed reduction was performed initially by milking the brachialis primarily laterally. While this was being done, I did apply extension, felt a reduction. I then, subsequently, flexed the elbow with pressure on the posterior aspect of the distal humerus. After the elbow was flexed, I subsequently, externally rotated and pronated the forearm. Overall, I actually had a very reasonable reduction. After this was performed, I felt that I could repeat this, so his left arm was prepped and draped in the usual sterile manner. Starting laterally, a small incision was made over the lateral epicondyle. Blunt dissection was taken down to the bone. One 0.064 mm K-wire was placed through the lateral epicondyle, across the fracture, engaging the medial column and medial cortex. Its position was confirmed on AP and lateral radiographs. A second K-wire was placed just posterior to this, extending proximally into the lateral column. This did also penetrate just to the anterior cortex. Position was confirmed on AP and lateral radiographs and had acceptable position, alignment, and reduction. After this was performed, the arm was again fully externally rotated. The medial epicondyle was felt. I did feel the proximal location of the ulnar nerve. An incision was taken through the skin. Blunt dissection was taken through subcutaneous tissue. I actually was able to find the nerve in this, so, subsequently, retracted posteriorly. Blunt dissection was made directly to the medial epicondyle. Under direct visualization, the K-wire was placed through the medial epicondyle, across the fracture and through the lateral column of the humeral metaphysis. Overall alignment and position were deemed acceptable. No tourniquet was used. With the arm under live fluoroscopy, I did extend the elbow to approximately 90 degrees. Of note, to maintain the reduction, I did hold his arm in full flexion and pronation and subsequently, Cobaned his arm in this position. Again, the Coban was released, the arm was taken to 90 degrees, and his fingers were pink, warm, with brisk refill. I utilized a Doppler and was able to get good Doppler radial and ulnar pulses. I was able to palpate a radial pulse. Medially, the wound was irrigated. The skin was closed with nylon sutures. Laterally, I did have to release the pin site and one suture was used to reapproximate the incision. Xeroform was placed. The pins were cut and bent. Soft roll was placed. He was placed in the posterior splint with reinforcement medially. He was awakened, extubated and taken to recovery uneventfully. His fingers again, after the splint was placed, were pink and demonstrate brisk capillary refill.

PLAN: We will keep Ryan overnight. I did inject his incision and pin sites both medially and laterally with a total of 12 cc of 0.25% Marcaine without epinephrine. We likely will be able to discharge him home tomorrow. He tolerated the above operative procedure with no known complications.

8-10B:

SERVICE CODE(S): _____

ICD-9-CM DX CODE(S): _____

ICD-10-CM DX CODE(S): _____

CASE 8-11

This is not the treatment of the injury.

8-11A OPERATIVE REPORT, SHOULDER

LOCATION: Outpatient, Hospital

PATIENT: Stan Hope

SURGEON: Mohamad Almaz, MD

PREOPERATIVE DIAGNOSIS: Left shoulder pain and numbness, past shoulder injury

POSTOPERATIVE DIAGNOSIS: Normal shoulder

PROCEDURE PERFORMED: Diagnostic arthroscopy, left shoulder

CLINICAL HISTORY: This is a 57-year-old with a 10-year-old rotator cuff tear injury to his left shoulder. The patient does heavy lifting for a living. For the past 6 months the patient has been experiencing pain in this shoulder with some numbness and tingling traveling down the arm. X-rays were normal. Decision was made to go in with an arthroscope to try and uncover a reason for this pain and numbness.

OPERATIVE REPORT: Under general anesthesia, the patient was laid in the beach-chair position on the operating room table. The left shoulder was examined and found to be stable. There is full range of motion of this shoulder also. The extremity was then prepped and draped in the usual fashion. A standard posterior arthroscopic portal was created and the camera was introduced. First the back of the joint was inspected and this did not show any evidence of damage. The anterior ligament structures were normal. The biceps attachment and its transit through the joint were normal. Subscapularis was intact with no abnormality. Old scarring of the rotator cuff was noted. But all looked as it should. Nothing abnormal was seen. The camera was then removed out of the glenohumeral joint and placed in the subacromial space. There was excellent visualization of this area. No abnormalities could be identified and there was no evidence of any impingements. The camera was then removed form the subacromial space. The area was then infiltrated with Marcaine. The posterior portal was then closed with absorbable sutures and Steri-Strips, and a Mepore dressing was placed on it. The arm was then placed in a sling; the patient awakened and was placed on her hospital bed and taken to the recovery room in good condition.

8-11A:

SERVICE CODE(S): _____

ICD-9-CM DX CODE(S): _____

ICD-10-CM DX CODE(S): _____

CASE 8-12

8-12A OPERATIVE REPORT, KNEE REPAIR

LOCATION: Inpatient, hospital

PATIENT: May Leigh

SURGEON: Mohamad Almaz, MD

PREOPERATIVE DIAGNOSIS: Osteoarthritis, left knee.

POSTOPERATIVE DIAGNOSIS: Same.

PROCEDURE PERFORMED: Left total knee arthroplasty.

ANESTHESIA: General.

ESTIMATED BLOOD LOSS: Minimal

Following satisfactory preoperative review and assessment and full discussion, the patient was brought to the operating room where under general anesthesia examination confirmed patient to demonstrate excellent appearance of her right total knee and increased valgus and crepitus of the left knee. The left knee was then elevated, scrubbed, prepped and draped in the usual fashion and utilizing a standard midline incision the subcutaneous tissues were dissected, the medial retinaculum was opened and the underlying knee joint identified with advanced osteoarthritic changes present. The distal femur, proximal tibia and patella were resected in the normal fashion allowing excellent fitting of a #2 femur, a #2½ tibia, an 8-tray insert, and a 31 patella. Excellent fit, stability, and range of motion were achieved. The knee joint was thoroughly waterpiked and irrigated, the tibia and femur securely cemented into position followed by the patella. Once again, excellent fit, stability, and range were achieved. The knee joint was drained with two deep suction Hemovacs. The medial retinaculum was closed with 0 Vicryl, subcutaneous closure with 2-0 Vicryl, cutaneous margins approximated with 4-0 Ethilon in vertical mattress fashion, and a sterile dressing was applied. The patient tolerated the procedure well and returned to PAR in satisfactory condition. There were no intraoperative complications. Sponge and needle count correct.

8-12A:

SERVICE CODE(S): _____

ICD-9-CM DX CODE(S): _____

ICD-10-CM DX CODE(S): _____

CASE 8-13

This is the initial treatment for this patient's chondromalacia.

8-13A OPERATIVE REPORT, DEBRIDEMENT

LOCATION: Outpatient, Hospital

PATIENT: Judy Rain

SURGEON: Mohamad Almaz, MD

PREOPERATIVE DIAGNOSIS: Chondromalacia, left knee

POSTOPERATIVE DIAGNOSIS: Chondromalacia, left knee, due to sudden overexertion

PROCEDURE PERFORMED: Arthroscopy, left knee, with debridement of chondromalacia

PROCEDURE: While under a spinal anesthetic the patient's knee was examined. She had a small effusion in her knee. Physical exam of her left knee showed her skin intact. Her collateral ligaments were intact. The Lachman's test was negative as was the pivot shift. McMurray's test was negative. She has a range of motion 0 to at least 125 degrees flexion. Her left knee was then prepped with Betadine and draped in a sterile fashion. An Esmarch bandage was used to exsanguinate the leg and a tourniquet time ended up being 27 minutes. Three portals were used for this procedure. The first was placed along the superior anterolateral aspect and a third along the inferior anteromedial aspect of the knee. We distended the knee with Lactated Ringer's solution. We examined the suprapatellar pouch and the medial and lateral gutters. She had significant chondromalacia starting at the patellofemoral joint. We did use shavers to trim and debride some of the chondromalacia on the trochlea. We then moved to the medial compartment and noted large areas of chondromalacia. We used a combination of basket forceps and the shaver to try to debride this large area. There was some bare bone found underneath this. The medial meniscus was intact. Examination showed that we found all of the areas of chondromalacia, and at this point we thoroughly irrigated the knee and looked for any remaining loose fragments. After removing the hardware we closed the skin incisions using 4-0 nylon suture. Sterile 4 × 4 dressings were applied followed by ABD pads and an Ace wrap. The tourniquet was released after 27 minutes of tourniquet time. The patient was then taken from the operating room in good condition breathing spontaneously. The final sponge and needle counts were correct. She will be sent home on aspirin, as well as some Keflex.

8-13A:

SERVICE CODE(S): _____

ICD-9-CM DX CODE(S): _____

ICD-10-CM DX CODE(S): _____

CASE 8-14

8-14A OPERATIVE REPORT, MENISCECTOMY

LOCATION: Outpatient, Hospital

PATIENT: Cathy Downs

SURGEON: Mohamad Almaz, MD

PREOPERATIVE DIAGNOSIS: Torn left medial meniscus, old

POSTOPERATIVE DIAGNOSIS: Torn left medial meniscus, old

PROCEDURE PERFORMED: Arthroscopy of the left knee with partial medial meniscectomy.

FINDINGS: The patient was found to have a horizontal tear involving the posterior one half of the medial meniscus. She had a previous partial meniscectomy in this area, but she seemed to have a horizontal tear in this area. This was in the location of her pain that she had preoperatively. The remainder of the knee looked very good. The articular surfaces throughout the knees were in excellent condition, and the anterior cruciate ligament was intact. The lateral meniscus was intact.

PROCEDURE: While under a general anesthetic, the patient's left knee was examined. No effusion was noted. She had three well-healed arthroscopy incisions. The collateral ligaments were intact. Lachman test was negative, as was the pivot shift. The McMurray's test was questionably positive medially with some crepitus. We then prepped the patient's left leg with Betadine and draped in a sterile fashion. An Esmarch bandage was used to exsanguinate the leg, and a tourniquet on the thigh was inflated to 300 mmHg. The total tourniquet time ended up being 25 minutes. Three portals were used for this procedure. The first was placed along the superior anterolateral aspect of the knee. The second was placed along the inferior anterolateral aspect and the third along the inferior anteromedial aspect of the knee. We distended the knee with lactated ringer solution. We examined the suprapatellar pouch and the medial and lateral gutters. No loose bodies were noted. The articular surface of the patella and the adjacent surface of the femur appeared to be in excellent condition. We then examined the medial compartment and probed the medial meniscus. She had a previous partial medial meniscectomy involving the posterior one half or so of the medial meniscus, but there appeared to be a horizontal tear within this posterior half of the medial meniscus. We eventually ended up performing an excision of this portion of the meniscus. We left the anterior one half of the meniscus intact. We excised the posterior one half of the meniscus back to what we felt was a stable rim using a combination of basket forceps and the shaver. At this point then, we thoroughly irrigated the knee. We then examined the notch area and probed the anterior cruciate ligament. It was intact. We then examined the lateral compartment and probed the lateral meniscus. It was intact. We examined the medial compartment once again finally, looking for any remaining loose fragments. We then drained the knee and removed the hardware. The skin incisions were left open, and sterile dressings were applied under a six-inch Ace wrap. The tourniquet was released after 25 minutes of tourniquet time. She tolerated the procedure well.

8-14A:

SERVICE CODE(S): _____

ICD-9-CM DX CODE(S): _____

ICD-10-CM DX CODE(S): _____

Respiratory System

CASE 9-1

Dr. Dawson admitted Don Barker to the hospital and prepared an admission history and physical. Dr. Grovedahl is a resident being supervised by Dr. Dawson. When completing the audit form for the admission service, place an "✗" on the form to indicate elements Dr. Dawson provided and a "✔" on the form to indicate elements Dr. Grovedahl provided. Dr. Grovedahl performed only a part of the service provided because Dr. Dawson also contributed to the service. Assume that the third-party payer requires the use of the HCPCS modifiers for those services provided in part by a resident.

9-1A ADMISSION HISTORY AND PHYSICAL (PHYSICIAN'S AND RESIDENT'S NOTES)

LOCATION: Inpatient, Hospital

PATIENT: Don Barker

PRIMARY CARE PHYSICIAN: Ronald Green, MD

ATTENDING PHYSICIAN: Gregory Dawson, MD

PHYSICIAN ADMISSION NOTES:

The patient is being admitted to the hospital with abdominal pain that has been going on for 2 weeks now. Testing shows the patient has an abdominal aortic aneurysm. Surgery will be consulted in on this. The patient also needed to be placed on a ventilator (ventilator dependent) in the Emergency Room on arrival due to acute respiratory failure. The patient also suffers from severe chronic obstructive lung disease, obstructive sleep apnea, may have a bit of an asthmatic or reversible component. He also has had some bloody diarrhea and there is the possibility of a colon resection. Patient is admitted to the ICU and I will be taking care of the patient's ventilator support. He is still hypotensive, has poor urine output.

For detailed review of the PAST MEDICAL, SOCIAL and FAMILY HISTORY and REVIEW OF SYSTEMS, please refer to my resident's note, Dr. Grovedahl, who has outlined as best he can as basically the patient is unconscious in a coma and what we got was from the chart from previous interviews. The important thing for past medical history is the COPD with probably an asthmatic component and underlying obstructive sleep apnea. He also has hyperlipidemia and obesity.

On exam, the patient is on a ventilator, with plateau pressures of a little over 40 with 02 sats that are just barely 90% and with some variation between 88 and 92. It is difficult for even 02 sat monitor to pick it up occasionally because there was hypotension and the vasoconstriction. He has blue feet, cold feet and I could not get pulses. Abdomen is soft and tender to the touch. Chest has diminished breath sounds but also clear and chest x-ray did not look bad either. Urine output was down. Neurologically, the patient was sedated and basically no response, at least when I was looking at him.

IMPRESSION: The patient is seriously ill and this could very well be his demise. The critical care time spent was an hour, spread over three separate visits, including multiple phone calls to update us on his lab, ventilator settings, and urine output. We adjusted the ventilator and when he gets back from surgery, if that is what the general surgeon decides to do for AAA, it will have to be adjusted again. We will put him on heparin. After surgery we will not want sequential devices on his legs because the vasculature is already tenuous. Hopefully we can get around having to do CRT if the patient starts making urine so will volume load him the best we can with albumin and hope for the best at this point.

RESIDENT'S ADMISSION NOTES

LOCATION: Inpatient, Hospital

PATIENT: Don Barker

PRIMARY CARE PHYSICIAN: Ronald Green, MD

ATTENDING PHYSICIAN: Gregory Dawson, MD

RESIDENT: Mandy Grovedahl, MD

CHIEF COMPLAINT: Abdominal pain, abdominal aortic aneurysm, respiratory failure

HISTORY OF PRESENT ILLNESS: The patient started having abdominal pain 2 weeks ago. Patient came into the EOD this morning via ambulance after being found unresponsive at his home by his wife, and CT scan reveals extremely large abdominal aortic aneurysm. Patient was placed on a ventilator to assist with the respiratory failure and we have contacted the general surgeon on call for the aneurysm. The patient is hypotensive with a systolic pressure in the 40s. The patient also received copious amounts of pressors predominantly phenylephrine with dopamine.

PAST MEDICAL HISTORY: Significant for an abdominal aortic aneurysm, chronic obstructive pulmonary disease, atherosclerotic heart disease, and hyperlipidemia.

PAST SURGICAL HISTORY:
1. Abdominal aortic aneurysm.
2. Appendectomy.
3. Tonsillectomy and adenoidectomy.
4. Knee surgery.
5. Umbilical hernia repair.
6. Back surgeries.

ALLERGIES: No known allergies.

HOME MEDICATIONS:
1. Zocor 40 mg p.o. q. day.
2. Tiazac 180 mg p.o. q. day.
3. Lasix 40 mg p.o. q. day.

4. Metoprolol 25 mg p.o. b.i.d.
5. Aspirin 1 p.o. q. day.
6. K-Lor 20 q. day.
7. Advair 50/100 b.i.d.
8. Albuterol and ipratropium nebulizers b.i.d.

CURRENT MEDICATIONS: Ancef; dopamine currently at 7 micrograms; Pepcid. The patient has been replaced with 16 millimoles of K-Phos.

SOCIAL HISTORY: The patient is a retired cabinet maker, consumes minimal amounts of alcohol, and quit smoking a few years ago.

FAMILY HISTORY: Father and brother both had abdominal aortic aneurysms.

REVIEW OF SYSTEMS: Not obtainable.

PHYSICAL EXAMINATION: TEMPERATURE of 36.8, HEART rate 135, BLOOD PRESSURE 101/40 with a mean arterial pressure of 59, RESPIRATORY rate 14, O_2 saturation 90%, on FIO_2 of 50%. GENERAL: The patient is unresponsive and intubated. RESPIRATORY: Coarse rales throughout, SIMV of 14, PEEP of 5.1, pressure support 10, peak airway pressure 42, mean airway pressure 20, tidal volume 800 with a minute volume of 10.8 liters. CARDIOVASCULAR: Regular rate and rhythm. Cardiac output 2.76, cardiac index 1.16, stroke volume 22.3, PAWP 24, SVRI 3090, PVRI 1030, CVP 21. ABDOMEN: The patient's abdomen is soft and tender. The patient also has recently had bloody stool. EXTREMITIES: No pedal pulses or popliteal pulses. Right foot is pale on the dorsal surface and a little purplish on the plantar surface. Left foot is a bit congested. Minimal pedal edema. FLUIDS: Urine over the last three hours, 1130, Neo-Synephrine at 1, dopamine at 7 micrograms, Sodium 148, potassium of 3.6, chloride 113, CO_2 of 22.3, BUN 15, creatinine 1.2, calcium 7.4, glucose 165, magnesium 2.0, phosphorus 2.8, white blood cell count 5.41, hemoglobin of 16.3, hematocrit of 45.2, platelets 46, PT 15.1, INR of 1.7, PTT 32.5. The pH is 7.38, PCO_2 of 42, PO_2 of 158, bicarb 24.8.

ASSESSMENT:
1. Very large abdominal aortic aneurysm.
2. Acute respiratory failure.
3. Severe COPD with diffusion of 43% of predicted and FEV-1 of 23% of predicted.
4. Pulseless leg.

PLAN: We will consult the general surgeon physician on call. We will decrease the patient's tidal volume to 500 mL, give the patient 3 liters of 5% albumin over the next 5 hours (first liter over 1 hour). We will place the patient on bi-level ventilation after he returns from the operating room. We will also obtain new set of labs when the patient returns from the OR. The patient was seen and evaluated independently and together with Dr. Dawson. Assessment and plan formulated by Dr. Dawson.

9-1A:

SERVICE CODE(S): _____

ICD-9-CM DX CODE(S): _____

ICD-10-CM DX CODE(S): _____

9-1B RADIOLOGY REPORT, CHEST

This chest x-ray is a single view (anteroposterior, front to back). It is the number of views that is reported. There are no films for comparison.

LOCATION: Inpatient, Hospital

PATIENT: Don Barker

PRIMARY CARE PHYSICIAN: Ronald Green, MD

ATTENDING PHYSICIAN: Gregory Dawson, MD

RADIOLOGIST: Morton Monson, MD

EXAMINATION OF: Chest

CLINICAL SYMPTOMS: Respiratory failure

PORTABLE CHEST: SINGLE VIEW: FINDINGS: An endotracheal tube is present. The tip lies just inferior to the inferior margin of the clavicular heads. A Swan-Ganz catheter is present. The tip overlies a proximal branch of the right pulmonary artery. There is what appears to be a nasogastric tube present. Tube is not well demonstrated below the level of the mid-chest. Radiographic technique causes significant limitation in visualization. Follow-up is suggested. The heart size appears within normal limits. The pulmonary vascular markings appear within normal limits. There is abnormal focal opacity present within both lower lung zones. That is greater on the right than on the left. Those opacities may relate to atelectasis, infiltrate, edema, or a combination thereof. Follow-up is recommended.

9-1B:

SERVICE CODE(S): _____

ICD-9-CM DX CODE(S): _____

ICD-10-CM DX CODE(S): _____

9-1C RADIOLOGY REPORT, CHEST

Dr. Monson suggested further imaging, and based on that recommendation, Dr. Dawson orders another chest x-ray, single view on the same day and Dr. Monson provided the interpretation and report.

LOCATION: Inpatient, Hospital

PATIENT: Don Barker

PRIMARY CARE PHYSICIAN: Ronald Green, MD

ATTENDING PHYSICIAN: Gregory Dawson, MD

RADIOLOGIST: Morton Monson, MD

EXAMINATION OF: Chest

CLINICAL SYMPTOMS: Respiratory failure

CLINICAL INFORMATION: Comparisons made on films on the same date. Pulmonary artery catheter is not seen. There is a right-sided IJ line, tip in the SVC. There is also an NG tube, tip not seen. Cardiac silhouette high normal in size. The lungs are hyperinflated. The bases of the lungs have been clipped off the film. Infrahilar opacities are strand-like in appearance, presumed related to crowding vessels. Limited study.

9-1C

SERVICE CODE(S): _____

ICD-9-CM DX CODE(S): _____

ICD-10-CM DX CODE(S): _____

9-1D THORACIC MEDICINE/CRITICAL CARE PROGRESS REPORT

LOCATION: Inpatient, Hospital

PATIENT: Don Barker

PRIMARY CARE PHYSICIAN: Ronald Green, MD

ATTENDING PHYSICIAN: Gregory Dawson, MD

HISTORY OF PRESENT ILLNESS: The patient had his AAA repaired last evening. The patient is back in the ICU on the ventilator. He is still unstable and fragile although he looks better then I thought he would look today.

REVIEW OF SYSTEMS: Unobtainable. The patient is intubated.

PHYSICAL EXAMINATION: Blood pressure 110/40. MAP 61. Sinus rhythm. Rate of 120 without any S3 or S4. No diastolic sounds, clicks, or rubs. No murmurs. So far, all the troponins have been negative. Rhythm regular. Lungs: Chest x-ray on him looked fairly decent. He had some basilar infiltrates. Blood gases have not returned yet. GI: Abdomen is nontender. He has a Vac-Pac in place for a large abdominal wound. I do not hear any bowel sounds. He does have an NG tube in place. In the last eight hours, there has been 100 mL removal. GU: Decreased urine output. Preop weight was 240 pounds. Today his weight is 268.9. Endocrine: He is on an insulin drip. Infectious diseases: So far, there is no sign of infection. He is on antibiotics. Neurologic: The patient is still sedated postop so he does not really respond. He does move all four extremities but it's more twitching than moving. Pupils equal round and react to light and conjugate.

DISPOSTION: The patient is in respiratory failure. We are mostly going to be watching fluids. He is hypotensive, so we will load him with albumin again. Tomorrow we will check an albumin level along with the rest of our lab to see where we are with the albumin. We are afraid to use that anymore. The effect of that lasts about a week and he was having some trouble with GI bleeding yesterday and I don't want to aggravate that. It took 45 minutes of critical care time for this patient. That was constant care at bedside.

9-1D:

SERVICE CODE(S): _____

ICD-9-CM DX CODE(S): _____

ICD-10-CM DX CODE(S): _____

9-1E THORACIC MEDICINE/CRITICAL CARE PROGRESS REPORT

LOCATION: Inpatient, Hospital

PATIENT: Don Barker

PRIMARY CARE PHYSICIAN: Ronald Green, MD

ATTENDING PHYSICIAN: Gregory Dawson, MD

HISTORY OF PRESENT ILLNESS: Mr. Barker had AAA repair 2 days ago and last evening the patient was brought back to surgery to look for damaged bowel because he developed bloody diarrhea. Blood cultures have grown out a large gram-positive rod (this is a rod-shaped bacteria). One out of two blood cultures came back positive. Sputum showed mixed flora with obvious inflammation of less than 10 squamous and greater than 25 white cells. Overnight the patient is doing fairly well yet is still critical. Patient is still on a ventilator. Cardiac output has been decent. Pulse has been decent. He has an albumin drip going as well. He is also semi-anticoagulated. His urine output has started to slide downwards.

PHYSICAL EXAMINATION: Blood pressure 120/50. Sinus tachycardia with a rate of 100 and cardiac index was good at 4.7 with a wedge of 27 at that point. Lungs: Chest has diminished breath sounds and a few scattered rales at the bases. Blood gases show a pCO_2 of 47, a pH of 7.34 and a pO_2 of 134, which is pretty decent. This is on bi-level of 30/0 and FIO_2 of 50% and we could probably wean that down some. GI: Abdomen is non-tender. He has a Vac-Pac in place for a large abdominal wound. I do not hear any bowel sounds. He does have an NG tube in place. In the last 8 hours, there has been 225 mL removal. GU: BUN 25, creatinine 1.7, and he had 72,068 mL in and 15,786 mL out. He weighs 315.7 pounds today. Baseline weight is 240. He has 75.7 extra pounds of fluid on board mostly third space I would guess. He does have some edema in his feet and the dorsum of his hands. Endocrine: Glucose is 77. We are not feeding him at this point and he does not really have any D5 going at all. Electrolytes: Sodium 137, potassium 3.9, chloride 103, CO_2 23.3, calcium 6.3, and ionized calcium 3.9, which is low, and this is in spite of actually replacing calcium. He has had some ventricular arrhythmias so we will make sure we replace that. Magnesium is 1.4 and phosphorus is 4.3. Hematology: White count is 2,080, which is somewhat low. Hemoglobin is 10, which is a little better than yesterday. We did transfuse him yesterday. Platelet count is 45,000. Infectious diseases: He has a temperature of 38° C but he tended to be hypothermic yesterday and now we have 37.8, 37.6 and we also have a large gram-positive rod growing out of the blood and multiple flora out of the sputum. He is on antibiotics. Neurologic: The patient is still somewhat sedated. He does move all four extremities.

IMPRESSION:
1. Respiratory failure
2. Sinus tachycardia
3. Anemia
4. Edema

DISPOSTION: I spent 1 hour and 30 minutes of constant critical care time with this patient. I do not think I will change the vent settings at all today. I think the patient is still too unstable. I will replace the calcium and have OT and PT start working with him. Rearrange antibiotics and get the infectious disease specialist involved with him. Right now we will stop the Cefazolin, add Zosyn and Vancomycin to the regimen. We will try to improve his urine output and perform follow-up electrolytes to make sure we do not make things worse with diuresis.

9-1E:

SERVICE CODE(S): _____

ICD-9-CM DX CODE(S): _____

ICD-10-CM DX CODE(S): _____

9-1F THORACIC MEDICINE/CRITICAL CARE PROGRESS NOTE

LOCATION: Inpatient, Hospital

PATIENT: Don Barker

PRIMARY CARE PHYSICIAN: Ronald Green, MD

ATTENDING PHYSICIAN: Gregory Dawson, MD

HISTORY OF PRESENT ILLNESS: Mr. Barker had AAA repair 3 days ago. Blood cultures have grown out a large gram-positive rod. Overnight the patient did poorly. His urine output is 0. He had CRRT started and he is hypotensive, requiring Levophed to support the blood pressure. We lost our Swan because he used that particular side for dialysis line. Patient is still on a ventilator.

PHYSICAL EXAMINATION: Cardiac: I do not have a cardiac output today but his blood pressure is 110/40. Atrial fibrillation with a rate of 120. No S3 or S4. No diastolic sounds, clicks, or rubs. Heart sounds are quite distant. Lungs: Chest x-ray shows increased infiltrates in both lungs. Chest has distant breath sounds with rales scattered at the lateral sides. PO_2 is 131 on 50% with bi-level of 30/0, pH is 7.34 with a PCO_2 of 39 and a release time of 24. GI: He has a Vac-Pac in place for a large abdominal wound. We are not feeding him at this point. GU: BUN 24, creatinine 2.5. He weighs 320 pounds today. Baseline weight is 240. He has 80 extra pounds of fluid on board mostly third space I would guess. Endocrine: Glucose is 73. Electrolytes: Sodium 137, potassium 4.6, chloride 104, CO_2 19.9, calcium 6.8, and ionized calcium 4, which is still low and we have to keep replacing that. Hematology: White count is 6,120. Hemoglobin is 10.7. Platelet count is 60,000. Infectious diseases: He is afebrile at 37. Neurologic: The patient is still sedated and does not respond to verbal stimulation. Pupils are equal, round, and react to light.

IMPRESSION:
1. Atrial fibrillation
2. Respiratory failure
3. Hypotension
4. Fluid overload

DISPOSTION: Continue the CRRT. His fluids do not include any glucose, so I will switch him to D-5 LR. I would like to be able to come down on the Levophed some, but it might be difficult because his blood pressure is just borderline; it is adequate, but only with a lot of support. The atrial fib is new. He had a dose of digoxin, and we might have to give him more digoxin as time goes on here. We will continue the antibiotics until we have a good idea of the bacteria from the blood. I spent 1 hour of constant critical care time with this patient.

9-1F:

SERVICE CODE(S): _____

ICD-9-CM DX CODE(S): _____

ICD-10-CM DX CODE(S): _____

9-1G DISCHARGE SUMMARY

LOCATION: Inpatient, Hospital

PATIENT: Don Barker

PRIMARY CARE PHYSICIAN: Ronald Green, MD

ATTENDING PHYSICIAN: Gregory Dawson, MD

The patient was admitted with acute respiratory failure and a large AAA. He was placed on a ventilator and when stabilized taken to the OR for repair of his aneurysm. As the days went on his case looked bleaker for a good prognosis. He developed gram-positive bacteremia and had no urine output to speak of. His weight increased by up to 80 pounds (fluid overload). Today we began having difficulty maintaining his blood pressure. We have tried to load him with Levophed and Dopamine. We just cannot keep him alive. We did speak to his family about code level and they have decided to make him a code level II at this point. It would be very difficult to resuscitate him with his gaping abdominal wound. Shortly after speaking to his family the patient developed bradycardia and was unresponsive to the epinephrine, Levophed, Dopamine, and the rest of the drugs we were using just for maintaining his blood pressure. We then lost his blood pressure completely. The patient was pronounced dead at 11:33 AM. His family has been informed and they will be visiting him shortly. The family pastor is with the patient.

9-1G:

SERVICE CODE(S): _____

ICD-9-CM DX CODE(S): _____

ICD-10-CM DX CODE(S): _____

CASE 9-2

Dr. Dawson requested an ENT consultation to assess the patient's ears for infection due to a fever the patient is having.

9-2A ENT CONSULTATION

LOCATION: Inpatient, Hospital

PATIENT: Nicole Ray

ATTENDING PHYSICIAN: Gregory Dawson, MD

CONSULTANT: Jeff King, MD

Thank you kindly for allowing me to see Nicole in consultation. She has had a fever and a cough, and a chest x-ray indicating an infiltrate in the right lung. She has had fevers. She has had an IV started and is on IV antibiotics. Whether or not some of the infection could be coming from the ears is unknown because of the amount of wax in the ears.

PREVIOUS SURGICAL HISTORY: This child has had a G-tube placed. Apparently the child has had a Nissen fundoplication.

MEDICATIONS: Please see chart.

ALLERGIES: None known.

REVIEW OF SYSTEMS: Currently undergoing genetic investigation for seizures

SOCIAL HISTORY: The child lives with the mother.

EXAMINATION: On exam, the patient appears well-nourished. She does not appear aware of her surroundings.

Examination of the salivary glands is within normal limits. Facial strength is within normal limits.

Using a currrette I did remove impacted wax from both ear canals. There is an effusion behind the left tympanic membrane. The right tympanic membrane appears normal. The left tympanic membrane does appear actively infected at this time.

The ears and nose on external inspection appear within normal limits. There are no suspicious lesions or masses detected. The nasal mucosa is within normal limits. The septum is relatively straight, and the turbinates are within normal limits.

The mucosa of the oral cavity is within normal limits. The hard and soft palates are within normal limits. The tongue, floor of the mouth, and posterior pharyngeal wall are within normal limits. The tongue is moving in a rhythmic fashion. The neck appears symmetric. No lymphadenopathy and no masses detected. The trachea is midline.

IMPRESSION: Left chronic otitis media with effusion, which is improving. Right tympanic membrane is normal. Impacted cerumen bilaterally.

PLAN: Keep taking current antibiotics. I will check on her tomorrow. Thank you kindly for allowing me to participate in her care.

9-2A:

SERVICE CODE(S): _____

ICD-9-CM DX CODE(S): _____

ICD-10-CM DX CODE(S): _____

CASE 9-3

You will be reporting only the physician portion of the service.

9-3A PULMONARY FUNCTION STUDY

LOCATION: Outpatient, Hospital

PATIENT: Kim Fields

PHYSICIAN: Gregory Dawson, MD

ENTRANCE DIAGNOSIS: Dyspnea on ascending hills and stairs. Frequent wheezing and productive cough in a patient with a 0.75-pack-year smoking history; quit 1 year ago. Gave good consistent effort.

INTERPRETATION:
1. Baseline spirometry is normal with maybe a hint of concavity towards the volume axis at the terminal portion of the curve. The spirometry does show only a 61% FEF25-75 indicating peripheral dysfunction, i.e., mild COPD/emphysema.
2. Baseline FEV1 of 3.02, which was 84% of predicted dropping to a low of 1.33 after only 24.5 cumulative units of methacholine. Five minutes later it was 1.78, both values, which are greater than 20% drop from baseline.
3. Baseline FEV25-75 was 2.50 dropping to 0. With the provocation doses 5 minutes later it was 0, both values which are greater than a 50% drop from baseline.
4. Ten minutes after bronchodilator, FEV1 rose to 2.89. The FEV25-75 rose to 2.12.

OVERALL IMPRESSION: This study demonstrates bronchial hyperactivity as well as reversibility with a clinical diagnosis of asthma. It would be interesting to see if this patient can turn her baseline to normal after a good month of intense bronchodilator therapy. She may have some underlying peripheral airway dysfunction from poorly controlled asthma and/or smoking. It would be nice to see what it is when she is as well controlled as we can get her.

9-3A:

SERVICE CODE(S): _____

ICD-9-CM DX CODE(S): _____

ICD-10-CM DX CODE(S): _____

CASE 9-4

Liz Charles presents to the outpatient hospital department for a sleep study.

9-4A SLEEP STUDY

LOCATION: Outpatient, Hospital

PATIENT: Liz Charles

PHYSICIAN: Gregory Dawson, MD

STUDY PERFORMED: Nocturnal polysomnogram without CPAP titration

ENTRANCE DIAGNOSIS: Somnolence

This is a fully attended, multichannel nocturnal polysomnogram, giving the patient 386.6 minutes in bed, 317 minutes asleep with 61 arousals through the night which is above the normal. It looks like she had some difficulty with sleep maintenance. She had sleep onset at 18.5 minutes, REM latency 171.5 minutes, again a little bit prolonged. She had 27 respiratory events through the night, a mixture of obstructive apneas and obstructive hypopneas with a respiratory disturbance index of 5.1. Anything over 5 is considered significant. The longest duration of any one event was 34 seconds. O_2 sat was between 76 and 95%, with 29% of the time spent with O_2 sats less than 88%. Heart rate varied between 55 and 113, somewhat varying with the obstructive events. The patient had grade 1-2 snoring noted, and respiratory disturbance events were most evident in REM while supine. All five stages of sleep were represented. Basically the only thing abnormal was a reduced amount of REM.

OVERALL IMPRESSION: This patient has significant obstructive sleep apnea based on the respiratory disturbance index of 5.1, which anything over 5 is considered significant, plus the amount of time that the patient spent hypoxic, at less than 88%. 29% of the time was spent that way. So I suspect that the patient does have significant obstructive sleep apnea. We will need a second sitting to do the CPAP titration.

The overall impression is obstructive sleep apnea.

9-4A:

SERVICE CODE(S): _____

ICD-9-CM DX CODE(S): _____

ICD-10-CM DX CODE(S): _____

CASE 9-5

9-5A OPERATIVE REPORT, SEPTOPLASTY, TURBINATE REDUCTION, AND TONSILLECTOMY

LOCATION: Inpatient, Hospital

PATIENT: Brad Nelson

PHYSICIAN: Gregory Dawson, MD

PREOPERATIVE DIAGNOSIS:
1. Septal deviation.
2. Bilateral inferior turbinate hypertrophy.
3. Nasal obstruction.
4. Chronic tonsillitis.

POSTOPERATIVE DIAGNOSIS: Same

PROCEDURES PERFORMED:
1. Septoplasty
2. Bilateral inferior turbinate outfracture
3. Tonsillectomy

ANESTHESIA: General endotracheal anesthesia

DESCRIPTION OF PROCEDURE: Following informed consent from the patient he is taken to the operating room and placed supine on the operating room table. The appropriate monitoring devices were placed on the patient and general anesthesia was induced. He was orally intubated without difficulty. He was draped in the usual sterile fashion.

The right and left nasal cavities were packed with Afrin-soaked gauze. It was removed after 5 minutes. The right and left nasal septum was injected with approximately 3 cc of Xylocaine with epinephrine on each side. Evaluation of the nasal cavity did indicate significant bilateral inferior turbinate hypertrophy. There was quite a significant left septal deviation and spur, mostly posteriorly on the left-hand side.

A #15 blade scalpel was used to make an incision on the anterior end of the left nasal septum. A mucoperiosteal and mucoperichondrial flap was then elevated. It was elevated over the septal spur and deviation on the left-hand side. The Freer elevator was then used to incise the cartilage and remove a 1 × 2 cm strip of cartilage from the posterior, inferior aspect of the nasal septum. Care was taken to maintain at least 1 and $^1/_2$ cm of anterior and dorsal nasal cartilage to provide tip support. This amount of cartilage was easily maintained. Once the strip of cartilage was removed, some of the bony vomer had to be removed using the small Wilde forceps. Following this the left nasal septum was significantly straighter.

The butter knife was then used to outfracture both left and right inferior turbinates. Following this the nasal airway was significantly improved. 4-0 Chromic catgut suture was used to close the anterior left nasal septum incision. Doyle splints were then placed into the right and left nasal cavities and sutured to the right nasal septum anteriorly.

The patient was repositioned for tonsillectomy. The McIvor mouth gag was placed. The left tonsil was removed by incising its mucous membranes superior and anterior, dissecting it down to its base, removing it with a tonsillar snare. A pack was placed. The right tonsil was removed in incising its mucous membranes superior and anterior, dissecting this tonsil down to its base and removing it with a tonsillar snare. Bismuth pack was placed. Packs were removed. The peritonsillar area was injected with 1% Xylocaine with epinephrine. Following this, electrocautery was used to obtain good hemostasis on both sides. The nasopharynx was examined, and no evidence of significant adenoids was noted. The oral cavity was washed well with saline. When good hemostasis was noted to be present in the tonsillar fossae, they were painted with viscous Xylocaine. The patient was then awakened from his anesthetic and returned to the recovery room in stable condition. Prognosis immediate and remote is good.

ESTIMATED BLOOD LOSS: 25 cc

PREOPERATIVE MEDICATION: Keflex 500 mg p.o. q.i.d. for 10 days. We will remove the stent in 2 weeks' time. I also provided a prescription for Percocet.

9-5A:

SERVICE CODE(S): _____

ICD-9-CM DX CODE(S): _____

ICD-10-CM DX CODE(S): _____

CASE 9-6

9-6A OPERATIVE REPORT, TRACHEOSTOMY

LOCATION: Inpatient, Hospital

PATIENT: Andrew McGregor

PHYSICIAN: Gregory Dawson, MD

PREOPERATIVE DIAGNOSIS:
1. Aspiration pneumonia
2. Ventilator dependent
3. Prolonged intubation with inability to extubate
4. Quadriplegia

POSTOPERATIVE DIAGNOSIS:
1. Aspiration pneumonia
2. Ventilator dependent
3. Prolonged intubation with inability to extubate
4. Quadriplegia

PROCEDURES PERFORMED: Tracheostomy, planned

ANESTHESIA: General endotracheal anesthesia

INDICATION: This is a 58-year-old male who has been ventilator dependent and has had prolonged intubation. Attempts at weaning off the ventilator have been unsuccessful. The patient is also being treated for aspiration pneumonia. He has quadriplegia.

DESCRIPTION OF PROCEDURE: After consent was obtained, the patient was taken to the operating room and placed on the operating room table in the supine position. After an adequate level of general endotracheal anesthesia was obtained, the patient was positioned for tracheostomy. The patient's neck was prepped with betadine prep and then draped in a sterile manner. A curvilinear incision was marked approximately a fingerbreadth above the sternal notch in an area just below the cricoid cartilage. This area was then infiltrated with 1% Xylocaine with 1:100,000 units epinephrine. After several minutes, sharp dissection was carried down through the skin and subcutaneous tissue. The subcutaneous fat was removed down to the strap muscles. Strap muscles were divided in the midline and retracted laterally. The cricoid cartilage was then identified. The thyroid gland was divided in the midline with the Bovie and then the two lobes retracted laterally. This exposed the anterior wall of the trachea. The space between the second and third tracheal ring was then identified. This was infiltrated with local solution. A cut was then made through the anterior wall. The endotracheal tube was then advanced superiorly. An inferior cut into the third tracheal ring was then made to make a flap. This was secured to the skin with 4-0 Vicryl suture. A #6 Shiley cuffed tracheotomy tube was placed. This was secured to the skin with ties as well as the tracheostomy strap. The patient was then turned over to anesthesia.

The patient tolerated the procedure well, there was no break in technique, patient was extubated and taken to the Medical Critical Care Unit in stable condition. Fluids administered 500 cc of RL. Estimated blood loss less than 5 cc.

9-6A:

SERVICE CODE(S): _____

ICD-9-CM DX CODE(S): _____

ICD-10-CM DX CODE(S): _____

CASE 9-7

9-7A OPERATIVE REPORT, ETHMOIDECTOMY, ANTROSTOMY, AND SPHENOIDOTOMY

LOCATION: Outpatient, Hospital

PATIENT: Tony Flaur

PHYSICIAN: Gregory Dawson, MD

PREOPERTIVE DIAGNOSIS:
1. Chronic sinusitis.
2. Nasal polyposis.
3. Septal deviation.

POSTOPERATIVE DIAGNOSIS: Same

PROCEDURE PERFORMED:
1. Bilateral image-guided intranasal antrostomy.
2. Bilateral image-guided total ethmoidectomy.
3. Bilateral image-guided intranasal sphenoidotomies.

ANESTHESIA: General endotracheal anesthesia

DESCRIPTION OF PROCEDURE: Tony is a 34-year-old woman seen in the office and diagnosed with the above condition. Decision was made in consultation with the patient to take her to the operating room to undergo the above-named procedure. Because of her septal deviation, we had to consent for her a possible septoplasty if access was not possible. She had a CT scan of the sinus performed on an outpatient basis. The images were reconstructed in the three-dimensional display that was used during stereotactic surgery.

She was admitted through the Same Day Surgery Program and taken to the operating room where she was administered a general anesthetic via intravenous injection. She was then intubated endotracheally. The nose was decongested with 4 ml of 4% cocaine solution on nasal pledgets. A small amount of Afrin was also used. The patient was draped in the usual fashion. The three-dimensional ray was placed on the chest and positioned. We entered our fiducial points into the computer and good accuracy was obtained. We then removed the patties from both sides of the nose and inserted the 4 mm endoscope. The right side had excellent access. The left side was extremely narrow. We felt, however, that we would be able to do this without septoplasty so decision was made to proceed. We started initially with the right side of the nose. The uncinate process was injected with 15 mg/kg Lidocaine with Epinephrine. Freer elevator was used to incise the uncinate process vertically. This was removed with a Wilde forceps. Curved tracking suction was used to identify the maxillary sinus ostium. Using the tracking microdebrider and the backbiting forceps, we removed materials to enlarge the left maxillary sinus opening. The ethmoid air cells were then penetrated with the microdebrider and we cleaned this out on both sides. The ground lamella was penetrated with the aid of the navigator and we cleaned out additional cells from this area. There was a lot of polypoid material. We moved superiorly along the fovea and cleaned out both anterior and posterior ethmoid air cells. We then entered the sphenoid sinus and enlarged this. Packing from the left was then removed and we placed the image-guided system into the nose. The curved tracking suction was used to identify the maxillary sinus ostium. This was enlarged with the microdebrider and the backbiting forceps. The posterior ethmoid air cells were entered in a similar fashion. We cleaned this out with the microdebrider using an image-guided system. We then entered the sphenoid sinus and enlarged this ostium. This side of the nose was then packed with the same material. The material was removed from both sides of the nose and a FloSeal was placed on either side. A mustache dressing was placed on the nose. The patient was then allowed to recover from the general anesthetic and taken to the Post Anesthesia Care Unit in stable condition. There were no complications during this procedure.

9-7A

SERVICE CODE(S): _____

ICD-9-CM DX CODE(S): _____

ICD-10-CM DX CODE(S): _____

CASE 9-8
9-8A EMERGENCY DEPARTMENT REPORT
9-8B THORACIC MEDICINE/CRITICAL CARE CONSULTATION
9-8C RADIOLOGY REPORT, CHEST
9-8D RADIOLOGY REPORT, CHEST
9-8E THORACIC MEDICINE/CRITICAL CARE PROGRESS REPORT
9-8F DISCHARGE SUMMARY

CASE 9-8

9-8A EMERGENCY DEPARTMENT REPORT

LOCATION: Inpatient, Hospital

PATIENT: Kelsey Lord

PHYSICIAN: Paul Sutton, MD

SUBJECTIVE: A 41-year-old female who presents with chief complaint of shortness of breath and chest pain. She awakened this morning with shortness of breath and substernal pressure sensation. It was very mild at onset, 5/10, but has progressively worsened throughout the day. It seems to radiate around to the back of her chest but does not radiate to the arms or into the jaw. She has other accompanying symptoms including nausea and dizziness and the feeling of hot and clamminess. No diaphoresis. She also has had intermittent numbness of the lips and hands today.

PAST MEDICAL HISTORY: The patient does have a history of panic disorder. She has never had a panic attack with symptoms such as this. Her panic attack usually consists of going into a sweat and being claustrophobic.

REVIEW OF SYSTEMS: Complete review of systems is performed. All are negative except for intermittent chest pains for the past couple of weeks. These episodes of chest tightness usually last about 5 minutes. Oftentimes, they are exertion related and relieved with rest. They never last longer than 5 minutes until the episode today.

SOCIAL HISTORY: Patient is married. She has 2 children. Both parents are alive and father and grandfather both have heart disease.

CARDIAC RISK FACTORS:
1. Hypercholesterolemia.
2. Cigarette smoking.
3. Family history of cardiovascular disease.

OBJECTIVE: This is initially a very anxious appearing 41-year-old female. Temperature is 37.4° C. Pulse: 68. Respiration: 17. Blood pressure: 148/64. Oxygen saturation: 100%. HEENT: Conjunctivae and lids are normal. Mouth well hydrated. Pharynx normal. Neck supple without lymphadenopathy. No thyromegaly. No jugular venous distention. Respirations are easy. Lungs clear to auscultation. Heart has a regular rate and rhythm. No murmurs or extra heart sounds heard. Chest wall is without deformities and no localizing tenderness. Abdomen is soft with normal bowel sounds. No hepatosplenomegaly. No pulsatile mass. No ventral hernia. Extremities: No peripheral edema noted. Skin: No rash seen. No nodules felt. Digits and nails are normal.

ASSESSMENT: Chest pain.

PLAN: The patient initially presented and appeared to be anxious, and we attempted to get a good EKG and could not get one secondary to her agitation. She was given Ativan 2 mg IV. Her chest tightness settled down from a 7 to a 3/10. An EKG was then possible and looked normal. Subsequent to this, we did give nitroglycerin, which further relieved this chest tightness away. The patient was also given 4 baby aspirin and started on heparin. The case was discussed with Dr. Dawson who will come in and consult on this case. Initial troponin I is mildly elevated to 0.08. The patient will be admitted for further workup and treatment.

9-8A:

SERVICE CODE(S): _____

ICD-9-CM DX CODE(S): _____

ICD-10-CM DX CODE(S): _____

9-8B THORACIC MEDICINE/CRITICAL CARE CONSULTATION

LOCATION: Inpatient, Hospital

PATIENT: Kelsey Lord

ATTENDING PHYSICIAN: Marvin Elhart, MD

CONSULTANT: Gregory Dawson, MD

Mrs. Lord is a 41-year-old lady who had an aortic valve replacement for severe aortic insufficiency secondary to Phen-Fen usage in her earlier years. She has some mitral regurgitation but it is really minimal. She had symptoms of chest pain and dizziness with the aortic insufficiency. She also has mild to moderate mitral regurgitation. She had the surgery done yesterday. This morning I was asked to see the patient because she was significantly short of breath and dyspneic. Chest x-ray showed increased pulmonary venous congestion. Echocardiogram did not really show much in the way of anything abnormal such as tamponade or clot in the pericardium. She really is not febrile at 37.3 now; earlier we had a 38.1 at midnight. She is quite sleepy, and she is on multiple medications to make her sleepy for her psychiatric problems. She is on Clonazepam, Prozac, Seroquel, Trazodone, Adderall, and Klonopin. The Trazodone can certainly cause significant problems with sedation. She was also on morphine PCA that has been stopped. Chest x-ray could be also ARDS or pneumonia but I think I favor congestive heart failure type problems. She seems to be responding to BiPAP at 15/5.

PAST MEDICAL HISTORY:
1. Bipolar disorder.
2. Panic disorder.
3. Attention-deficit disorder.

PAST SURGICAL HISTORY: Tubal ligation.

ALLERIGIES: The chart says she does not have any allergies.

REVIEW OF SYSTEMS: Unable to attain due to the patient being so sleepy and sedated.

FAMILY HISTORY & SOCIAL HISTORY: Please refer to the EOD note by Dr. Paul Sutton.

PHYSICAL EXAMINATION: Patient is very sleepy and lethargic. She will answer questions but immediately falls asleep and tends to mumble. HEENT otherwise is benign. There is no blood in the nose or throat. NECK is supple without JVD. LUNGS have end-inspiratory rales bilaterally. HEART shows a regular rhythm with a metallic click of the aortic valve replacement. I do not hear an S3. I cannot hear any murmurs. ABDOMEN is benign. Bowel sounds are present. Nontender. No hepatosplenomegaly. EXTREMITIES show no edema, rashes, clubbing, cyanosis or tremor. LYMPHATIC SYSTEM: No nodes in the neck or clavicular area.

IMPRESSION: Acute hypoxic respiratory failure. Hopefully, it is just due to sedation and maybe some congestive heart failure but she seems to be responding to BiPAP 15/5. She does wake up enough to answer some questions. One has to worry about a pulmonary embolus also because it seemed to come on relatively quickly after postop. Echocardiogram was the first thing that was done and cardiac problems do not seem to be the cause of this. I will try to get the CT scan tomorrow with PE technique. Today will just use the weight-based heparin protocol, put her on BiPAP in the ICU and see if she turns the corner. I would certainly like to avoid intubation if possible, but, of course, that is always a possibility. Will have her on Zosyn for possible pneumonia. Two blood cultures have already been collected and will try to get a sputum.

9-8B:

SERVICE CODE(S): _____

ICD-9-CM DX CODE(S): _____

ICD-10-CM DX CODE(S): _____

9-8C RADIOLOGY REPORT, CHEST
This x-ray was taken after the patient had aortic bypass surgery.

LOCATION: Inpatient, Hospital

PATIENT: Kelsey Lord

ATTENDING PHYSICIAN: Marvin Elhart, MD

RESPIRATORY CARE: Gregory Dawson, MD

RADIOLOGIST: Morton Monson, MD

EXAMINATION OF: Chest

CLINICAL SYMPTOMS: Aortic insufficiency; status post aortic valve replacement

PORTABLE CHEST: Sternotomy. Mediastinal drains/thoracostomy tubes. Endotracheal tube tip above the carina. No cardiac enlargement. Pulmonary vascularity upper limits of normal and slightly less prominent. Area of infiltrate or atelectasis in the right infrahilar region. Mild elevation, right hemidiaphragm. No definite pleural effusions. Cardiac valvular prosthesis.

9-8C:

SERVICE CODE(S): _____

ICD-9-CM DX CODE(S): _____

ICD-10-CM DX CODE(S): _____

9-8D RADIOLOGY REPORT, CHEST
This x-ray is compared to the x-ray in Case 9-8C.

LOCATION: Inpatient, Hospital

PATIENT: Kelsey Lord

ATTENDING PHYSICIAN: Marvin Elhart, MD

RESPIRATORY CARE: Gregory Dawson, MD

RADIOLOGIST: Morton Monson, MD

EXAMINATION OF: Chest

CLINICAL SYMPTOMS: Congestive heart failure; s/p AVR

PORTABLE CHEST X-RAY FINDINGS: Comparison is made to the portable chest from 12/6 at 2:20 AM. Sternotomy with cardiac valvular prosthesis and mediastinal drain/thoracostomy tubes. NG tube. Endotracheal tube tip above the carina. Cardiac enlargement is unchanged. Pulmonary vascularity within normal limits and stable. Scattered atelectasis and fibrosis in both costophrenic angles. Area of infiltrate or atelectasis in the retrocardiac region of the left lower lobe is not appreciably changed.

9-8D:

SERVICE CODE(S): _____

ICD-9-CM DX CODE(S): _____

ICD-10-CM DX CODE(S): _____

9-8E THORACIC MEDICINE/CRITICAL CARE PROGRESS REPORT

LOCATION: Inpatient, Hospital

PATIENT: Kelsey Lord

ATTENDING PHYSICIAN: Marvin Elhart, MD

RESPIRATORY CARE: Gregory Dawson, MD

Mrs. Lord is a critically ill 41-year-old lady. After an aortic valve replacement, she is in respiratory distress. She came close to being intubated last night. She is on BiPAP continuously to keep her O_2 sats up. Overnight, she came even closer to being intubated. She was noted to be bronchospastic. She did respond to treatment with bronchodilators and Verapamil to control the rate. It seemed to control things enough that we avoided intubation. That was a fair amount of time spent last night taking care of her.

PHYSICAL EXAMINATION/REVIEW OF SYSTEMS:
1. CARDIAC SYSTEM REVIEW: Blood pressure this morning is 110s /40s. Sinus tach is around 90. On exam, you can hear the mechanical valve that is an aortic stenosis type murmur but it is really soft in the right second interspace.
2. PULMONARY SYSTEM REVIEW: On BiPAP of 12/5, PO_2 was on 58, PCO_2 was 44, pH of 7.43. She had some rhonchi and rales scattered about everywhere. Chest x-ray showed bilateral pulmonary opacities probably improved compared to yesterday. We are still not sure exactly what those are. She is being treated for infection as well as congestive heart failure and hopefully, we are trying to get a CAT scan today, PE technique but I don't know if we can do that or not. She is being treated for that as well.
3. GI: She is not eating but good bowel sounds, nontender abdomen.
4. GU: Over the last 8 hours, she had 805 in and 1,047 out. BUN is 11 with a creatinine of 0.5.
5. ENDOCRINE: Glucose is 109.
6. ELECTROLYTES: Sodium is 135, potassium is 4.4, chloride is 97, CO_2 is 28.2, calcium is 8.2, magnesium is 1.9, phosphorus is 2.6.
7. HEMATOLOGY: White count is 15,410. Hemoglobin is 8.9. Platelets are 149,000 and she is anticoagulated on a Heparin drip at this point.
8. INFECTIOUS DISEASE: She had elevated white count, this could be for many reasons. She is not febrile. The highest temp recorded in 24 hours was 37.6° C Blood

cultures are negative. Urine cultures showed an Enterococcus, only 2,000. She is on Zosyn. This is day 2 of Zosyn.
9. NEUROLOGICAL: The patient does awaken and follows some commands. She is a lot less sleepy than yesterday.

DISPOSITION: More Lasix, continue watching. Change the Verapamil to a long-acting one. One can get rid of the Xopenex and put her back on Atrovent and Albuterol at this point with Pulmicort Respules. She is already on systemic Solu-Medrol q. 6, 20 mg and try to redo the BiPAP as she may eventually go on a ventilator and I am still not sure exactly why she went into pulmonary edema, which is what it looks like mostly to me.

9-8E:

SERVICE CODE(S): _____

ICD-9-CM DX CODE(S): _____

ICD-10-CM DX CODE(S): _____

9-8F DISCHARGE SUMMARY

LOCATION: Inpatient, Hospital

PATIENT: Kelsey Lord

ATTENDING PHYSICIAN: Marvin Elhart, MD

RESPIRATORY CARE: Gregory Dawson, MD

DISCHARGE DIAGNOSES:
1. S/P AVR
2. Congestive heart failure.

OPERATIONS OR PROCEDURES PERFORMED DURING THIS ADMISSION:
1. Cardiac catheterization and coronary angiography.
2. Aortic valve replacement.
3. Mechanical intubation and ventilation.

HISTORY OF PRESENT ILLNESS: Mrs. Lord is a 41-year-old woman who presented to the Emergency Room because of chest pain and shortness of breath. She never had trouble like that in the past. She did have some abdominal pain the week prior but denied any history of shortness of breath or chest pain. She was admitted through the Emergency Room for further evaluation and treatment. She was started on IV Heparin and nitroglycerin. The following day she was taken to the cath lab where cardiac catheterization and coronary angiography were performed. The results of that evaluation revealed normal pulmonary artery pressures with a pulmonary capillary wedge pressure of 12. Her ejection fraction was calculated to be 63%. There appeared to be significant mitral insufficiency. There was no coronary artery disease. There also appeared to be significant aortic insufficiency. Mrs. Lord was taken to the OR and under general anesthesia and cardiopulmonary bypass, a severely insufficient aortic valve was removed and replaced with a 21 mm St. Jude medical mechanical prosthesis. Transesophageal echocardiography during surgery revealed only 1+ mitral insufficiency and therefore nothing was done with the mitral valve. She tolerated the procedure fairly well. She was extubated on the evening of surgery. She was transferred from the Intensive Care Unit to a telemetry bed on the first postop day. Her diet and activity level were advanced. She was started on Coumadin. On the third postop day she developed some respiratory distress. She was eventually transferred back to the medical ICU. Her chest x-ray revealed cardiomegaly with congestive changes. There were bilateral pulmonary opacities seen. There was a small right apical pneumothorax. The overall picture looked like congestive heart failure. She was treated with diuretics and pulmonary toilet. Her condition deteriorated somewhat and she was eventually intubated on the fifth postop day. She did receive two units of packed red blood cells in the ICU. With additional pulmonary toilet and diuresis, her respiratory status improved and she was eventually extubated a couple of days later. She was transferred back to a telemetry bed. Over the next couple of days her diet and activity level were steadily advanced. At the time of discharge she was ambulating ad lib in the hallways without difficulty although she did fatigue somewhat easily. Her surgical wounds were clean, dry and healing quite nicely. She remained in a normal sinus rhythm. Her INR at the time of discharge was 1.6 but her Coumadin dose had been increased from 5 to 7.5 mg each day.

DISCHARGE MEDICATIONS:
1. Aspirin 81 mg p.o. daily.
2. Strattera 18 mg p.o. daily.
3. Pulmicort inhaler as directed.
4. Seroquel 100 mg p.o. q.h.s.
5. Coumadin 7.5 mg p.o. daily.
6. Oxycodone/acetaminophen 5/325, 1-2 tablets p.o. q. 6-8h. p.r.n.
7. Ambien 5 mg p.o. q.h.s. p.r.n. sleep.

The patient will get her protime checked as an outpatient. Discharge instructions were given regarding activity level, diet, sleep and emotions.

9-8F:

SERVICE CODE(S): _____

ICD-9-CM DX CODE(S): _____

ICD-10-CM DX CODE(S): _____

CASE 9-9

LOCATION: Outpatient, Hospital

PATIENT: Kevin Hendrickson

PHYSICIAN: Gregory Dawson, MD

PREOPERATIVE DIAGNOSIS: Hemoptysis

POSTOPERATIVE DIAGNOSIS: Same

PROCEDURE PERFORMED: The patient was intubated prior to the procedure. Informed consent as obtained from the patient's wife who agreed for the procedure. The bronchoscope was passed with an endotracheal tube, 8.5 size. Then Lidocaine was utilized for lubrication for the endotracheal tube. Video monitoring was utilized through endoscopic technique. With the bronchoscope into the endotracheal tube, the left upper, lingula, and lower lobe regions for the subsegmental branches were visualized. They were cleaned with cold saline. There were no endobronchial lesions on the left side. Then the right upper lobe bronchus to segmental branches was visualized, and there were no endobronchial lesions or bleeding from any particular segment. Then the right mid-lobe branches up to medial and lateral branches up to segmental branches were visualized and no bleeding was noted and no endobronchial lesions either. Then right lower lobe bronchus up to subsegmental branches was visualized including the superior segmental bronchus. The anterior segment of the left lower lobe was showing evidence of active bleeding after washing with all the saline. After cold saline irrigation, the bleeding was able to be controlled. Then local epinephrine was also administered to cause local vasoconstriction. Specimens were collected to send for cytology to rule out malignancy and also to rule out any infectious etiology. The procedure was uneventful. Bleeding seemed to be controlled with cold saline irrigation administrations.

Pathology Report Later Indicated: See Report 9-9B

9-9A:

SERVICE CODE(S): _____

ICD-9-CM DX CODE(S): _____

ICD-10-CM DX CODE(S): _____

9-9B PATHOLOGY REPORT, CYTOLOGY

LOCATION: Outpatient, Hospital

PATIENT: Kevin Hendrickson

PHYSICIAN: Gregory Dawson, MD

PATHOLOGISTS: Morton Monson, MD

CLINICAL HISTORY: Hemoptysis

SPECIMEN RECEIVED: Bronchial wash, right lower lobe

GROSS DESCRIPTION: 20 mL opaque red fluid specimen

SPECIMEN ADEQUACY: Specimen satisfactory for cytologic evaluation

DIAGNOSIS: No cytologic evidence of malignancy

9-9B:

SERVICE CODE(S): _____

ICD-9-CM DX CODE(S): _____

ICD-10-CM DX CODE(S): _____

CHAPTER 10

Urinary, Male Genital, and Endocrine Systems

CASE 10-1

10-1A OPERATIVE REPORT, NEPHROSTOMY TUBE EXCHANGE

The patient in this case requires routine exchange of a previously placed nephrostomy tube. The diagnosis is the reason for the service, which in this case will be a V code /Z code. No radiological guidance was used during the procedure.

LOCATION: Outpatient, Hospital

PATIENT: Gene Udder

SURGEON: Ira Avilla, MD

EXAMINATION OF: Left nephrostomy tube exchange

CLINICAL SYMPTOMS: Routine exchange of nephrostomy tube

LEFT NEPHROSTOMY TUBE EXCHANGE HISTORY: This is a 76-year-old male with hydronephrosis, needing routine exchange of the nephrostomy tube.

FINDINGS: Informed consent was obtained. The patient was placed prone on the angiographic table and has preexisting left nephrostomy tube. The back was prepped and draped in the usual sterile fashion. A 0.035 Bentson guidewire was advanced through the nephrostomy tube. The tube was exchanged for a 5 French Berenstein catheter, which allowed wire placement into the proximal ureter. The wire was exchanged for a 0.035 Amplatz guidewire. Berenstein was exchanged for a new 16 French Cook nephrostomy tube whose pigtail was formed within the central renal pelvis. The tube was secured to the skin with 2-0 Ethilon suture.

The patient did not receive conscious sedation. However, his pulse oximeter and vital signs were monitored throughout the exam. There were no complications. He tolerated the procedure well and left the Radiology Department in stable condition.

IMPRESSION: Successful and uncomplicated exchange of left nephrostomy tube.

Make sure to check
evolve
learning system
for the latest
content updates

10-1A:

SERVICE CODE(S): _____

ICD-9-CM DX CODE(S): _____

ICD-10-CM DX CODE(S): _____

10-1B RADIOLOGY REPORT, NEPHROSTOGRAM

During the nephrostomy tube placement in Case 10-1A, Dr. Monson was performing a pre- and post-nephrostogram. Code Dr. Monson's radiology service for this.

LOCATION: Outpatient, Hospital

PATIENT: Gene Udder

SURGEON: Ira Avilla, MD

RADIOLOGIST: Morton Monson, MD

EXAMINATION OF: Nephrostogram

CONTRAST: Hand injection of contrast through the nephrostomy tube

CLINICAL SYMPTOMS: Check placement of the nephrostomy tube

NEPHROSTOGRAM HISTORY: This is a 76-year-old male with hydronephrosis, needing routine exchange of the nephrostomy tube.

FINDINGS PRE LEFT NEPHROSTOGRAM: Nephrostogram obtained demonstrates a preexisting 16 French nephrostomy tube within an upper pole calyx. Mild hydronephrosis is seen. No filling defects are identified. Ureteral coils are present.

FINDINGS POST LEFT NEPHROSTOGRAM: Final nephrostogram obtained demonstrates mild hydronephrosis. The new nephrostomy tube is present in the main renal pelvis with the tip of the pigtail into the ureteral pelvic junction. No contrast extravasation of filling defects are seen.

10-1B:

SERVICE CODE(S): _____

ICD-9-CM DX CODE(S): _____

ICD-10-CM DX CODE(S): _____

CASE 10-2

10-2A OPERATIVE REPORT, ESWL

LOCATION: Outpatient, Hospital

PATIENT: Allen Athens

SURGEON: Ira Avilla, MD

PREOPERATIVE DIAGNOSIS: Right renal calculus with stent

POSTOPERATIVE DIAGNOSIS: Right renal calculus with stent

PROCEDURE PERFORMED: Right ESWL, cystoscopy, stent removal

CLINICAL NOTE: This gentleman has had a large stone burden bilaterally, he is now here for his third and hopefully, final ESWL treatment to these stones. He has no further stones left in the left kidney. He has one residual stone in the right with the stent in situ.

PROCEDURE NOTE: The patient was placed on the lithotripsy table, and administered a general anesthetic. The stone was targeted, shock head engaged. Total of 2400 shocks at maximum kV of 24 were administered to the stone. Good fragmentation was noted. The patient was then prepped and draped in the supine position. The urethra was anesthetized with 2 % Xylocaine jelly. The patient was cystoscoped with the flexible instrument; stent was visualized, grasped and removed intact. He tolerated the procedure well, and was transferred to the recovery room in good condition. He will be seen in six weeks' time for follow-up KUB and to make arrangements for metabolic workup.

10-2A:

SERVICE CODE(S): _____

ICD-9-CM DX CODE(S): _____

ICD-10-CM DX CODE(S): _____

CASE 10-3

10-3A OPERATIVE REPORT, URETHROPEXY

LOCATION: Outpatient, Hospital

PATIENT: Irene Ash

SURGEON: Ira Avilla, MD

PREOPERATIVE DIAGNOSIS: Incontinence

POSTOPERATIVE DIAGNOSIS: Incontinence

PROCEDURE PERFORMED: Urethropexy

CLINICAL NOTE: The patient is a 60-year-old woman who has been suffering from stress incontinence for quite some time now. She has made the decision to proceed with surgery to correct this situation.

PROCEDURE: The patient was brought to the operating room and placed on the operating table in the supine position and prepped and draped. A small horizontal incision is made in the abdomen just above the symphysis pubis. The bladder was then suspended by placing sutures bilaterally at the mid-portion of the urethra 1 cm lateral and at the bladder neck 2 cm lateral. The sutures were then suspended to the Cooper's ligament bilaterally. The urethra was then elevated to the horizontal position. One finger could be passed between the urethra and the symphysis anteriorly. Hemostasis was achieved and the incision was then closed in layers. The patient was turned over to the recovery area in stable condition.

10-3A:

SERVICE CODE(S): _____

ICD-9-CM DX CODE(S): _____

ICD-10-CM DX CODE(S): _____

CASE 10-4

In the following case Dr. Avilla provided **both** *the cystoscopic and fluoroscopic examination of the kidney.*

10-4A OPERATIVE REPORT, CYSTOSCOPY

LOCATION: Outpatient, Hospital

PATIENT: Eileen Lab

SURGEON: Ira Avilla, MD

PREOPERATIVE DIAGNOSIS: Left ureteral calculus

POSTOPERATIVE DIAGNOSIS: Left ureteral calculus

PROCEDURE PERFORMED: Cystoscopy, bilateral retrograde pyelograms, left ureteroscopy, stone extraction.

PROCEDURE: The patient was given a general laryngeal mask anesthetic, prepped and draped in the lithotomy position. The patient was cystocoped using a 21 French instrument. There was no evidence of urethral or bladder abnormality. Bilateral retrograde pyelograms were performed that showed normal collecting system of the right-hand side. There was only a minimal suggestion of a filling defect in the distal ureter on the left. There was minimal dilation of the left collecting system, and clear urine could be seen effluxing from both orifices. Because her symptoms were so classic for a stone, I decided to ureteroscope the patient anyway. A stiff Terumo guidewire was advanced up the ureter under fluoroscopic control and then followed this with a 7 French rigid short ureteroscope without prior ureteral dilation. Just at the level of Waldeyer's fascia, a stone was visualized. This was entrapped in a helical basket and withdrawn under visual guidance. Repeat ureteral inspection showed no evidence of abrasion or edema; therefore, it was decided not to stent the patient. The bladder was drained and cystoscope withdrawn. B&O suppository was placed rectally. She tolerated the procedure well and was transferred to the recovery room in good condition. She will be discharged later today. Follow-up will be arranged for ultrasound in 3 months' time.

10-4A:

SERVICE CODE(S): _____

ICD-9-CM DX CODE(S): _____

ICD-10-CM DX CODE(S): _____

CASE 10-5

Nick Latin has been experiencing left renal colic for the past week. He does have a ureteral stone, and Dr. Avilla is going to perform a cystoscopy and place a ureteral stent to help his ureter stay open. Fluoroscopic guidance was used by Dr. Avilla to help make sure placement of the stent was in the correct location.

10-5A OPERTATIVE REPORT, STENT INSERTION

LOCATION: Outpatient, Hospital

PATIENT: Nick Latin

SURGEON: Ira Avilla, MD

PREOPERATIVE DIAGNOSIS: Left ureteral calculus

POSTOPERATIVE DIAGNOSIS: Left ureteral calculus

PROCEDURE PERFORMED: Cystoscopy, left retrograde pyelogram, under fluoroscopic control insertion of left ureteral stent.

CLINICAL NOTE: Mr. Latin is a 74-year-old male who presents with a 1-week history of left renal colic. He has an 8- to 9-mm stone above the pelvic brim on the left-hand side. There is associated hydronephrosis. (This indicates that the hydronephrosis is a manifestation of the ureter calculus.) He has noticed also slight increase in his serum creatinine over the last week. It was 1.3 at the beginning of the week. Yesterday it was 1.9 and this morning 1.8. He has been pain free overnight but the stone is so large that I think it highly unlikely that he would pass it on his own; therefore, I have recommended manipulation today.

PROCEDURE: The patient was given a general endotracheal anesthetic, prepped and draped in the lithotomy position. A 21 French cystoscope was passed into the bladder under direct vision. Urethra was normal. Sphincter was intact. Prostate had been previously removed. Inspection of the bladder neck closed. The suture line runs up between the ureters and as a result his left ureter has been pulled over to the right-hand side. There is really no trigone left. Both ureters are within 1 cm of each other on the right side in the base of the bladder.

A retrograde pyelogram was performed using contrast and fluoroscopic control and the stone was identified at the level of L4 on the right hand side. Also, the ureter took a very lateral route below and then over the pelvic brim.

It took some time to carefully manipulate a guidewire up the left ureter and beyond the stone using fluoroscopic control. I felt it unsafe to try and ureteroscope this gentleman because of the location of the ureter; it was almost as if he had a crossed trigonal reimplant on that side. I did not think we would be able to safely negotiate the ureter with a rigid or even flexible ureteroscopy. Therefore, we decided to simply stent the patient and subsequently treat him with ESWL. The 810 Amplatz stent positioning system was introduced under fluoroscopic control. A 30 cm 7 French stent was then placed in the usual fashion. Bladder was drained and a B&O suppository placed in the usual fashion. The patient tolerated the procedure well. He was transferred to the recovery room in good condition.

10-5A:

SERVICE CODE(S): _____

ICD-9-CM DX CODE(S): _____

ICD-10-CM DX CODE(S): _____

CASE 10-6

10-6A OPERATIVE REPORT, RESECTION HEMANGIOMA

LOCATION: Outpatient, Hospital

PATIENT: George Lund

SURGEON: Ira Avilla, MD

PREOPERATIVE DIAGNOSIS: Mass of the penis

POSTOPERATIVE DIAGNOSIS: Large hemangioma with vascular malformation, penis

PROCEDURE PERFORMED: Resection of the large penile hemangioma

CLINICAL NOTE: This is a 25-year-old man who presents with a 2-month history of pain on the dorsal penile area. Ultrasound showed this to be a solid mass. No flow was seen within it. It is thought to possibly be a sarcoma. It is a soft mass and it may be vascular. Resection will be done to determine what we are dealing with.

OPERATIVE NOTE: The patient was placed under general anesthesia via endotracheal tube. The patient was prepped and draped in the supine position. An incision was made on the dorsal side of the penile shaft, overlying the mass. Just below the skin, a large vein was encountered. Bleeding was controlled with ligation using 3-0 chromic ligatures. The mass was seen and was approximately 9 cm long. Under closer inspection this was noted to be a hemangioma coming from the superficial veins from Buck's fascia. Care and mobilization were taken and all perforating vessels were individually ligated with chromic ligature. Photographs were taken during the procedure showing the extreme vascularity of the lesion. Frozen section was taken and this showed no malignancy present. After the mass was resected it left a large cavity in the base of the patient's penile shaft. The subcutaneous tissues were closed with 4-0 chromic and the skin was closed with subcuticular Dexon. A compression dressing was applied. The patient tolerated the procedure well and was transferred to the recovery room in stable condition.

Pathology Report Later Indicated: Benign hemangioma

10-6A:

SERVICE CODE(S): _____

ICD-9-CM DX CODE(S): _____

ICD-10-CM DX CODE(S): _____

CASE 10-7

Azoospermia is the absence of sperm and can be caused by many conditions, including neoplasm of the testes. Biopsies of the testis can be accomplished by means of percutaneous biopsy or open incision biopsy. Code the following service provided by Dr. Avilla.

10-7A OPERATIVE REPORT, BIOPSY

LOCATION: Outpatient, Hospital

PATIENT: Mark Flom

SURGEON: Ira Avilla, MD

PREOPERATIVE DIAGNOSIS: Azoospermia

POSTOPERATIVE DIAGNOSIS: Azoospermia

PROCEDURE PERFORMED: Bilateral incisional biopsy of the testes

PROCEDURE: The patient was given general mask anesthesia and prepped and draped in the supine position. Bilateral testicular cord blocks were done using a mixture of 0.5% Marcaine and 2% Xylocaine with epinephrine. Half was applied to each side. We began on the right side and a scrotal incision was made. The tunica vaginalis was identified and opened, and a stay stitch was placed in the testis. A small incision was made. The tubules were delivered, resected, and sent for permanent section. The testis was then closed with a 3-0 chromic, and the scrotal sac was closed with 3-0 chromic. The identical procedure was then performed on the left side. The patient tolerated the procedure well and dressings were applied. Scrotal support was applied. A discharge prescription for Tylenol no. 3 was given.

Pathology Report Later Indicated: Benign testicular tissue

10-7A:

SERVICE CODE(S): _____

ICD-9-CM DX CODE(S): _____

ICD-10-CM DX CODE(S): _____

CASE 10-8

10-8A OPERATIVE REPORT, RESECTION HYDROCELE

LOCATION: Outpatient, Hospital

PATIENT: Donald Styel

SURGEON: Ira Avilla, MD

PREOPERATIVE DIAGNOSIS: Left hydrocele, left scrotal mass

POSTOPERATIVE DIAGNOSIS: Left hydrocele

PROCEDURE PERFORMED: Resection of hydrocele sac, left testicular cord, left scrotum, and resection of left paratesticular mass.

CLINICAL NOTE: This is a 78-year-old gentleman who has developed a hydrocele and has a left scrotal mass. We have discussed different options and he has decided he would like this surgically taken care of. The patient has been marked earlier for surgery.

OPERATIVE NOTE: The patient was given a general endotracheal anesthetic, prepped and draped in the supine position. A midline scrotal incision was made and the testis delivered. Two hydroceles were identified, one of the testis and one of the cord. The hydrocele of the cord was resected. Hemostasis was achieved with electrocautery. The hydrocele sac of the scrotum was also opened and resected. Once opening this, there was a very dark 1.5 cm lesion separate from the epididymis and testis in the region of the testicular cord. This was mobilized, isolated, and resected intact. It did not appear to have a blood supply or be in association with any of the cord or testicular structures. This was sent separately for pathologic identification. Once hemostasis was achieved the testis was returned to the scrotum. A $1/4$ inch Penrose drain was left through a separate stab wound and sutured to the skin with 2-0 Prolene. The scrotum was closed in two layers with a 3-0 chromic. Dressings applied. Scrotal support applied. The patient was transferred to the recovery room in good condition.

10-8A:

SERVICE CODE(S): _____

ICD-9-CM DX CODE(S): _____

ICD-10-CM DX CODE(S): _____

CASE 10-9

Jonathon Wend's prostate biopsy indicated carcinoma of the prostate. Dr. Avilla has scheduled a prostatectomy.

10-9A OPERATIVE REPORT, PROSTATECTOMY

LOCATION: Inpatient, Hospital

PATIENT: Jonathon Wend

SURGEON: Ira Avilla, MD

PREOPERATIVE DIAGNOSIS: Carcinoma of the prostate

POSTOPERATIVE DIAGNOSIS: Carcinoma of the prostate

PROCEDURE PERFORMED: Radical retropubic prostatectomy, plastic repair of bladder neck, bilateral pelvic lymph node dissection.

CLINICAL NOTE: This gentleman was found to have adenocarcinoma of the prostate after presenting with a rising PSA and abnormal digital rectal examination.

OPERATIVE NOTE: The patient was given an epidural anesthetic. Unfortunately, analgesia was incomplete and therefore he was converted to a general endotracheal anesthetic. A 20 French catheter was inserted into the bladder and a lower abdominal midline incision made. The Omni retractor was used for exposure. Bilateral pelvic lymphadenectomy was performed. The obturator nerves were identified and spared. There was no gross abnormality of the lymph nodes and therefore they were sent for permanent section. The superficial venous complex was identified, cauterized, and divided. The endopelvic fascia was opened bilaterally. The puboprostatic ligaments were divided sharply. The dorsal venous complex was then surrounded with a McDougal clamp, ligated distally with #1 silk and oversewn proximally with 2-0 chromic. It was then divided using electrocautery. The urethra was incised anteriorly, the catheter withdrawn, clamped, divided and the urethra divided posteriorly. A left nerve-sparing procedure was performed and the nerves were dissected off the prostate under direct visual guidance. The right neurovascular bundle was taken widely using clips and chromic ties. Lateral pedicles were taken with 0 chromic ties. The bladder neck was opened anteriorly, then divided posteriorly after the ureteric orifices were identified. The seminal vesicles were clipped and divided near their bases. A small amount of seminal vesicle tissue was left on the right hand side. The ampullae of the vas were also clipped and divided. Hemostasis was achieved with 2-0 chromic suture ligatures. The bladder neck was then closed in a tennis racquet fashion using 2-0 chromic and the mucosa everted using 4-0 chromic. The urethra was re-anastomosed to the bladder neck using 2-0 Monocryl sutures over a 20 French Foley catheter in the usual fashion. A Jackson-Pratt drain was left through a left lower quadrant stab wound and sutured to the skin with 2-0 Prolene. The fascia was closed with #1 Vicryl, subcutaneous tissue with 3-0 Vicryl and skin with 4-0 subcuticular Dexon and Dermabond. Estimated blood loss was 750 cc. Sponge and needle counts were reported as correct. The patient remained hemodynamically stable intraoperatively.

Pathology Report Later Indicated: Malignant, primary prostate cancer

10-9A:

SERVICE CODE(S): _____

ICD-9-CM DX CODE(S): _____

ICD-10-CM DX CODE(S): _____

CASE 10-10

10-10A OPERATIVE REPORT, CRYOABLATION OF PROSTATE
This case demonstrates the use of cryoablation.

LOCATION: Outpatient, Hospital

PATIENT: Wes Flanders

SURGEON: Ira Avilla, MD

PREOPERATIVE DIAGNOSIS: Recurrent carcinoma of the prostate

POSTOPERATIVE DIAGNOSIS: Recurrent carcinoma of the prostate

PROCEDURE PERFORMED: Cryoablation of the prostate

CLINICAL NOTE: This is a 53-year-old gentleman who has undergone radiation therapy for adenocarcinoma of the prostate. Unfortunately, he developed problems again and underwent a needle biopsy and recurrence of his cancer was found. Options were discussed with the patient and he has opted to proceed with cryoablation. He has been told of the risk of incontinence and possible rectal injury. He understands and still chooses to proceed with the surgery.

PROCEDURE: The patient was given a general endotracheal anesthetic and was prepped and draped in the lithotomy position. An 18-French Foley catheter was placed in the bladder. A transrectal probe was introduced. Prostate volume was returned at 27.5 g. A six-probe freeze was selected. Using quick stick method, sheaths were placed using ultrasound guidance. Following placement of the sheaths, temperature probes were then placed in the left and right neurovascular bundles, apex, external sphincter, and Denonvilliers fascia. A two-cycle probe freeze was performed. The first cycle was a very rapid freeze and the second cycle was a more prolonged freeze. The external sphincter temperature never reached less than 0° C. The freeze was monitored both digitally and radiographically with ultrasound. The probes were then withdrawn after the full thaw. Two active thaw cycles were undertaken. The perineal incisions were then closed with 3-0 plain catgut subcuticular sutures. The catheter was left in. The patient tolerated the procedure well and was transferred to the recovery room in good condition.

10-10A:

SERVICE CODE(S): _____

ICD-9-CM DX CODE(S): _____

ICD-10-CM DX CODE(S): _____

CASE 10-11

10-11A OPERATIVE REPORT, THYROIDECTOMY

LOCATION: Inpatient, Hospital

PATIENT: Andrea Slim

SURGEON: Gary Sanchez, MD

PREOPERATIVE DIAGNOSIS: Right thyroid nodule

POSTOPERATIVE DIAGNOSIS: Right thyroid nodule

PROCEDURE PERFORMED: Right thyroid total lobectomy

OPERATIVE NOTE: With the patient under general anesthesia the neck was prepped and draped in a sterile manner. A standard collar incision was made with sharp dissection carried down through the platysma. Hemostasis was maintained with the electrocautery and clamps and ligatures of 3-0 silk. Superior and inferior flaps were created and when we established a plane in-between sternohyoid and sternothyroid, particularly on the right side. We then were able to elevate the sternothyroid off the thyroid gland using the electrocautery with careful dissection. With this accomplished we then exposed the isthmus of the thyroid gland. We took down vessels leading into the isthmus from top and below using clamps and ligature of 2-0 silk. With this accomplished, we were able to dissect the isthmus off the trachea and divide the isthmus between suture ligatures of 2-0 silk. We then turned our attention to mobilizing the gland upwards. We were able to identify the recurrent nerve on the right and the right and superior parathyroids that were all preserved out of the field. We rotated the gland to take the inferior and superior pole vessels using clamps and ligatures of 2-0 silk and some hemoclips. Once we had this accomplished we could definitely see the course of the nerve and the parathyroid gland. We then removed the entire specimen. Hemostasis maintained in the bed using some Avitene. Specimen was submitted to pathology and the diagnosis is read as Hurthle cell adenoma on pathology, benign. We made sure hemostasis was intact and then closed the midline structures of the neck using 3-0 silk. The platysma and subcutaneous tissue was closed using 3-0 Vicryl. The skin was closed using staples. A standard thyroid dressing was applied. The patient tolerated the procedure well and was discharged from the operating room in stable condition. At the end of the procedure all sponges and instruments are accounted for.

Pathology Report Later Indicated: Benign adenoma of thyroid gland

10-11A:

SERVICE CODE(S): _____

ICD-9-CM DX CODE(S): _____

ICD-10-CM DX CODE(S): _____

CHAPTER 11

Female Genital System and Maternity Care/Delivery

Make sure to check **evolve** learning system **for the latest content updates**

CASE 11-1

Dr. Green's patient, Margaret Hill, is seen in consultation by Dr. Martinez for post-menopausal bleeding. She has also been experiencing chronic cholecystitis with cholelithiasis.

11-1A CONSULTATION, POSTMENOPAUSAL BLEEDING

LOCATION: Inpatient, Hospital

PATIENT: Margaret Hill

ATTENDING PHYSICIAN: Ronald Green, MD

CONSULTANT: Andy Martinez, MD

Mrs. Hill is an 87-year-old Caucasian female who has been having difficulty with postmenopausal bleeding. She also has been experiencing right upper quadrant abdominal pain, nausea, and vomiting. The patient was found to have chronic cholecystitis with cholelithiasis. The patient also has chronic lymphocytic leukemia. She has been having difficulty with diarrhea also. The patient is now being seen for possible laparoscopic, possible open cholecystectomy.

PAST MEDICAL HISTORY: Patient has a history of chronic lymphocytic leukemia.

ALLERGIES: To sulfa.

GYNECOLOGY EXAMINATION: Mrs. Hill is an 87-year-old Caucasian female who appears in no acute distress. CHEST: Lungs are clear. No rales or rhonchi were heard. HEART: Regular rhythm. ABDOMEN: Normal bowel sounds. The patient does have tenderness in the RUQ area with deep palpation. No guarding or rebound tenderness.

Breasts: Negative for masses, discharge, or tenderness. Breasts are pendulous and symmetrical. Pelvic: Adult female genitalia, vagina, and uterus sounded to 4 inches and the cervix descends to the opening.

IMPRESSION:
1. Postmenopausal bleeding.
2. Chronic cholecystitis with cholelithiasis.
3. Chronic lymphocytic leukemia.

PLAN: The patient has been counseled for hysteroscopy with possible D&C. Dr. Sanchez will be consulted regarding a possible laparoscopic procedure for the patient's gallbladder problems, possible open cholecystectomy. She has consented to the D&C operation. The patient will undergo surgery today.

11-1A:

SERVICE CODE(S): _____

ICD-9-CM DX CODE(S): _____

ICD-10-CM DX CODE(S): _____

11-1B OPERATIVE REPORT, HYSTEROSCOPY

Dr. Martinez schedules a hysteroscopy for Margaret. Before the procedure, Dr. Sanchez consulted with Margaret and the decision was made to remove her gallbladder during the same operative session. The hysteroscopy was performed by Dr. Martinez (11-1B) and the cholecystectomy will be performed by Dr. Sanchez (11-1C).

LOCATION: Inpatient, Hospital

PATIENT: Margaret Hill

ATTENDING PHYSICIAN: Ronald Green, MD

SURGEON: Andy Martinez, MD

PREOPERATIVE DIAGNOSIS: Postmenopausal bleeding

POSTOPERATIVE DIAGNOSIS: Postmenopausal bleeding

PROCEDURE PERFORMED: Hysteroscopy with fractional dilatation and curettage

ANESTHESIA: General endotracheal

ESTIMATED BLOOD LOSS: Less than 25 cc

IRRIGATION: 400 cc used, 400 cc recovered

FLUIDS: 1,000 cc

FINDINGS: Uterus sounded to 4 inches and the cervix descends to the opening. The patient has a second-degree cystocele and a first-degree rectocele with gaping introitus.

PROCEDURE: The patient was prepped and draped in the lithotomy position under general endotracheal anesthesia and the bladder was straight catheterized. A weighted speculum was placed in the vagina and the anterior lip of the cervix was grasped with a single-toothed tenaculum. The Kevorkian curet was then used to obtain endocervical curettings. The uterus was then sounded to a depth of 4 inches. The cervical os was then dilated to allow passage of the hysteroscope. The hysteroscope was then used to document intrauterine morphology. There was an endometrial polyp present. The cervical os was then serially dilated further to allow passage of a sharp curet. Stone polyp forceps were used to remove the endometrial polyp. The sharp curet was then used to sample the endometrial cavity, with scant return of tissue. The tenaculum was removed from the cervix. The tenaculum site was oversewn with 3-0 chromic figure-of-eight suture. The weighted speculum was removed from the vagina. All sponges and needles were accounted for at the completion of the procedure. The patient tolerated the procedure well and when she left my care she was doing well. The patient was then turned over to Dr. Sanchez for the gallbladder surgery.

Pathology Report Later Indicated: Benign endometrial polyp

11-1B:

SERVICE CODE(S): _____

ICD-9-CM DX CODE(S): _____

ICD-10-CM DX CODE(S): _____

11-1C OPERATIVE REPORT, CHOLECYSTECTOMY

Dr. Sanchez removes the gallbladder during the same operative session as the hysteroscopy performed by Dr. Martinez. Report the services of Dr. Sanchez.

LOCATION: Inpatient, Hospital

PATIENT: Margaret Hill

ATTENDING PHYSICIAN: Ronald Green, MD

SURGEON: Gary Sanchez, MD

PREOPERATIVE DIAGNOSIS: Chronic cholecystitis and cholelithiasis

POSTOPERATIVE DIAGNOSIS: Chronic cholecystitis and cholelithiasis

PROCEDURE PERFORMED: Laparoscopic cholecystectomy

INDICATION: Mrs. Hill has been having RUQ pain with nausea and vomiting and diarrhea. The patient was found to have chronic cholecystitis with cholelithiasis and she was taken to the operating room.

PROCEDURE: The patient received Ancef 1 gram intravenously preoperatively. She was prepped and draped in the usual manner. An infraumbilical incision was made; the abdomen was entered under direct vision. Two stay sutures of 0 Vicryl were placed on either side of the incision. The Hasson sheath was then inserted. The abdomen was then inflated with CO_2 gas. Three additional ports were then placed. The hilum of the gallbladder was then dissected free. The cystic duct and cystic arteries were identified. The cystic duct was clipped with three white clips and divided. The cystic arteries were clipped with three white clips and divided. There was another small branch of the artery encountered up on the gallbladder bed. This was also clipped with three white clips and divided. The gallbladder was then dissected free from the gallbladder bed using hook cautery. The specimen was placed in a bag and brought out through a lateral port. The lateral port fascia was approximated with 0 Vicryl sutures. The operative area was thoroughly irrigated and the incisions were then closed with 3-0 Vicryl sutures for the subcutaneous tissues and a 4-0 Vicryl subcuticular stitch for the skin. Steri-Strips were applied. Incisions were then injected with 0.5% Marcaine with Epinephrine. The patient tolerated the operation and returned to Recovery in stable condition.

Pathology Report Later Indicated: See Report 11-1D

11-1C:

SERVICE CODE(S): _____

ICD-9-CM DX CODE(S): _____

ICD-10-CM DX CODE(S): _____

11-1D PATHOLOGY REPORT

LOCATION: Inpatient, Hospital

PATIENT: Margaret Hill

ATTENDING PHYSICIAN: Ronald Green, MD

SURGEON: Gary Sanchez, MD

PATHOLOGIST: Grey Lonewolf, MD

CLINICAL HISTORY: Chronic cholecystitis and cholelithiasis

SPECIMEN RECEIVED: Gallbladder and contents.

GROSS DESCRIPTION: The specimen is labeled with the patient's name and "gallbladder and contents" and consists of an unopened 7 × 4 cm gallbladder with somewhat roughened serosal surface. The wall is distended with bile and numerous multifaceted green stones ranging from microscopic to 1.5 cm in greatest dimension.

MICROSCOPIC DESCRIPTION: Sections show gallbladder showing chronic inflammatory infiltrates in the wall.

DIAGNOSIS: Chronic cholecystitis and cholelithiasis.

11-1D:

SERVICE CODE(S): _____

ICD-9-CM DX CODE(S): _____

ICD-10-CM DX CODE(S): _____

CASE 11-2

11-2A OPERATIVE REPORT, HYSTERECTOMY

LOCATION: Inpatient, Hospital

PATIENT: Brenda Black

ATTENDING PHYSICIAN: Andy Martinez, MD

SURGEON: Andy Martinez, MD

PREOPERATIVE DIAGNOSIS: Marked atypical endometrium hyperplasia

POSTOPERATIVE DIAGNOSIS: Marked atypical endometrium hyperplasia

PROCEDURE PERFORMED: Total abdominal hysterectomy with lysis.

FINDINGS: Small bowel adherent to anterior abdominal wall, ovaries and tubes absent bilaterally.

PROCEDURE: The patient was prepped and draped in the supine position under general endotracheal anesthesia with Foley catheter indwelling. A vertical incision was made in the lower abdomen. The fascia was divided in the midline and the peritoneum was entered in a sharp manner and the incision extended vertically. Pelvic washings were obtained for cytology. The patient had the small bowel that was adherent to the right lateral side wall, which may have been impacted by an abdominal retractor. The small bowel was then lifted and a window was noticed between the small bowel and the peritoneum and this was incised with Metzenbaum scissors without difficulty. The bowel was then packed out of the operative field using a self-retaining retractor and laparotomy sponges. The uterus was then grasped and elevated. There were no tubes and ovaries noted bilaterally. The round ligaments were cross-clamped, divided, and ligated with 0 Vicryl suture ligature. The bladder flap was created using sharp and blunt dissection and reflected inferiorly. The uterine vessels were then skeletonized, doubly clamped and divided and ligated with 0 Vicryl suture ligature times two. The bladder flap was advanced from the operative field. The broad ligaments were cross-clamped, divided, and ligated with 0 Vicryl suture ligature in a stepwise fashion down to uterosacral cardinal ligament complex. The vagina was entered from the right side. The vagina was incised immediately adjacent to the cervix, and the surgical specimen was removed intact and sent out for frozen pathologic evaluation. The vaginal angles were sutured to the uterosacral cardinal ligament complex for support using 0 Vicryl modified Richardson suture. The vaginal cuff was whip stitched using Vicryl interlocking suture. The vaginal cuff was reapproximated using 0 Vicryl interrupted figure-of-eight sutures. The operative site was inspected, irrigated and was hemostatic. The right ureter could be easily traced throughout its course. The left ureter was more obscure but did not appear to be involved in the surgical site. After irrigation, the sponge and instruments were removed from the abdominal cavity. The omentum was brought down anteriorly. The fascia and peritoneum were reapproximated using 0 Vicryl interrupted internal retention sutures. The fascia was then reapproximated using 0 PDS continuous suture. At the completion of suturing with the PDS, the 0 Vicryl internal retention were then secured. The operative site was irrigated. The Bovie was used for hemostasis. The skin was reapproximated with staples. A pressure dressing was applied. All sponge and needles were accounted for at the completion of the procedure. The patient left the operating room in apparent good condition having tolerated the procedure well. The Foley catheter was patent and draining clear yellow urine at the completion of the procedure.

Pathology Report Later Indicated:
1. Hyperplasia of uterus endometrium
2. Intramural leiomyoma of uterus (this is a benign tumor)
3. Endometrial polyp
4. Nabothian cyst of cervix
5. Adenomyosis of uterus

11-2A:

SERVICE CODE(S): _____

ICD-9-CM DX CODE(S): _____

ICD-10-CM DX CODE(S): _____

11-2B DISCHARGE SUMMARY

LOCATION: Inpatient, Hospital

PATIENT: Brenda Black

ATTENDING PHYSICIAN: Andy Martinez, MD

DISCHARGING SERVICE: Gynecology

CLINICAL HISTORY:
1. Endometrial hyperplasia.
2. Intramural leiomyoma.
3. Endometrial polyp.
4. Nabothian cyst.
5. Adenomyosis.

PRINCIPLE PROCEDURES: Total abdominal hysterectomy

PATHOLOGY: Uterus weighed 275 grams. Uterus hysterectomy:
1. Complex endometrial hyperplasia with two endometrial polyps. No myometrial invasion is present.
2. Fibrovascular adhesions uterine serosa.
3. Focal Nabothian cyst, cervix.
4. Uterine leiomyoma, intramural.
5. Adenomyosis, focal.
6. Attached left adnexa with intact round ligament.

IDENTIFICATION AND HPI: The patient is a 72-year-old married white female, gravida 1-para 1-0-0-1, LMP postmenopausal, pap August, mammogram August.

CHIEFT COMPLAINT: Atypical adenomatous hyperplasia with atypia.

HISTORY OF PRESENT ILLNESS: The patient had a pelvic ultrasound, which demonstrated uterus to measure $10.5 \times 6.8 \times 6.7$ cm, it was retroflexed and prominent in size for the patient's age. Abnormal appearance of the central endometrial echo, which measured 7.6 mm and is heterogeneous with scattered hyperechoic areas. The patient subsequently had hysteroscopy with D&C, which demonstrated complex hyperplasia with atypia. The patient was then scheduled for TAH/BSO.

HOSPITAL COURSE: The patient's diet and ambulation were increased as tolerated. The patient was discharged postoperative day three in stable ambulatory condition with instructions to return to the clinic in 5 days for staple removal and 2 weeks for incision check and 4 weeks for postop evaluation.

DISCHARGE MEDICATIONS: Motrin 600 mg, quantity 30, Colace, quantity 18. The patient will continue home meds.

Discharge hemoglobin is 10.4, discharge creatinine is 0.5.

11-2B:

SERVICE CODE(S): _____

ICD-9-CM DX CODE(S): _____

ICD-10-CM DX CODE(S): _____

CASE 11-3

Tara reports for a tubal ligation shortly after delivering her child. Report Dr. Sanchez's service.

11-3A OPERATIVE REPORT, STERILIZATION

LOCATION: Inpatient, Hospital

PATIENT: Tara Loud

ATTENDING PHYSICIAN: Andy Martinez, MD

SURGEON: Gary Sanchez, MD

PREOPERATIVE DIAGNOSIS: Desire for sterilization

POSTOPERATIVE DIAGNOSIS: Desire for sterilization

PROCEDURE PERFORMED: Bilateral tubal ligation, modified Pomeroy technique

ANESTHESIA: General

INDICATION: The patient is a 32-year-old gravida 3, para 3, who underwent spontaneous vaginal delivery yesterday, and affirmed her request for permanent sterilization. Risks and benefits of surgery were discussed with the patient and she elected to proceed with the surgery.

TECHNIQUE: The patient was taken to the operating room where epidural anesthesia was found to be inadequate, and she was therefore given general anesthesia, prepped and draped in the normal sterile fashion. An approximately 15 mm transverse infra-umbilical incision was made with the scalpel and blunt dissection to the fascia was made with Kelly clamp. The fascia was grasped between two Kocher clamps, tented up, and entered sharply. The incision was extended bilaterally for about 10 mm. Then the peritoneum was identified, grasped with two hemostats, tented up, and entered sharply to expose the uterus. Then the right fallopian tube was identified, grasped with a Babcock clamp, walked out to its fimbriated end, re-grasped approximately 3 cm from the corneal region, and the avascular portion of the mesosalpinx was identified and perforated under the fallopian tube with a Mosquito and a length of 0 plain gut was drawn back through the proximal followed by distal ends, and an approximately 3 cm segment of tube was tied and the intervening segment of fallopian tube was excised. The luminal ends were identified and found to be hemostatic. Then a similar procedure was carried out on the left. Following this, the fascia was closed in a running fashion with 0 Vicryl, and the skin was reapproximated with 4-0 Vicryl in subcuticular stitch. The patient tolerated the procedure well. Sponge, lap, and needle counts were correct. The patient was taken to recovery in stable condition.

11-3A:

SERVICE CODE(S): _____

ICD-9-CM DX CODE(S): _____

ICD-10-CM DX CODE(S): _____

CASE 11-4

Dr. Martinez admits a patient who will undergo a cesarean section.

11-4A ADMISSION HISTORY AND PHYSICAL

LOCATION: Inpatient, Hospital

PATIENT: Lisa Logan

ATTENDING PHYSICIAN: Andy Martinez, MD

CHIEF COMPLAINT: Spontaneous rupture of the membranes

SUBJECTIVE: This is a 22-year-old G1, P0, with estimated date of confinement of 7/21 based on ultrasound at 19 weeks, putting her at a 38½ estimated gestational age, that was transferred here because of intermittent late decelerations. The patient was seen earlier this morning with spontaneous rupture of membranes that was clear at approximately 7 AM with re-confirmation of rupture of membranes with Nitrazine positive. The patient was subsequently admitted, IV started and the patient had a vasovagal type syncopal episode with decelerations to 104 beats per minute for greater than 1 minute shortly thereafter. Approximately an hour later, there was another late deceleration to the 90s according to notes. Pitocin was used to augment patient's labor, started at 9:30 AM and stopped at noon prior to transport. There were notes of adequate contractions at that point. The patient was subsequently transferred to our facility via ambulance because of intermittent late decelerations.

LABORATORY STUDIES: Rubella immune, VDR negative, negative hepatitis antigen, HIV, and cultures, and Group B Strep negative at 36 weeks.

PAST MEDICAL HISTORY: Essentially noncontributory.

ALLERGIES: No known allergies.

MEDICATIONS: Prenatal vitamins.

FAMILY HISTORY: From charts there is remote thrombophlebitis history. Grandfather and grandmother had cancer.

SOCIAL HISTORY: The patient smokes, down to 5 cigarettes per day at this point, had occasional alcohol use early in pregnancy according to notes. Denies any other drug use and has been taking prenatal vitamins. She is single.

REVIEW OF SYSTEMS: The patient denies any headaches, abdominal pain, swelling, visual changes, but she does note feeling contractions shortly after her spontaneous rupture of membranes and increased after Pitocin was started.

PHYSICAL EXAMINATION: Vital signs: Blood pressure of 111/66, Temperature of 36.6° C, Heart rate 74, Respiratory rate 20. Fetal heart tones 130s to 150s. Appearance: 22-year-old female who appears stated age, alert, and oriented, and appropriately answering questions. Lung sounds were distant but clear to auscultation bilaterally. Heart: Regular rate and rhythm. S1, S2. Abdomen: Leopold's maneuvers were indeterminate. Extremities: There was trace edema, deep tendon reflexes brisk, 4/4 with no noted clonus. Vaginal exam reveals 3-4 cm, 80% effacement and 0 station. External fetal monitoring revealed a fetal heart rate of 120s to 150s with reactivity, contractions occurring every 3-4 minutes.

ASSESSMENT: Spontaneous rupture of the membranes and attempt to augment. Intermittent decelerations and no cesarean section coverage at this time.

PLAN: Currently we will observe the patient, watch fetal heart rate monitoring in relation to contractions and expect delivery.

11-4A:

SERVICE CODE(S): _____

ICD-9-CM DX CODE(S): _____

ICD-10-CM DX CODE(S): _____

11-4B OPERATIVE REPORT, CESAREAN SECTION

Lisa was given Pitocin but it failed to cause any more cervical change and she remained dilated 3-4 cm. Due to deceleration of fetal heart tones Dr. Sanchez decided to take Lisa to surgery to deliver her baby by cesarean section.

LOCATION: Inpatient, Hospital

PATIENT: Lisa Logan

ATTENDING PHYSICIAN: Andy Martinez, MD

SURGEON: Gary Sanchez, MD

PREOPERATIVE DIAGNOSIS:
1 Spontaneous rupture of the membranes.
2. Failure to progress.

POSTOPERATIVE DIAGNOSIS:
1. Spontaneous rupture of the membranes.
2. Failure to progress.

PROCEDURE PERFORMED: Primary low transverse cesarean section.

ANESTHESIA: Epidural with Duramorph.

ESTIMATED BLOOD LOSS: 700 cc

FLUIDS: 3000 cc crystalloid

URINE OUTPUT: 90

COMPLICATIONS: None

FINDINGS: A single viable male infant, Apgar's 7 at 1 minute, 9 at 5 minutes, weight 2656 gm (5 pounds 13.7 ounces).

INDICATIONS: Lisa is a 22-year-old, G1, who presented to her primary obstetrician with ruptured membranes at 38 weeks and was found to have intermittent late decelerations. She was transported here. Pitocin was used to attempt to cause cervical change; however; despite nine hours of attempting to adjust Pitocin without causing late deceleration, she remained at 3 to 4, 90 and 0. The baby began to experience late decelera-tions and patient elected to proceed with cesarean. Risks and benefits of surgery were discussed with the patient.

FINDINGS AT THE TIME OF SURGERY included single viable male infant, left occiput transverse position, with cord around the neck × 1, normal tubes and ovaries, normal uterine contour.

TECHNIQUE: The patient was taken to the operating room, where epidural anesthesia was dosed. She was prepped and draped in a normal sterile fashion, and anesthesia was found to be adequate. A Pfannenstiel skin incision was made with the scalpel and carried through to the underlying fascia, which was nicked in the midline, and the fascial incision was extended bilaterally with Mayo scissors. The superior aspect of the fascial incision was grasped with Kocher clamps, tented up, and the underlying rectus muscles were dissected off with sharp dissection. The inferior aspect of the fascial incision was likewise grasped with Kocher clamps, tented up, and the underlying rectus and pyramidalis muscles were dissected off with sharp dissection. The rectus muscles were separated in the midline, and the incision was extended superiorly and inferiorly, with good visualization of the bladder. The peritoneum was grasped with hemostat, tented up, and entered sharply. The peritoneal incision was extended superiorly and inferiorly with good visualization of the bladder. The rectus muscles were separated in the midline. The bladder blade was inserted. The vesicouterine peritoneum was grasped with pickup, entered sharply, and the incision was extended bilaterally with Metzenbaum scissors. The bladder flap was created digitally. The bladder blade was reinserted. The uterus was transcribed in a transverse manner with the scalpel and extended with bandage scissors. The fetus in left occiput posterior presentation was delivered into the incision, and the fetus was bulb suctioned on the abdomen after delivery. Cord gases were cut and sent. The fetus was handed to NICU after the cord was clamped and cut. The placenta was extracted manually. The uterus was exteriorized, cleared of clots and debris, and the angles of the uterine incision were grasped with ring forceps, and the incision was closed with 0 Vicryl in a running locked fashion, a second imbricating layer was used to achieve hemostasis. The bladder flap was closed with 2-0 Vicryl in a running fashion. The posterior cul-de-sac was copiously irrigated. The uterus was replaced within the abdominal cavity. The pelvic cavity was then copiously irrigated and cleared of clots and debris. Then, the rectus diathesis was closed with 2-0 Vicryl in a running fashion. The fascia was closed with 0 Vicryl in a running fashion, using two sutures beginning at the angles and meeting in the midline. The subcuticular space was closed with 2-0 Vicryl interrupted sutures. The skin was reapproximated with staples. The patient tolerated the procedure well. Sponge, lap and needle counts were correct, and she was taken to recovery in stable condition.

11-4B:

SERVICE CODE(S): _____

ICD-9-CM DX CODE(S): _____

ICD-10-CM DX CODE(S): _____

11-4C DISCHARGE SUMMARY

LOCATION: Inpatient, Hospital

PATIENT: Lisa Logan

ATTENDING PHYSICIAN: Andy Martinez, MD

PRINCIPLE DIAGNOSIS: Intrauterine pregnancy 38 weeks' gestation, delivered.

ADDITIONAL DIAGNOSES:
1. Spontaneous rupture of the membranes
2. Repetitive late decelerations.
3. Failure to progress.

PRINCIPLE PROCEDURE: Primary low transverse Cesarean section.

INDICATION: The patient is a 22-year-old gravida 1 who underwent spontaneous rupture of membranes and presented to her primary obstetrician. She developed intermittent repetitive late decelerations and was transferred to our facility for lack of cesarean coverage where she was originally admitted. On a low dose of Pitocin, the baby had reactive tracing, but when Pitocin was increased because she was not progressing in labor, the baby, again, began to develop repetitive variables and she was offered cesarean section for delivery of the infant. She underwent cesarean section of a viable 5 pound 13.7 ounce infant with Apgars of 7 at 1 minute and 9 at 9 minutes with the cord around the neck times one, and returned to recovery in stable condition. By later on postoperatively day zero, she was ambulating with active bowel sounds. She was passing flatus by postoperative day one and tolerating a regular diet. She remained afebrile with stable vital signs. She continued to do well and by postoperative day two, she requested discharge.

DISPOSITION: Discharge to home.

CONDITION AT DISCHARGE: Good.

FOLLOW-UP with her primary OB physician for staple removal and postoperative care.

DISCHARGE MEDICATIONS:
1. Percocet 5/325 mg 1-2 p.o. q.4h. p.r.n.
2. Ibuprofen 600 mg 1 p.o. q.6h. p.r.n., dispense 30 with no refills.
3. Iron sulfate 1 p.o. b.i.d., take with food.

DISCHARGE HEMOGLOBIN: 9.5.

PATHOLOGY: No pathologic diagnosis.

11-4C:

SERVICE CODE(S): _____

ICD-9-CM DX CODE(S): _____

ICD-10-CM DX CODE(S): _____

CHAPTER *12*

Nervous System

Make sure to check
evolve
learning system
**for the latest
content updates**

CASE 12-1

The following craniectomy is for the purpose of removal of an atraumatic epidural hematoma. This patient has a history of recurrent atraumatic fractures with craniectomies for evacuation. You will note there is a fracture area in the report; however, this fracture is due to previous craniectomies and not considered a traumatic fracture.

12-1A OPERATIVE REPORT, OSTEOPLASTIC CRANIECTOMY

LOCATION: Inpatient, Hospital

PATIENT: Jake Ark

ATTENDING PHYSICIAN: Timothy Pleasant, MD

SURGEON: Timothy Pleasant, MD

PREOPERATIVE DIAGNOSIS: Left epidural hematoma, atraumatic

POSTOPERATIVE DIAGNOSIS: Left epidural hematoma, atraumatic

PROCEDURE PERFORMED: Craniectomy, removal of epidural hematoma

ANESTHESIA: General

PREOP NOTE: I think there was some family involved, we got telephone consent. I told anesthesia that this was a lifesaving procedure that I would, under the Good Samaritan law, operate on this individual and write on the chart that he needed emergency surgery. Consent was asked for craniectomy from some relatives. I do not know who they were.

PROCEDURE: Under general anesthesia the patient's head was prepped and draped in the usual manner. The patient was placed in the head outrigger and we then prepped and shaved his head. An inverted U-shaped incision was done over the left posterior parietal area. The skin was incised. We saw the skin and hematoma above when we encountered the fracture. There was a free fragment of the fracture, I elevated this and there was a large epidural hematoma there. We evacuated some, stopped the bleeder on the meninges, and then proceeded to irrigate the wound well. I then beeswaxed the bony edges, achieved hemostasis, tacked up the dura with 2-0 Vicryl and was satisfied that we would now close the scalp. I placed a Hemovac drain in the wound, closed the scalp and galea in layers with 0-Vicryl and surgical staples on the skin. A dressing was applied. The patient was discharged to the recovery room.

12-1A:

SERVICE CODE(S): _____

ICD-9-CM DX CODE(S): _____

ICD-10-CM DX CODE(S): _____

CASE 12-2

The removal of this tumor is conducted through a U-shaped incision and burr hole.

12-2A OPERATIVE REPORT, CRANIOTOMY

LOCATION: Inpatient, Hospital

PATIENT: Shawn Moore

ATTENDING PHYSICIAN: Timothy Pleasant, MD

SURGEON: Timothy Pleasant, MD

PREOPERATIVE DIAGNOSIS: Parietal left brain tumor

POSTOPERATIVE DIAGNOSIS: Parietal left brain tumor

PROCEDURE PERFORMED: Craniotomy with removal of tumor

The Stealth was utilized for localization of the tumor. Coordinated in real-time with the MRI, which had been done the previous day.

PROCEDURE: The head was placed into the Mayfield pins. Fiducials having been placed on the head, the Stealth was then utilized to mark topographically the area of the tumor. The scalp was then marked for our skin incision. This having been done, the fiducials were removed and the head was prepped and draped in the usual manner. An inverted U-shaped incision was made over the site of the tumor and the burr hole was done. The bone flap was then elevated. The dura was incised so that the flap came down on the sinus. Having exposed the brain and having utilized the navigator to localize the tumor, we now incised over the tumor, got into the tumor. This was grayish tissue, hard, gritty. This was sent for frozen section. This came back as gemistocytic astrocytoma so this was, in my opinion, a glioblastoma multiforme. I then removed the tumor with the coagulator and the Bovie. This came out very nicely. We utilized the Stealth probe to make sure that we had gone deep enough and around the cavity of the tumor. Remembering that this was on the left side, we did not want to produce a deficit but stayed within the context of the tumor, achieved adequate hemostasis after the tumor cavity had been cleaned out of its tumor. I then placed a piece of Gelfoam over the raw surface of the brain, and we then closed the dura with 4-0 Nurolon. We then re-applied the bone flap with screws and a small burr hole cover. A Hemovac drain was placed above the bone, and the scalp was approximated with 2-0 Vicryl on the galea and surgical staples on the skin. A dressing was applied. The patient was discharged to the recovery room.

Pathology Report Later Indicated: Malignant neoplasm of brain

12-2A:

SERVICE CODE(S): _____

ICD-9-CM DX CODE(S): _____

ICD-10-CM DX CODE(S): _____

CASE 12-3

This is a re-do craniectomy. This patient has a recurrent atraumatic epidural hematoma as seen on CT scan. This is the same patient from Case 12-1.

12-3A OPERATIVE REPORT, RE-DO CRANIECTOMY

LOCATION: Inpatient, Hospital

PATIENT: Jake Ark

ATTENDING PHYSICIAN: Timothy Pleasant, MD

SURGEON: Timothy Pleasant, MD

PREOPERATIVE DIAGNOSIS: Recurrent atraumatic epidural hematoma

POSTOPERATIVE DIAGNOSIS: Recurrent atraumatic epidural hematoma

PROCEDURE PERFORMED: Re-do craniectomy, enlargement of previous craniectomy and removal of clot and tacking of dura.

ANESTHESIA: General

PREOP NOTE: This patient who had his epidural hematoma removed a couple of days ago had a repeat CT scan. There is re-accumulation here. I have decided to take him back to surgery and enlarge the craniectomy and possibly get at a bleeder that may have been missed or maybe re-accumulation from the scalp, which was quite oozy.

PROCEDURE: Under general anesthesia, the patient was placed in the outrigger with the left side up. The staples were removed. The previous incision was incised and there was obvious clot. I removed the clot. I enlarged the craniectomy with the craniotome. There were some surface bleeders on the dura. I utilized Gelfoam in the corners underneath the bone. I then tacked up the dura with 4-0 Nurolon utilizing about 6-8 tacking sutures and was satisfied the clot had been removed and there was no active bleeding. I then placed a Hemovac drain in the wound, closed the wound in layers utilizing 0 Vicryl on the galea with surgical staples on the skin. Dressing was applied. The patient was discharged to the SCCU.

12-3A:

SERVICE CODE(S): _____

ICD-9-CM DX CODE(S): _____

ICD-10-CM DX CODE(S): _____

CASE 12-4

12-4A OPERATIVE REPORT, SHUNT REMOVAL AND REPLACEMENT

LOCATION: Inpatient, Hospital

PATIENT: Cory Rhode

ATTENDING PHYSICIAN: Timothy Pleasant, MD

SURGEON: Timothy Pleasant, MD

PREOPERATIVE DIAGNOSIS: Hydrocephalus and myelomeningocele

POSTOPERATIVE DIAGNOSIS: Hydrocephalus and myelomeningocele

PROCEDURE PERFORMED: Placement of left ventriculoperitoneal shunt

INDICATION: This is a 4-month-old child who presented with a bacterial shunt infection. The shunt was externalized, and after the spinal fluid was sterilized with antibiotics, it was electively decided to place a new shunt on the opposite side.

PROCEDURE: The patient was taken to the operating room and underwent induction of general endotracheal anesthesia in the supine position. At that point, the left side of the head was shaved, and the left head, neck, and abdomen were prepped and draped. A 3 cm midline skin incision was made just above the umbilicus after infiltrating the skin with ¼% Xylocaine without Epinephrine. The skin and subcutaneous tissues were sharply divided using blunt dissection with the Senn retractors. The midline fascia was identified. This was cut with a #15 blade. The properitoneal fat was dissected bluntly out of the way and the peritoneum was grasped with a hemostat. It was cut with the scissors, and hemostats were applied around the peritoneum. A red rubber catheter was placed into the peritoneal cavity. I next made a horseshoe-shaped incision in the left occipital region and reflected the scalp flap. I then burred a 0.50-cm diameter hole in the left occipital region. The dura was coagulated and incised with a #11 blade, as was the pia/arachnoid. I then made a subcutaneous tunnel from the scalp down to the abdomen and passed the peritoneal catheter. Prior to doing this, I flushed it with normal saline. I used a low profile Delta I level valve and connected this to the distal catheter. I flushed the valve with normal saline prior to connecting it. I secured this with a silk ligature. I then took a ventricular catheter with a stylet in place and passed it into the occipital horn. I felt an ependymal pop and then withdrew the stylet and advanced the catheter a total length of 8 cm. Copious CSF spontaneously flowed. I then connected this to the valve and I pulled the distal tubing so that the valve would lie nicely in the subcutaneous pocket in the left occipital region. The connections were all secured with 3-0 silk. The catheter was tacked down at its exit point of the skull with 3-0 silk. I then placed the distal tubing into the peritoneal cavity after verifying that there was good flow while pumping the shunt. I then closed the pursestring suture in the abdomen. I closed the abdomen in layers with interrupted 3-0 and 2-0 Vicryl. The skin was closed with a running 4-0 Prolene stitch. Benzoin and ¼ inch Steri-Strips were placed. The galea was closed with interrupted 3-0 Vicryl on the scalp, and the skin on the scalp was closed with 4-0 chromic. Bacitracin and a dressing were applied. The patient tolerated the procedure well without apparent complications. Sponge, instrument and needle counts were correct times two. He was taken to the recovery room in stable condition. I would note that after the shunt was placed, I snipped the suture and removed the ventriculostomy from the right occipital region. There were no complications.

12-4A:

SERVICE CODE(S): _____

ICD-9-CM DX CODE(S): _____

ICD-10-CM DX CODE(S): _____

CASE 12-5

12-5A OPERATIVE REPORT, PUMP IMPLANTATION

LOCATION: Inpatient, Hospital

PATIENT: Brian Hoople

ATTENDING PHYSICIAN: Timothy Pleasant, MD

SURGEON: Timothy Pleasant, MD

PREOPERATIVE DIAGNOSIS: Patient with multiple sclerosis with spasticity

POSTOPERATIVE DIAGNOSIS: Patient with multiple sclerosis with spasticity

PROCEDURE PERFORMED: Placement of a catheter and baclofen pump

ANESTHESIA: General

INDICATION: Patient is a 42-year-old male who has severe muscle spasticity now for a few months. Patient has a decubitus ulcer that needs debridement but this cannot be done due to the uncontrolled movement of the patient. A pump will be placed to try to control this.

PROCEDURE: The patient was brought to the operating room and placed under general anesthesia. The patient's spine, side, and right abdomen were prepped and draped in the usual manner. The skin incision was then made over the spinal process of L2, L3, and L4 and got down to the fascia. I then inserted a spinal needle into the subarachnoid space, and got good backflow and then proceeded to place the catheter into the subarachnoid space. I had good CSF flow. I then put a clamp on it and began anchoring of the tubing by securing the tubing to the plastic insert that holds it to the fascia in the paramedian area. This was secured with 2-0 silk. I then went to the anterior right quadrant and made an incision for acceptance of the pump. The pump was the placed in the pocket after using blunt dissection. I then passed the tubing from the posterior to the anterior incision using the trocar. I then had good CSF flow. I connected this to the baclofen pump anchoring it with sutures. I anchored the pump with two sutures to the fascia and began closure of the wounds. The wounds were closed watertight with 2-0 plain in the subcuticular tissue; the skin was closed with surgical staples. A dressing was applied. The patient was taken to the recovery room in stable condition.

12-5A:

SERVICE CODE(S): _____

ICD-9-CM DX CODE(S): _____

ICD-10-CM DX CODE(S): _____

CASE 12-6

Prior to surgery for laminectomies and foraminotomies, Dr. Pleasant orders an x-ray.

I2-6A RADIOLOGY REPORT, LUMBAR SPINE

LOCATION: Inpatient, Hospital

PATIENT: Aaron Marriot

ATTENDING PHYSICIAN: Timothy Pleasant, MD

RADIOLOGIST: Morton Monson, MD

EXAMINATION OF: Lumbar spine

CLINICAL SYMPTOMS: Low back pain

SINGLE VIEW SPINE: For the purpose of this examination there are presumed to be five lumbar type vertebral bodies. Posterior metallic markers are thus at the L4-5 level.

I2-6A:

SERVICE CODE(S): _____

ICD-9-CM DX CODE(S): _____

ICD-I0-CM DX CODE(S): _____

I2-6B OPERATIVE REPORT, LAMINOTOMIES AND FORAMINOTOMIES

LOCATION: Inpatient, Hospital

PATIENT: Aaron Marriot

ATTENDING PHYSICIAN: Timothy Pleasant, MD

SURGEON: Timothy Pleasant, MD

PREOPERATIVE DIAGNOSIS: Displacement of L3-4 on the right

POSTOPERATIVE DIAGNOSIS: Displacement of L3-4 on the right

PROCEDURE PERFORMED: Laminotomy, foraminotomy, and removal of a disc at L3-4

ANESTHESIA: General

PREOP NOTE: This patient has been counseled regarding his disc, regarding the inability to relieve his pain, the necessity for further surgery, fusion, the complications of persistent pain, pseudomeningocele and infection. He consents to go ahead with surgery because of the intractable pain.

DESCRIPTION OF PROCEDURE: Under general anesthesia the patient was placed in prone position. The back was prepped and draped in the usual manner. An incision was made in the skin extending through the subcutaneous tissue, lumbodorsal fascia divided. The erector spini muscles were bluntly dissected from the lamina of L3-4, the interspace was localized via x-ray. I then performed a generous laminotomy, foraminotomy and looked at the L3-4 disc space laterally. There was a hole in the annulus. We entered the disc space and then removed much degenerating material medially and laterally, took it down with curets, took it down with various pituitary rongeurs and cleaned out the disc space. Irrigated the wound well. Then closed the wound in layers utilizing double knotted 0 chromic on the lumbodorsal fascia with 0 Vicryl and 2-0 plain in the subcutaneous tissue and surgical staples on the skin and dressing was applied. The patient was discharged to the recovery room.

12-6B:

SERVICE CODE(S): _____

ICD-9-CM DX CODE(S): _____

ICD-10-CM DX CODE(S): _____

12-6C DISCHARGE SUMMARY

LOCATION: Inpatient, Hospital

PATIENT: Aaron Marriot

ATTENDING PHYSICIAN: Timothy Pleasant, MD

SURGEON: Timothy Pleasant, MD

DIAGNOSIS: L3-4 disc herniation

HOSPITAL COURSE: Mr. Marriot is a 48-year-old gentleman who was experiencing severe back pain. He was found to have a herniation of L3-4 disc on CT scan. He went through epidural steroid injections and other conservative treatment without any success. After risks, benefits, and alternatives were explained, he elected to undergo surgery. He had a pre-op evaluation and was admitted for surgery. He underwent the surgical procedure. His postoperative course has been uneventful. He was discharged home to follow up in our office in 1 week. On discharge, his incision was clean, dry, and intact without signs or symptoms of infection. His pain was well-controlled with oral medication. He has no bowel or bladder dysfunction.

PRINCIPLE PROCEDURE: Laminotomy, foraminotomy, and removal of disc at L3-4 on the right.

12-6C:

SERVICE CODE(S): _____

ICD-9-CM DX CODE(S): _____

ICD-10-CM DX CODE(S): _____

CASE 12-7

12-7A RADIOLOGY REPORT, DISC REPAIR

LOCATION: Inpatient, Hospital

PATIENT: Sarah Malone

ATTENDING PHYSICIAN: Timothy Pleasant, MD

RADIOLOGIST: Morton Monson, MD

EXAMINATION OF: Lumbar spine

CLINICAL SYMPTOMS: Lumbar laminectomy; herniation of L3-L4 disc

CROSSTABLE LATERAL LUMBAR SPINE-INTRAOPERATIVE SPOT FILMS DURING LUMBAR LAMINECTOMY: FINDINGS: The films are grossly under-penetrated. There is a comparison from 12/19. Very limited study. The posterior metallic markers are believed to be at the lumbosacral junction but that is assuming, for the purposes of this examination, only five lumbar-type vertebral bodies.

12-7A:

SERVICE CODE(S): _____

ICD-9-CM DX CODE(S): _____

ICD-10-CM DX CODE(S): _____

12-7B OPERATIVE REPORT, RE-DO LAMINOTOMY AND FORAMINOTOMY, L4-5

LOCATION: Inpatient, Hospital

PATIENT: Sarah Malone

ATTENDING PHYSICIAN: Timothy Pleasant, MD

SURGEON: Timothy Pleasant, MD

PREOPERATIVE DIAGNOSIS: Herniation of L4-5 on the right

POSTOPERATIVE DIAGNOSIS: Herniation of L4-5 on the right

PROCEDURE PERFORMED: Re-do laminotomy, foraminotomy, L4-5 on the right

ANESTHESIA: General

PROCEDURE: Under general anesthesia, the patient was placed in the prone position. The back was prepped and draped in the usual manner. An incision was made extending through subcutaneous tissue. The lumbodorsal fascia was divided. The erector spinae muscles were bluntly dissected from the lamina of L4-5. The L4-5 interspace was localized via x-ray. We enlarged the laminotomy and foraminotomy, saw the extruded fragment, and removed it. We entered the disc space and removed much degenerating material. We decompressed the nerve root, satisfied there were no other free fragments. I irrigated the wound well. I put a Hemovac drain in the wound and closed the wound in layers utilized double knotted 0 chromic on the lumbodorsal fascia, 0 Vicryl and 2-0 plain in the subcutaneous tissue, and surgical staples on the skin. A dressing was applied. The patient was discharged to the recovery room.

Pathology Report Later Indicated: See Report 12-7C

12-7B:

SERVICE CODE(S): _____

ICD-9-CM DX CODE(S): _____

ICD-10-CM DX CODE(S): _____

12-7C PATHOLOGY REPORT

LOCATION: Inpatient, Hospital

PATIENT: Sarah Malone

ATTENDING PHYSICIAN: Timothy Pleasant, MD

SURGEON: Timothy Pleasant, MD

PATHOLOGIST: Grey Lonewolf, MD

CLINICAL HISTORY: Disc herniation

SPECIMEN RECEIVED: Lumbar disc

GROSS DESCRIPTION: Received in a container labeled "disc" are fragments of pink-gray to white cartilaginous tissue totaling 2 gm. The specimen is totally submitted.

MICROSCOPIC DIAGNOSIS: Intervertebral disc fragments, L4-5, excision: Fibrocartilage with cystic degeneration and fragmentation

12-7C:

SERVICE CODE(S): _____

ICD-9-CM DX CODE(S): _____

ICD-10-CM DX CODE(S): _____

12-7D RADIOLOGY REPORT, LUMBAR SPINE MRI

LOCATION: Inpatient, Hospital

PATIENT: Sarah Malone

ATTENDING PHYSICIAN: Timothy Pleasant, MD

SURGEON: Timothy Pleasant, MD

RADIOLOGIST: Morton Monson, MD

EXAMINATION OF: Lumbar spine MRI

CLINICAL SYMPTOMS: Herniated lumbar disc

LUMBAR SPINE MRI WITH CONTRAST: TECHNIQUE: Post-contrast axial images were acquired from L1-S1. No prior studies are provided for comparison.

FINDINGS: The conus is normal.

At L1-2, there is an enhancing peripherally left anterolateral epidural soft-tissue process. There is no enhancement abnormality within the disc space.

At L2-3, normal disc and disc space noted.

At L3-4, there is enhancing granulation tissue. There is a mild bulge of the disc. Mild spurring of the disc space.

At L4-5, there is a right laminotomy and foraminotomy with a small fluid collection in the surgical bed.

At L5-S1, there is mild degenerative facet disease of the disc. Disc bed looks normal.

IMPRESSION: Disc L4-5 shows the laminotomy and foraminotomy with just a small fluid collection in the disc bed. All other discs look fairly normal with just some mild degenerative changes.

12-7D:

SERVICE CODE(S): _____

ICD-9-CM DX CODE(S): _____

ICD-10-CM DX CODE(S): _____

CASE 12-8

This is a case to challenge your coding abilities. Reference the "Procedure Performed" section of the report to identify the number of procedures to be coded, noting that there are two segments to report for the fixation and fusion. Then read the report and ensure that the procedures are those identified in the "Procedure Performed" section. There will be a code for the cervical fracture repair, spinal fixation, arthrodesis of the posterior cervical vertebra, application of cranial halo, autograft for the spinal surgery, bone graft harvesting, and evoked potential testing. Assume this is the initial care of this fracture.

12-8A OPERATIVE REPORT, HALO VEST PLACEMENT AND REPAIR

LOCATION: Inpatient, Hospital

PATIENT: Terry Rake

ATTENDING PHYSICIAN: Timothy Pleasant, MD

SURGEON: Timothy Pleasant, MD

PREOPERATIVE DIAGNOSIS: Unstable C4 fracture with deformity of the spine

POSTOPERATIVE DIAGNOSIS: Unstable C4 fracture with deformity of the spine

PROCEDURE PERFORMED:
1. Halo vest placement.
2. Posterior segmental fixation C3 to C5 with Halifax clamps.
3. Open repair of the cervical fracture (first-listed procedure).
4. Fusion of the posterior cervical spine from C3 to C5 utilizing one autograft and an iliac crest graft.
5. Evoked potential monitoring.

ANESTHESIA: General endotracheal

PROCEDURE: The patient is taken to the OR and placed under general anesthesia. After the patient was intubated, the patient was placed in a four-pin halo vest. This was accomplished by maintaining in-line cervical traction using standard technique and chest rolls. The posterior cervical region and the area surrounding the iliac crest were then shaved, prepped for harvest, and draped in sterile fashion. The iliac crest was harvested first through a standard incision. Then a split-thickness graft was harvested making sure a large amount of cancellous bone was included in the harvest. The harvest sites were then closed in layers and hemostasis was ensured. The posterior cervical region was then incised and sharp dissection was carried down through the subcutaneous tissue. The fascia was then dissected from C3 through C5. This was done very cautiously and carefully. Then the superior aspect of the hemilamina of C5 was carefully exposed with curettes. Halifax clamps were then attached from C3 through C5. The area of the fracture of disc C4 was seen. The Halifax clamp construct was assembled and was noted to be secure. The lamina was then decorticated with a cutting burr and the cancellous and cortical bones were used to finish the posterior fusion. Halifax clamps ensured the correct alignment of the slight deformity. Throughout the procedure evoked potential monitoring was performed. Hemostasis was achieved and patient only had minimal blood loss. The wound was then closed in layers and the skin was stapled with surgical staples.

12-8A:

SERVICE CODE(S): _____

ICD-9-CM DX CODE(S): _____

ICD-10-CM DX CODE(S): _____

CASE 12-9

12-9A ELECTROENCEPHALOGRAM REPORT

LOCATION: Outpatient, Hospital

PATIENT: Ken Robb

REQUESTING PHYSICIAN: Ronald Green, MD

PHYSICIAN: Timothy Pleasant, MD

Mr. Robb is a 74-year-old, right-handed male who had an EEG performed with tin electrodes and collodion paste. No sedation was given. The time of last meal was noon. This was not sleep-deprived. The EEG was performed in awake, drowsy and pre-sleep states. Photic stimulation was performed. Hyperventilation was now performed.

MEDICATIONS:
1. Flunisolide
2. Budesonide
3. Ipratropium
4. Aspirin
5. Digoxin
6. Furosemide
7. Metoprolol
8. Pantoprazole
9. Prednisone
10. Ramipril
11. Temazepam
12. Terazosin
13. Heparin

INDICATION: Unconsciousness episode question subclinical seizure or epileptiform activity.

DESCRIPTION: Background rhythm of the EEG is approximately 8-9 cycle activities although at times it is intermittently intermixed with slower rhythms. The wave-forms do attenuate with eye opening. There is a significant amount of movement and muscle artifact during the recording. Photic stimulation of 1-25 Hertz did not activate the record. There are 2-3 episodes of 3 cycles per second slowing that last maybe 1 to 1.5 seconds, most were seen in the frontal leads. The patient does transition somewhat to drowsiness and may be part of drowsiness.

IMPRESSION: This is a mildly abnormal EEG secondary to intermittent slower rhythms. This can be seen in individuals who have global encephalopathy such as seen with infection, hypoxia or medication effect. Additionally, the patient is transitioning to drowsiness and may be a component of that transition state. There is no specific focal or epileptiform activity noted otherwise.

12-9A:

SERVICE CODE(S): _____

ICD-9-CM DX CODE(S): _____

ICD-10-CM DX CODE(S): _____

CASE 12-10

This is a nerve conduction study in which each study (motor nerve and sensory nerve) is reported separately.

12-10A ELECTRODIAGNOSTIC EVALUATION SUMMARY REPORT

LOCATION: Outpatient, Hospital

PATIENT: Eve Lu

REQUESTING PHYSICIAN: Ronald Green, MD

PHYSICIAN: Timothy Pleasant, MD

CLINICAL SYMPTOM: Arm numbness and pain

Motor Nerve Study

Left Median Nerve

Rec Site: APB STIM SITE	Lat (ms)	Norm Lat	Amp (mV)	Dist (mm)	C.V. (m/s)	Norm C.V.
Wrist	4.2	4.2	3.9	64		
Elbow	7.9		.156	224	57.0	49

Left Ulnar Nerve

Rec Site: ADM	Lat (ms)	Norm Lat	Amp (mV)	Dist (mm)	C.V. (m/s)	Norm C.V.
Wrist	2.9	3.8	11.0	58		
Below Elbow	6.2		5.1	234	64.0	52
Above Elbow	8.7		.671	126	68.5	

Sensory Nerve Study

Left Median Nerve

Rec Site: Index STIM SITE	Lat (ms)	Norm Lat	Amp (uV)	Dist (mm)	C.V. (m/s)	Norm C.V.
Wrist	3.4	3.8	25.8	136	41.8	50

Left Ulnar Nerve

Rec Site: 5th digit STIM SITE	Lat (ms)	Norm Lat	Amp (uV)	Dist (mm)	C.V. (m/s)	Norm C.V.
Wrist	3.1	3.5	4.6	112	38.2	52

Left Median-MP Nerve

Rec Site: Wrist STIM SITE	Lat (ms)	Norm Lat	Amp (uV)	Dist (mm)	C.V. (m/s)	Norm C.V.
Midpalm	1.8	2.2	37.0	58	37.6	

SUMMARY/INTERPRETATION:

FINDINGS:

1. Normal left median nerve sensory conduction studies. Including both antidromic and orthodromic techniques.
2. Normal left ulnar nerve sensory and motor conduction study.

IMPRESSION: Normal left upper extremity nerve conduction study.

12-10A:

SERVICE CODE(S): _____

ICD-9-CM DX CODE(S): _____

ICD-10-CM DX CODE(S): _____

CHAPTER 13

Eye and Auditory Systems

CASE 13-1

Make sure to check
evolve
learning system
**for the latest
content updates**

Dr. Wimer uses a B-scan ultrasound to assess the status of Melinda's retina while performing an eye examination. The ultrasound is reported in addition to the examination. There is an E code that will be assigned to this case as this is the initial episode of care. Report the medications given to the patient intramuscularly and intravenously with HCPCS codes. Report the medication administration as well. Do not report the drops, ointment, or patch.

13-1A CLINIC PROGRESS NOTE, EYE EXAMINATION

LOCATION: Outpatient, Clinic

PATIENT: Melinda Child

PHYSICIAN: Rita Wimer, MD

INDICATIONS: Contusion, eyelid

Today, I saw Melinda, a 23-year-old, a new patient to me, who was standing by her boyfriend when he was cutting a piece of wood with a table saw. The piece of wood went flying and unfortunately hit Melinda in the left eye. She has severe pain and has no vision right now in that eye. She was seen in the ER after it happened. She was sent right over to see me. Her right eye has 20/20 vision. In the left eye the patient had bare light perception. The pressure was 37, and there was 33% hyperemia and a vitreous hemorrhage. B-scan showed no detachment or separation of the optic nerve. I administered 60 mg of Toradol IM and started her on Cosopt 2 drops twice a day and Iopidine 1% two drops twice a day and gave her 500 of Diamox IV push. Just after a few minutes her pressure dropped in her eye to 26, and the vision improved somewhat. I placed atropine ointment for a soothing and numbing feeling and placed a TobraDex patch over her eye. I am placing her on strict bed rest and no work. We will see her again in 24 hours.

13-1A:

SERVICE CODE(S): _____

ICD-9-CM DX CODE(S): _____

ICD-10-CM DX CODE(S): _____

CASE 13-2

Phacoemulsification is used in the following cataract surgery.

13-2A OPERATIVE REPORT, SENILE CATARACTS

LOCATION: Outpatient, Hospital

PATIENT: Guy Parker

ATTENDING PHYSICIAN: Rita Wimer, MD

SURGEON: Rita Wimer, MD

PREOPERATIVE DIAGNOSIS: Senile nuclear cataract, right eye

POSTOPERATIVE DIAGNOSIS: Senile nuclear cataract, right eye

PROCEDURE PERFORMED: Cataract extraction by phacoemulsification, right eye (Model AR40E, +21.5 diopters, serial #90402)

ANESTHESIA: Topical

ESTIMATED BLOOD LOSS: Minimal

COMPLICATIONS: None

PROCEDURE: In the OR, a drop of lidocaine 4%-MPF was applied to the eye. The patient was prepped and draped in the usual sterile fashion for an intraocular procedure of the right eye. A lid speculum was placed. A Weck-cel soaked with lidocaine 4%-MPF was placed at the limbus both in the area of the planned phaco incision and planned side-port incision. A keratome was used to enter the chamber at the arcade. A small amount of preservative-free lidocaine 1% was injected into the anterior chamber. The aqueous was exchanged with viscoelastic material and a side-port incision was made with a 15 degree angle blade. A continuous tear capsulotomy was made with a 15 degree angle blade. A continuous tear capsulotomy was made with a bent needle and the Utrata forceps. The nucleus was hydrodissected. Phacoemulsification was used to remove the nucleus using an ultrasound time of 2 minutes, 22 seconds, and effective phaco time 5.93 seconds. Irrigation and aspiration was used to remove the remaining cortical material. The capsule was polished and vacuumed as indicated. A small additional amount of non-preserved lidocaine 1% was again injected into the anterior chamber. The chamber was deepened with viscoelastic and the posterior chamber intraocular lens was injected into the capsule bag and dialed into position. The remaining viscoelastic material was removed with irrigation and aspiration. The globe was pressurized and the cornea was hydrated to ensure a good seal. The wound was tested and found to be watertight. Zymar and Pred Forte 1% drops were placed on the surface of the eye. The patient left the operating room in stable condition without complications having tolerated the procedure well.

13-2A:

SERVICE CODE(S): _____

ICD-9-CM DX CODE(S): _____

ICD-10-CM DX CODE(S): _____

CASE 13-3

13-3A OPERATIVE REPORT, BLEPHAROPLASTY

LOCATION: Outpatient, Hospital

PATIENT: Peter Win

ATTENDING PHYSICIAN: Rita Wimer, MD

SURGEON: Rita Wimer, MD

PREOPERATIVE DIAGNOSIS:
1. Entropion, right lower lid.
2. Chronic eye pain.
3. Chronic conjunctivitis.
4. Chronic exposure keratitis.
5. #2, #3, and #4 secondary to #1

POSTOPERATIVE DIAGNOSIS:
1. Entropion, right lower lid.
2. Chronic eye pain.
3. Chronic conjunctivitis.
4. Chronic exposure keratitis.
5. #2, #3, and #4 secondary to #1

PROCEDURE PERFORMED: Tarsal wedge resection right lower lid

ANESTHESIA: MAC

INDICATIONS: This 75-year-old white male has had multiple suffering episodes of red, sore, painful, infected and irritated eye secondary to entropion of his right lower lid. He was counseled for repair to relieve his symptoms.

PROCEDURE: After the patient was prepped and draped in the usual sterile fashion for ophthalmic surgery, the area we marked was infiltrated with Xylocaine 2% with 0.75% Marcaine and bicarbonate. A 6-mm equilateral triangle base-down was made on the tarsal surface of the right lower lid, the middle one-third, and a 12-mm equilateral triangle base-up was made in the right lateral canthus inferior to the lesion. The tarsal plate triangle was taken first from the inside with a chalazion clamp exposed to control bleeding. A 6-mm triangle was removed, saving the superior point only. This was closed with interrupted 5-0 chromic gut sutures tied anteriorly and one tied posteriorly. The skin surface, anterior side, was closed with two 5-0 chromic sutures. The 12-mm equilateral triangle at the right lower lateral canthus was then cut with a #15 Bard Parker blade down to the fascia. The skin and muscle were cut away. Cautery was used, and this was closed with interrupted 4-0 silk. Maxitrol ointment, Telfa pad and patch were applied. The patient was sent to the recovery room. There were no complications.

13-3A:

SERVICE CODE(S): _____

ICD-9-CM DX CODE(S): _____

ICD-10-CM DX CODE(S): _____

CASE 13-4

This patient is in for removal of his pressure equalization tubes. This is done in an outpatient setting.

13-4A OPERATIVE REPORT, TUBE REMOVAL

LOCATION: Outpatient, Hospital

PATIENT: Chad Allen

ATTENDING PHYSICIAN: Jeff King, MD

PREOPERATIVE DIAGNOSIS: Obstructed PE tubes

POSTOPERATIVE DIAGNOSIS: Same

PROCEDURE PERFORMED: Removal of PE tubes

ANESTHESIA: General

OPERATIVE NOTE: The patient is a 9-year-old male who has had PE tubes in for a prolonged period. Recently, he has had problems with recurrent infections and fluid. He has granulation on both tubes. A decision was made to remove these in the operating room.

PROCEDURE: He was admitted through the same-day surgery program and taken to the operating room, where general anesthetic was administered via inhalation. A 4-mm speculum was inserted in the right ear. Wax was removed from the canal. The tube was visualized. Using cup forceps, this tube was removed. There was granulation tissue around the opening. Two drops of Cortisporin were applied. The speculum was removed and inserted in the left ear. Again, wax was removed from the canal. The PE tube was removed with cup forceps. Again, granulation tissue seemed to close the perforation nicely. Two drops of Cortisporin were applied. The speculum was removed. The patient was allowed to recover from the general anesthetic and taken to the postanesthesia care unit in stable condition. There were no complications noted during the procedure.

13-4A:

SERVICE CODE(S): _____

ICD-9-CM DX CODE(S): _____

ICD-10-CM DX CODE(S): _____

CASE 13-5

In the following case, a myringotomy and a tonsillectomy/adenoidectomy (the most resource-intense) are performed on a 14-year-old.

13-5A OPERATIVE REPORT, TONSILLECTOMY, ADENOIDECTOMY, AND MYRINGOTOMY

LOCATION: Outpatient, Hospital

PATIENT: Terri Laffe

ATTENDING PHYSICIAN: Jeff King, MD

SURGEON: Jeff King, MD

PREOPERATIVE DIAGNOSIS:
1. Chronic adenotonsillitis.
2. Adenotonsillar hypertrophy.
3. Chronic serous otitis media.

POSTOPERATIVE DIAGNOSIS:
1. Chronic adenotonsillitis.
2. Adenotonsillar hypertrophy.
3. Chronic serous otitis media.

PROCEDURE PERFORMED:
1. Bilateral myringotomies.
2. Tonsillectomy.
3. Adenoidectomy.

PROCEDURE: The patient was admitted through the same-day surgery program and taken to the OR. A general endotracheal anesthesia was administered. A 4-mm speculum was then inserted in the right ear, and wax was removed from the canal. A small incision was made and a small amount of fluid was removed. The same was then performed on the left ear. The patient was then turned 90 degrees. A McIvor mouth gag was inserted. The patient's tonsils were touching in the midline. The left tonsil was removed by snare technique, and then bismuth packs were placed. The right tonsil was removed by snare technique, and then bismuth packs were placed. Adenoids were removed with the use of adenotome curettement and biopsy forceps. Nasopharynx was both visually examined and palpated to be sure the adenoids have been removed, and then bismuth packs were placed. Packs were serially removed, and electrocautery was used to attain hemostasis in all three areas. The nasal and oral cavities were washed well with saline. All three areas were reexamined, and when good hemostasis was present, they were painted with viscous Xylocaine. The patient was then awakened from his anesthetic and returned to the recovery room in stable condition.

13-5A:

SERVICE CODE(S): _____

ICD-9-CM DX CODE(S): _____

ICD-10-CM DX CODE(S): _____

CASE 13-6

Report the ENT surgeon's procedures.

13-6A OPERATIVE REPORT, MYRINGOTOMIES WITH TYMPANOSTOMY TUBE PLACEMENT

LOCATION: Outpatient, Hospital

PATIENT: Lynn Welsh

ATTENDING PHYSICIAN: Jeff King, MD

SURGEON: Jeff King, MD

PREOPERATIVE DIAGNOSIS: Chronic otitis media with effusion, bilateral eustachian tube dysfunction

POSTOPERATIVE DIAGNOSIS: Chronic otitis media with effusion, bilateral eustachian tube dysfunction

PROCEDURE PERFORMED: Bilateral myringotomies and tympanostomy tube placement

ANESTHESIA: General anesthetic by inhalational mask technique

PROCEDURE: Following informed consent from the parents, the child was taken to the operating room and placed supine on the operating table. The appropriate monitoring devices were placed on the patient. General anesthesia was induced. It was maintained by inhalational mask technique. The right ear was initially evaluated. Wax was removed. A radial incision was made at the 6 o'clock position on the right tympanic membrane. A large amount of thick mucoid effusion was suctioned. A tube was placed. Topical antibiotic drops were then applied. The patient then had the left ear evaluated. Wax was removed. A radial incision was made at the 6 o'clock position on the left tympanic membrane. A large amount of mucoid effusion was suctioned from behind the left tympanic membrane. A tube was then placed. Topical antibiotic drops were then applied. The patient was then allowed to recover from general anesthesia. She was transferred to the recovery room in good condition. She tolerated the procedure well.

13-6A:

SERVICE CODE(S): _____

ICD-9-CM DX CODE(S): _____

ICD-10-CM DX CODE(S): _____

CHAPTER 14

Anesthesia

CASE 14-1

Make sure to check
evolve learning system
for the latest
content updates

Anesthesia by: MDA and CRNA. Anesthesiologist was medically directing 4 concurrent cases.

14-1A OPERATIVE REPORT, ANESTHESIA

LOCATION: Inpatient, Hospital

PATIENT: Sebastian Webb

SURGEON: Larry Friendly, MD

PREOPERATIVE DIAGNOSIS: Perirectal fistula

POSTOPERATIVE DIAGNOSIS: Perirectal fistula

PROCEDURE PERFORMED: Perirectal fistulectomy

ANESTHESIA: General anesthesia

INDICATIONS FOR SURGERY: This is a normal healthy 65-year-old male who has had a draining perirectal fistula. He is now being admitted for incision of this fistula.

DESCRIPTION OF PROCEDURE: The patient is placed in a jackknife position. He was prepped and draped in a sterile fashion. General anesthesia was given. The fistula tract was in the 3 o'clock position. This was completely excised. The tract continued over the 5 o'clock position. This tract was made into one incision and all of the inflamed tissue was also excised. The rectum was then dilated up and examined. There was one tract that was seen directly draining into the rectum. The inflamed tissue that was on the outer skin area was also completely excised. The area was then thoroughly irrigated. Hemostasis was achieved with use of cautery. The wound was then left open and dressings were applied. The patient tolerated the procedure and was then turned over to recovery in stable condition.

14-1A:

PHYSICIAN CODE: _____

CRNA CODE: _____

CASE 14-2

Unless stated otherwise, assume "normal, healthy patient." Anesthesia by: MDA and CRNA. Anesthesiologist was medically directing 4 concurrent cases.

14-2A OPERATIVE REPORT, ANESTHESIA

INDICATIONS FOR SURGERY: This is a 28-year-old healthy male who has had some problems with sleep apnea and breathing through his nose. He is now admitted for repair of his deviated septum with bilateral inferior turbinate reduction and removal of his tonsils.

LOCATION: Inpatient, Hospital

PATIENT: Don Albet

SURGEON: Gregory Dawson, MD

PREOPERATIVE DIAGNOSIS:
1. Septal deviation
2. Bilateral inferior turbinate hypertrophy
3. Tonsillar hypertrophy

POSTOPERATIVE DIAGNOSIS:
1. Septal deviation
2. Bilateral inferior turbinate hypertrophy
3. Tonsillar hypertrophy

PROCEDURE PERFORMED:
1. Septoplasty
2. Bilateral inferior turbinate reduction
3. Tonsillectomy

ANESTHESIA: General anesthesia

SURGICAL FINDINGS: The patient had a fairly significant left septal deviation. Some of this was anterior. He also had posteriorly on the left-hand side contact between the posterior left nasal septum and the left lateral nasal wall from a bony spur. The inferior turbinates bilaterally were grossly hypertrophic. The tonsils were extremely hypertrophied. Many crypts were present.

DESCRIPTION OF PROCEDURE: After informed consent the patient was taken to the operating room and placed in the supine position. He was draped in the usual fashion. The nose was packed bilaterally with Afrin-soaked gauze. Right and left nasal septum were each injected with 3 cc of 1% Xylocaine with Epinephrine. Some of the nose hairs were trimmed. The Afrin soaked gauze was removed bilaterally. An incision was made at the anterior end of the right nasal septum. A mucoperichondral flap was identified. This was elevated on the right nasal septum. No perforations occurred during this. Taking care to leave a good 1 cm of anterior septal cartilage, an incision was made through the right side of the septal cartilage at its base. Through this incision, a left mucoperichondrial flap was then elevated. We also elevated a mucoperiosteal flap on the left-hand side with the freer elevator. A strip of cartilage was removed from the inferior end of the septal cartilage at its junction with the maxillary crest. A portion of the anterior inferior left-sided septal deviation was due to the deviation of the left maxillary crest. A 4-mm osteotome was used to remove this deviated portion. The bony vomer was deviated to the left-hand side with a spur in contact with the left lateral nasal wall and I did remove this with Wilde forceps. The strip of cartilage removed was approximately 2 cm in length and 1 cm in height. At least a cm of nasal dorsal strut and anterior strut was maintained. This was to provide good tip support, which was present at the end of the case. Following removal of the cartilage and the maxillary crest, the septum was significantly straighter. There was still a small amount of anterior left septal deviation, but significantly less. The anterior inferior edges of the turbinates bilaterally were then cauterized with needlepoint cautery. Following this, a butter knife was used to out-fracture the turbinates bilaterally. This gave a significant improvement in the nasal airway. There was a small mucosal tear posteriorly on the left-hand side, which would serve as a drainage site to prevent hematoma formation beneath the mucosal flap. The anterior end of the right nasal septum was then closed using interrupted 4-0 chromic catgut. I then placed Doyle nasal splints bilaterally. The patient was then repositioned for tonsillectomy. The McIvor out gag was placed and we were able to visualize the tonsils. They were extremely large with many crypts on them. Attention was first focused on the left tonsil. The retractor was placed in the superior pole, and the tonsil was retracted toward the midline. Then, using the harmonic scalpel at power level III, the tonsil was removed. Hemostasis was achieved from spot suction cautery. Similar procedure was then performed on the left tonsil. The tonsillar fossa was then irrigated and hemostasis was achieved. Infiltration of 1% Xylocaine with 1:100,000 units of epinephrine were placed in the retromolar and soft palate areas bilaterally. Tension on the mouth gag was then released. Reinspection showed no active bleeding. The patient was then allowed to recover from general anesthesia. He tolerated the procedure well. He was transferred to the recovery room in good condition. He will go home on Keflex 500 mg po q.i.d. He has a prescription for Percocet for pain. He is going to be using nasal saline rinses until I see him again in 2 weeks. At that time we will be removing the stents. He will get in touch with my office if he is having any other problems.

14-2A:

PHYSICIAN CODE: _____

CRNA CODE: _____

CASE 14-3

The procedure is circumcision. Anesthesia by: CRNA.

14-3A OPERATIVE REPORT, ANESTHESIA

LOCATION: Outpatient, Hospital

PATIENT: Stephen Void

SURGEON: Ira Avilla, MD

PREOPERATIVE DIAGNOSIS: Phimosis

POSTOPERATIVE DIAGNOSIS: Phimosis

PROCEDURE PERFORMED: Circumcision

ANESTHESIA: General mask anesthesia

PROCEDURE: This 18-month-old normal healthy fellow was placed on a standard circumcision board. General mask anesthesia was applied. He was prepped in the standard procedure with Betadine. The foreskin was retracted. We then used a Gomco clamp and removed the foreskin. Vaseline gauze was applied. There were no complications. He tolerated the procedure well. The patient was transferred to the recovery room in good condition.

14-3A:

CRNA CODE: _____

Answers to Every Other Case

Chapter 1
Evaluation and Management Services

CASE 1-1

1-1A EMERGENCY DEPARTMENT SERVICES

Professional Services: 99283 (Evaluation and Management, Emergency Department)
ICD-9-CM DX: 837.1 (Dislocation, ankle, open), **910.0** (Injury, superficial, chin, abrasion without mention of infection), **916.0** (Injury, superficial, leg, abrasion without mention of infection), **E906.8** (Stepped on by animal [not being ridden])
ICD-10-CM DX: S93.04XA (Dislocation, ankle), **S00.81xA** (Abrasion, chin), **S70.312A** (Abrasion, thigh), **W55.89A** (Stepped on, by, animal [not being ridden] NEC)

Facility Services: 837.1 (Dislocation, ankle, open), **910.0** (Injury, superficial, chin, abrasion without mention of infection), **916.0** (Injury, superficial, leg, abrasion without mention of infection), **E906.8** (Stepped on by animal)

CASE 1-3

1-3A PROGRESS NOTE

Professional Services: 99233 (Evaluation and Management, Hospital)
ICD-9-CM DX: 786.52 (Pain[s], pleura/pleural/pleuritic), **742.2** (Pain[s], low back), **162.9** (Neoplasm, lung, Malignant, Primary), **496** (Disease/diseased, pulmonary, diffuse obstructive, chronic), **305.1** (Tobacco abuse)
ICD-10-CM DX: R07.89 (Pain[s], pleura, pleural, pleuritic), **M54.5** (Pain[s], low back), **C34.90** (Neoplasm, lung, Malignant Primary), **J44.9** (Disease, airway, obstructive, lung [chronic]), **F17.210** (Dependence, drug, nicotine, cigarettes)

Facility Services: This is an inpatient stay. The entire record would need to be reviewed before coding. No inpatient codes are assigned in the workbook.

CASE 1-5

1-5A CONSULTATION

Professional Services: 99252 (Evaluation and Management, Consultation), **99356** (Evaluation and Management, Prolonged Services), **99357** (Evaluation and Management, Prolonged Services)
ICD-9-CM DX: 250.10 (Diabetes/diabetic, ketosis/ketoacidosis, unspecified type), **578.9** (Bleeding, gastrointestinal), **401.9** (Hypertension, Unspecified)
ICD-10-CM DX: E68.10 (Diabetes, due to underlying condition, with, ketoacidosis), **K92.2** (Bleeding, gastrointestinal), **I10** (Hypertension)

Facility Services: This is an inpatient stay. The entire record would need to be reviewed before coding. No inpatient codes are assigned in the workbook.

CASE 1-7

1-7A ICU NOTE

Professional Services: 99291 (Evaluation and Management, Critical Care)
ICD-9-CM DX: 518.81 (Failure/failed, respiration/respiratory, acute), **514** (Edema/edematous, lung), **410.71** (Infarct/infarction, myocardium/myocardial, initial episode), **427.31** (Fibrillation, atrial)
ICD-10-CM DX: J96.0 (Failure/failed, respiratory, acute), **J81.0** (Edema, lung), **I21.4** (Infarction, myocardium, non Q wave), **I48.0** (Fibrillation, atrial)

Facility Services: This is an inpatient stay. The entire record would need to be reviewed before coding. No inpatient codes are assigned in this workbook.

CASE 1-9

1-9A OFFICE VISIT

Professional Services: 99213 (Evaluation and Management, Office and Other Outpatient)
ICD-9-CM DX: 250.01 (Diabetes/diabetic [mellitus], type 1, controlled), **455.6** (Hemorrhoids)
ICD-10-CM DX: E10.9 (Diabetes, type 1), **I84.20** (Hemorrhoids)

Facility Services: No facility service provided.

CASE 1-11

1-11A HOSPITAL SERVICES

Professional Services: 99468 (Evaluation and Management, Neonatal Critical Care)
ICD-9-CM DX: 770.6 (Tachypnea, newborn), **765.16** (Prematurity, 1500-1749 grams), **765.26** (Newborn, gestation, 31-32 weeks completed), **V30.00** (Newborn, single, hospital, without mention of cesarean)
ICD-10-CM DX: P22.1 (Tachypnea, newborn), **P07.31** (Preterm, infant, newborn), **P05.16** (Small for dates [infant], with weight of, 1500-1749 grams), **Z38.00** (Newborn [infant] [liveborn], born in hospital)

Facility Services: This is an inpatient stay. The entire record would need to be reviewed before coding. No inpatient codes are assigned in this workbook.

1-11B NICU PROGRESS NOTE

Professional Services: 99469 (Evaluation and Management, Neonatal Critical Care)
ICD-9-CM DX: 765.16 (Prematurity, 1500-1749 grams), **765.26** (Newborn, gestation, 31-32 weeks completed), **770.6** (Tachypnea, newborn), **785.2** (Murmur), **275.41** (Hypocalcemia), **781.3** (Hypotonia/hypotonicity/hypotony), **V30.00** (Newborn, single, hospital, without mention of cesarean)
ICD-10-CM DX: P05.16 (Small for dates [infant], with weight of, 1500-1749 grams), **P07.31** (Preterm, infant, newborn), **P22.1** (Tachypnea, newborn), **R01.1** (Murmur), **P71.1** (Hypocalcaemia, neonatal), **P94.2** (Hypotonia, congenital), **Z38.00** (Newborn [infant] [liveborn], born in hospital)

Facility Services: This is an inpatient stay. The entire record would need to be reviewed before coding. No inpatient codes are assigned in this workbook.

1-11C NICU PROGRESS NOTE

Professional Services: 99478 (Evaluation and Management, Low Birthweight Infant)
ICD-9-CM DX: 765.16 (Prematurity, 1500-1749 grams), **765.26** (Newborn, gestation, 31-32 weeks completed), **781.3** (Hypotonia/hypotonicity/hypotony), **774.2** (Hyperbilirubinemia, neonatal, of prematurity), **769** (Hyaline membrane disease), **V30.00** (Newborn, single, hospital, without mention of cesarean)
ICD-10-CM DX: P05.16 (Small for dates [infant], with weight of, 1500-1749 grams), **P07.31** (Preterm, infant, newborn), **P59.9** (Jaundice, newborn), **P94.2** (Hypotonia, congenital), **P22.0** (Disease, hyaline), **Z38.00** (Newborn [infant] [liveborn], born in hospital)

Facility Services: This is an inpatient stay. The entire record would need to be reviewed before coding. No inpatient codes are assigned in this workbook.

CASE 1-13

1-13A OFFICE VISIT

Professional Services: 99215 (Evaluation and Management, Office or Other Outpatient)
ICD-9-CM DX: 401.9 (Hypertension/hypertensive, unspecified), **733.01** (Osteoporosis, postmenopausal), **272.4** (Hyperlipidemia), **300.4** (Anxiety, depression), **794.39** (Findings, abnormal, without diagnosis, stress test), **414.00** (Arteriosclerosis/arteriosclerotic coronary)
ICD-10-CM DX: I10 (Hypertension), **M81.0** (Osteoporosis, postmenopausal), **E78.5** (Hyperlipidemia), **F41.8** (Anxiety, depression), **R94.39** (Findings, abnormal, without diagnosis, stress test), **I25.10** (Arteriosclerosis/arteriosclerotic coronary [artery])

Facility Services: No facility services were provided.

Chapter 2

Medicine

CASE 2-1

2-1A CHART NOTE

Professional Services: 90746 (Vaccines, Hepatitis B), **90471** (Immunization Administration, One Vaccine/Toxoid)
ICD-9-CM DX: V05.3 (Vaccination, prophylactic, hepatitis)
ICD-10-CM DX: Z23 (Immunization, encounter for)

Facility Services: No facility services provided.

CASE 2-3

2-3A INITIAL HOSPITAL CARE

Professional Services: 99221 (Evaluation and Management, Hospital)
ICD-9-CM DX: 584.9 (Failure/failed, renal, acute), **585.9** (Failure/failed, renal, chronic), **285.21** (Anemia, in, chronic kidney disease)
ICD-10-CM DX: N17.9 (Failure/failed, renal, acute), **N18.9** (Failure/failed, renal, chronic), **D63.1** (Anemia, in, chronic renal failure)

Facility Services: This is an inpatient stay. The entire record would need to be reviewed before coding. No inpatient codes are assigned in the workbook.

2-3B Dialysis

Professional Services: 90945 (Dialysis, Peritoneal)
ICD-9-CM DX: 584.9 (Failure/failed, renal, acute), **585.9** (Failure/failed, renal, chronic), **514** (Edema/edematous, lung)
ICD-10-CM DX: N17.9 (Failure/failed, renal, acute), **N18.9** (Failure/failed, renal, chronic), **J81.1** (Edema, lung)

Facility Services: This is an inpatient stay. The entire record would need to be reviewed before coding. No inpatient codes are assigned in this workbook.

2-3C DIALYSIS PROGRESS NOTE

Professional Services: 90945 (Dialysis, Peritoneal)
ICD-9-CM DX: 584.9 (Failure/failed, renal, acute), **585.9** (Failure/failed, renal, chronic), **514** (Edema/edematous, lung), **799.02** (Hypoxia), **796.2** (Elevation, blood pressure, reading, no diagnosis of hypertension)
ICD-10-CM DX: N17.9 (Failure/failed, renal, acute), **N18.9** (Failure/failed, renal, chronic), **J81.1** (Edema, lung), **R09.01** (Hypoxia), **R03.0** (Elevation, blood pressure)

Facility Services: This is an inpatient stay. The entire record would need to be reviewed before coding. No inpatient codes are assigned in this workbook.

2-3D DIALYSIS PROGRESS NOTE

Professional Services: 90945 (Dialysis, Peritoneal)
ICD-9-CM DX: 584.9 (Failure/failed, renal, acute), **585.9** (Failure/failed, renal, chronic), **276.8** (Findings, abnormal without diagnosis, potassium, deficiency)
ICD-10-CM DX: N17.9 (Failure/failed, renal, acute), **N18.9** (Failure/failed, renal, chronic), **E87.6** (Findings, abnormal, potassium deficiency)

Facility Services: This is an inpatient stay. The entire record would need to be reviewed before coding. No inpatient codes are assigned in this workbook.

2-3E DIALYSIS PROGRESS NOTE

Professional Services: 99231 (Evaluation and Management, Hospital)
ICD-9-CM DX: 584.9 (Failure/failed, renal, acute), **585.9** (Failure/failed, renal, chronic), **996.56** (Complications, mechanical, catheter, dialysis, peritoneal)
ICD-10-CM DX: N17.9 (Failure/failed, renal, acute), **N18.9** (Failure/failed, renal, chronic), **T85.621** (Complication[s], catheter, intraperitoneal dialysis, mechanical, malposition)

Facility Services: This is an inpatient stay. The entire record would need to be reviewed before coding. No inpatient codes are assigned in this workbook.

2-3F DIALYSIS PROGRESS NOTE

Professional Services: 90945 (Dialysis, Peritoneal)
ICD-9-CM DX: 584.9 (Failure/failed, renal, acute), **585.9** (Failure/failed, renal, chronic), **275.3** (Hyperphosphatemia)
ICD-10-CM DX: N17.9 (Failure/failed, renal, acute), **N18.9** (Failure/failed, renal, chronic), **E83.39** (Hyperphosphatemia)

Facility Services: This is an inpatient stay. The entire record would need to be reviewed before coding. No inpatient codes are assigned in this workbook.

2-3G DIALYSIS PROGRESS NOTE

Professional Services: 90945 (Dialysis, Peritoneal)
ICD-9-CM DX: 584.9 (Failure/failed, renal, acute), **585.9** (Failure/failed, renal, chronic)
ICD-10-CM DX: N17.9 (Failure/failed, renal, acute), **N18.9** (Failure/failed, renal, chronic)

Facility Services: This is an inpatient stay. The entire record would need to be reviewed before coding. No inpatient codes are assigned in this workbook.

2-3H Discharge Summary

Professional Services: 99238 (Evaluation and Management, Hospital, Discharge)
ICD-9-CM DX: 585.9 (Failure/failed, renal, chronic), **285.21** (Anemia, in, chronic kidney disease), **514** (Edema/edematous, lung), **276.6** (Overload, fluid), **518.81** (Failure/failed, respiration/respiratory, acute), **276.2** (Acidosis, metabolic)
ICD-10-CM DX: N18.9 (Failure/failed, renal, chronic), **D63.1** (Anemia, in, chronic renal failure), **J81.1** (Edema, lung), **E87.7** (Overload, fluid), **J96.0** (Failure, respiration/respiratory, acute), **E87.2** (Acidosis, metabolic)

Facility Services: This is an inpatient stay. The entire record would need to be reviewed before coding. No inpatient codes are assigned in this workbook.

CASE 2-5

2-5A ULTRASOUND, LOWER EXTREMITIES

Professional Services: 93970-26 (Vascular Studies, Venous Studies, Extremity)
ICD-9-CM DX: 453.41 (Thrombosis/thrombotic, lower extremity, deep vessel, acute, femoral)
ICD-10-CM DX: I82.411 (Thrombosis, femoral)

Facility Services: 93970 (Vascular Studies, Venous Studies, Extremity); **453.41** (Thrombosis, lower extremity, deep vessel, acute, femoral)

CASE 2-7

2-7A PHYSICAL THERAPY EVALUATION

Professional Services: 97001 (Physical Medicine/Therapy/Occupational Therapy, Evaluation)

ICD-9-CM DX: V57.1 (Admission, for, physical therapy NEC), **457.1** (Lymphedema)
ICD-10-CM DX: Z51.89 (Admission [for], aftercare), **I97.2** (Lymphedema, surgical, postmastectomy [syndrome])

Facility Services: No facility services provided.

2-7B PHYSICAL THERAPY EVALUATION

Professional Services: 97001 (Physical Medicine/Therapy/Occupational Therapy, Evaluation), **97110×1** (Physical Medicine/Therapy/Occupational Therapy, Procedures, Therapeutic Exercises, [one or more areas, each 15 minutes])
ICD-9-CM DX: V57.1 (Admission, for, physical therapy NEC), **719.41** (Pain[s], joint, shoulder), **V58.78** (Aftercare, following surgery, of, musculoskeletal system)
ICD-10-CM DX: M25.511 (Pain[s], joint, shoulder, right), **Z47.89** (Aftercare, following surgery, orthopedic NEC)

Facility Services: No facility services provided.

2-7C PHYSICAL THERAPY EVALUATION

Professional Services: 97002 (Physical Medicine/Therapy/Occupational Therapy, Evaluation); **97110×1** (Physical Medicine/Therapy/Occupational Therapy, Procedures, Therapeutic procedure, [one or more areas, each 15 minutes])
ICD-9-CM DX: V57.1 (Admission/Encounter for physical therapy), **719.46** (Pain[s], joint, knee), **V58.78** (Aftercare, following surgery, of, musculoskeletal system)
ICD-10-CM DX: Z51.89 (Admission [for], aftercare), **M25.511** (Pain[s], joint, shoulder, right), **Z47.89** (Aftercare, following surgery, orthopedic NEC)

Facility Services: No facility services provided.

Chapter 3
Radiology

CASE 3-1

3-1A RADIOLOGY REPORT

Professional Services: 71010-26 (X-ray, Chest)
ICD-9-CM DX: 785.51 (Shock, cardiogenic)
ICD-10-CM DX: R57.0 (Shock, cardiogenic)

Facility Services: 71010 (X-ray, Chest); **785.51** (Shock, cardiogenic)

CASE 3-3

3-3A RADIOLOGY REPORT, KNEE

Professional Services: 73560-RT (X-ray, Knee)
ICD-9-CM DX: 719.46 (Pain[s], joint knee)
ICD-10-CM DX: M25.561 (Pain[s], joint, knee)

Facility Services: No facility services were provided.

CASE 3-5

3-5A CT SCAN, BRAIN

Professional Services: 70450-26 (CT Scan, Without Contrast, Brain)
ICD-9-CM DX: 780.97 (Change, mental status), **781.0** (Involuntary movement, abnormal)
ICD-10-CM DX: R41.82 (Change [in], mental status), **R25.9** (Involuntary movement, abnormal)

Facility Services: 70450 (CT Scan, Brain, Without Contrast); **780.97** (Change, mental status), **781.0** (Involuntary movements, abnormal)

CASE 3-7

3-7A CT SCAN, ABDOMEN AND PELVIS

Professional Services: 74150-26 (CT Scan, Without Contrast, Abdomen), **72192-26** (CT Scan, Without contrast, Pelvis)
ICD-9-CM DX: 567.22 (Abscess, peritoneum/peritoneal), **575.8** (Distention, gallbladder)
ICD-10-CM DX: K65.1 (Abscess, peritoneum), **K82.8** (Distention, gallbladder)

Facility Services: 74150 (CT Scan, Abdomen, Without contrast), **72192** (CT Scan, Pelvis, Without Contrast); **567.22** (Abscess, peritoneum), **575.8** (Distention, gallbladder)

CASE 3-9

3-9A CT SCAN, ABDOMEN AND PELVIS

Professional Services: 74150-26 (CT Scan, Without Contrast, Abdomen), **72192-26** (CT Scan, Without Contrast, Pelvis)
ICD-9-CM DX: 038.9 (Septicemia/septicemic), **995.91** (Sepsis), **511.9** (Effusion, pleural/pleurisy/pleuritic/pleuro-pericardial), **518.89** (Nodule[s], lung, solitary)
ICD-10-CM DX: R78.81 (Septicemia), **A41.9** (Sepsis), **J90** (Effusion, pleural), **J98.4** (Nodule[s], lung, solitary)

Facility Services: 74150 (CT Scan, Without Contrast, Abdomen), **72192** (CT Scan, Without Contrast, Pelvis); **995.91** (Sepsis), **511.9** (Effusion, pleural), **518.89** (Nodule[s], lung, solitary)

CASE 3-11

3-11A ULTRASOUND, ABDOMEN

Professional Services: 76705-26 (Ultrasound, Abdomen, Limited)
ICD-9-CM DX: 574.20 (Cholelithiasis, without mention of obstruction)

ICD-10-CM DX: K80.20 (Calculus, gallbladder)

Facility Services: 76705 (Ultrasound, Abdomen, Limited); **574.20** (Cholelithiasis, without mention of obstruction)

CASE 3-13

3-13A ULTRASOUND, RENAL

Professional Services: 76770-26 (Ultrasound, Retroperitoneal, Limited)
ICD-9-CM DX: 788.5 (Anuria), **593.2** (Cyst, kidney, acquired), **592.0** (Calculus/calculi/calculous, kidney)
ICD-10-CM DX: R34 (Anuria), **N28.1** (Cyst, kidney, acquired), **N20.0** (Calculus, kidney)

Facility Services: 76770 (Ultrasound, Retroperitoneal, Limited); **788.5** (Anuria), **593.2** (Cyst, kidney, acquired), **592.0** (Calculi, kidney)

CASE 3-15

3-15A VENTILATION-PERFUSION LUNG SCAN

Professional Services: 78588-26 (Nuclear Medicine, Lung, Imaging Ventilation)
ICD-9-CM DX: 786.50 (Pain[s], chest), **728.87** (Weak/weakness, muscle, generalized)
ICD-10-CM DX: R07.9 (Pain[s], chest), **M62.81** (Weakness, muscle)

Facility Services: 78588 (Nuclear Medicine, Lung, Imaging Ventilation); **786.50** (Pain[s], chest), **728.87** (Weakness, muscle, generalized)

Chapter 4
Pathology and Laboratory

CASE 4-1

4-1A THERAPEUTIC DRUG ASSAYS AND DRUG MONITORING
Professional Services:

1. **80166** (Drug Assays, Doxepin)
2. **80150** (Drug Assays, Amikacin)
3. **80188** (Drug Assays, Primidone)
4. **80176** (Drug Assays, Lidocaine)
5. **80172** (Drug Assays, Gold)
6. **80196** (Drug Assays, Salicylate)
7. **80164** (Drug Assays, Dipropylacetic acid [valproic acid])
8. **80170** (Drug Assays, Gentamicin)

CASE 4-3

4-3A IMMUNOHEMATOLOGY
Professional Services:

1. **86157** (Agglutinin, Cold)
2. **86277** (Antibody, Growth hormone)
3. **86580** (Tuberculosis, Intradermal)
4. **86593** (Syphilis Test)

CASE 4-5

4-5A TRANSFUSION MEDICINE
Professional Services:

1. **86985** (Splitting, Blood Products)
2. **86850** (Red Blood Cell, Antibody)

CASE 4-7

4-7A CYTOPATHOLOGY AND CYTOGENIC STUDIES
Professional Services:

1. **88147** (Cytopathology, Smear, Cervical)
2. **88235** (Culture, Amniotic Fluid, Chromosome Analysis)

Chapter 5
Integumentary System

CASE 5-1

5-1A OPERATIVE REPORT, DEBRIDEMENT

Professional Services: 11043 (Debridement, Skin, Subcutaneous Tissue)
ICD-9-CM DX: 707.14 (Ulcer/ulcerated/ulcerating/ulceration/ulcerative, ischemic, heel), **041.11** (Infection/infected/infective, staphylococcus aureus)
ICD-10-CM DX: L97.413 (Ulcer, lower limb, heel, right, with, muscle necrosis), **B95.6** (Infection, staphylococcal aureus)

Facility Services: This is an inpatient stay. The entire record would need to be reviewed before coding. No inpatient codes are assigned in this workbook.

CASE 5-3

5-3A OPERATIVE REPORT, LIPOMA

Professional Services: 21931 (Excision, Tumor, Back/Flank)
ICD-9-CM DX: 214.8 (Lipoma, other specified sites)

ICD-10-CM DX: D17.39 (Lipoma, site classification, skin, specified site)

Facility Services: 21931 (Excision, Tumor, Back/Flank); **214.8** (Lipoma, skin, other specified site)

CASE 5-5

5-5A OPERATIVE REPORT, EXCISION MELANOMA

Professional Services: 11606 (Excision, Lesion, Skin, Malignant), **12032-51** (Repair, Skin, Wound, Intermediate)
ICD-9-CM DX: 172.5 (Melanoma, chest wall)
ICD-10-CM DX: C43.59 (Melanoma, skin, chest wall)

Facility Services: 11606 (Excision, Lesion, Skin, Malignant), **12032** (Repair, Skin, Wound, Intermediate); **172.5** (Melanoma, chest wall)

CASE 5-7

5-7A OPERATIVE REPORT, LACERATION

Professional Services: 12052 (Repair, Wound, Intermediate)
ICD-9-CM DX: 873.42 (Wound, open, forehead), **E821.0** (Accident, off road type motor vehicle)
ICD-10-CM DX: S01.80xA (Wound, head, specified site), **V19.9xxA** (Accident, transport, pedal cyclist)

Facility Services: 12052 (Repair, Wound, Intermediate); **873.42** (Wound, open, forehead), **E821.0** (Accident, off road type motor vehicle)

CASE 5-9

5-9A OPERATIVE REPORT, SCAR REVISION, DERMABRASION

Professional Services: 13132 (Wound, Repair, Complex), **13133 × 3** (Wound, Repair, Complex)
ICD-9-CM DX: 701.4 (Scar/scarring, keloid)
ICD-10-CM DX: L91.0 (Scar, keloid)

Facility Services: 13132 (Wound, Repair, Complex), **13133** (Wound, Repair, Complex); **701.4** (Scar, keloid)

CASE 5-11

5-11A OPERATIVE REPORT, EXCISION BASAL CELL CARCINOMA

Professional Services: 11602 (Excision, Lesion, Skin, Malignant)
ICD-9-CM DX: 173.7 (Neoplasm, skin, calf, Malignant, Primary)
ICD-10-CM DX: C44.72 (Neoplasm, skin, calf, left, Malignant Primary)

Facility Services: 11602 (Excision, Lesion, Skin, Malignant); **173.7** (Neoplasm, skin, calf, Malignant, Primary)

5-11B PATHOLOGY REPORT

Professional Services: 88305 (Pathology, Surgical, Gross and Micro Exam, Level IV)
ICD-9-CM DX: 173.7 (Neoplasm, skin, calf, Malignant, Primary)
ICD-10-CM DX: C44.72 (Neoplasm, skin, calf, left, Malignant Primary)

CASE 5-13

5-13A OPERATIVE REPORT, ABDOMINOPLASTY

Professional Services: 15830 (Abdominoplasty), **15847** (Abdominoplasty, excision)
ICD-9-CM DX: 701.9 (Redundant/redundancy, abdominal)
ICD-10-CM DX: E65 (Redundant, panniculus [abdomen])

Facility Services: This is an inpatient stay. The entire record would need to be reviewed before coding. No inpatient codes are assigned in this workbook.

CASE 5-15

5-15A OPERATIVE REPORT, BREAST MASS

Professional Services: 19101-RT (Excision, Breast, Biopsy)
ICD-9-CM DX: 174.4 (Neoplasm, breast, upper-outer quadrant, Malignant, Primary)
ICD-10-CM DX: C50.412 (Neoplasm, breast, upper-outer, right, Malignant Primary)

Facility Services: 19101-RT (Excision, Breast, Biopsy); **174.4** (Neoplasm, breast, upper-outer quadrant, Malignant, Primary)

5-15B PATHOLOGY REPORT

Professional Services: 88305 (Pathology, Surgical, Gross and Micro Exam, Level IV)
ICD-9-CM DX: 174.4 (Neoplasm, breast, upper-outer quadrant, Malignant, Primary)
ICD-10-CM DX: C50.41 (Neoplasm, breast, upper-outer, right, Malignant Primary)

Facility Services: 88305 (Pathology, Surgical, Gross and Micro Exam, Level IV); **174.4** (Neoplasm, breast, upper-outer quadrant, Primary, Malignant)

CASE 5-17

5-17A OPERATIVE REPORT, MAMMOPLASTY

Professional Services: 19318-50 (Mammoplasty, Reduction)
ICD-9-CM DX: 611.1 (Hypertrophy/hypertrophic, breast), **611.81** (Ptosis, breast), **V50.1** (Admission, for, breast, augmentation or reduction)

ICD-10-CM DX: N62 (Hypertrophy, breast), **N64.8** (Disorder, breast, specified NEC), **Z41.1** (Admission, plastic surgery, cosmetic)

Facility Services: This is an inpatient stay. The entire record would need to be reviewed before coding. No inpatient codes are assigned in this workbook.

Chapter 6
Cardiovascular System

CASE 6-1

6-1A CORONARY ARTERY BYPASS

Professional Services: 33533 (Coronary Artery Bypass Graft (CABG), Arterial), **33518** (Coronary Artery Bypass Graft, Arterial-Venous), **33508** (Vein, Endoscopic Harvest for Bypass Graft)
ICD-9-CM DX: 414.01 (Arteriosclerosis/arteriosclerotic, coronary, native artery)
ICD-10-CM DX: I25.10 (Arteriosclerosis, coronary, native artery)

Facility Services: This is an inpatient stay. The entire record would need to be reviewed before coding. We will not be assigning codes on inpatients.

CASE 6-3

6-3A ADENOSINE CARDIOLITE STRESS TEST

Professional Services: 93016 (Stress Tests, Cardiovascular), **93018** (Stress Tests, Cardiovascular)
ICD-9-CM DX: 786.50 (Pain[s], chest), **V45.82** (Status [post], percutaneous transluminal coronary angioplasty)
ICD-10-CM DX: R07.9 (Pain[s], chest), **Z98.61** (Status [post], angioplasty, coronary artery)

Facility Services: 93017 (Stress Tests, Cardiovascular, tracing only); **786.50** (Pain, chest), **V45.82** (Status, percutaneous transluminal coronary angioplasty)

6-3B RADIOLOGY REPORT, PERFUSION SCAN

Professional Services: 78452 (Stress Tests, Myocardial Perfusion Imaging)
ICD-9-CM DX: 786.50 (Pain[s], chest), **780.99** (Hypokinesia)
ICD-10-CM DX: R07.9 (Pain[s], chest), **R68.89** (Symptoms NEC)

Facility Services: 78452 (Stress Tests, Myocardial Perfusion Imaging), **786.50** (Pain[s], chest), **780.99** (Hypokinesia)

6-3C ECHO DOPPLER REPORT

Professional Services: 93306-26 (Echocardiography, Transthoracic)

ICD-9-CM DX: 786.50 (Pain[s], chest), **424.0** (Insufficiency/insufficient, mitral [valve]), **397.0** (Endocarditis, tricuspid [valve])
ICD-10-CM DX: R07.9 (Pain[s], chest), **I34.0** (Insufficiency, mitral), **I36.8** (Endocarditis, tricuspid, nonrheumatic)

Facility Services: 93306 (Echocardiography, Transthoracic), **786.50** (Pain[s], chest), **424.0** (Insufficiency, mitral [valve]), **397.0** (Endocarditis, tricuspid [valve])

CASE 6-5

6-5A EMERGENCY AND OUTPATIENT RECORD

Professional Services: 99285 (Evaluation and Management, Emergency Department)
ICD-9-CM DX: 786.50 (Pain[s], chest), **786.05** (Short/shortening/shortness, breath), **V45.82** (Status [post], angioplasty).
ICD-10-CM DX: R07.9 (Pain[s], chest), **R06.02** (Breath, shortness), **Z98.61** (Status [post], angioplasty)

Facility Services: This is an inpatient stay. The entire record would need to be reviewed before coding. We will not be assigning codes on inpatients.

6-5B RADIOLOGY REPORT, CHEST

Professional Services: 71010-26 (X-Ray, Chest)
ICD-9-CM DX: 786.50 (Pain[s], chest)
ICD-10-CM DX: R07.9 (Pain[s], chest)

Facility Services: This is an inpatient stay. The entire record would need to be reviewed before coding. We will not be assigning codes on inpatients.

6-5C INITIAL HOSPITAL CARE

Professional Services: 99221 (Evaluation and Management, Hospital)
ICD-9-CM DX: 786.50 (Pain[s], chest), **414.01** (Arteriosclerosis/arteriosclerotic, coronary, native artery), **412** (Infarct/infarction, myocardium/myocardial, healed or old), **401.9** (Hypertension/hypertensive, Unspecified), **V45.82** (Status, percutaneous transluminal coronary angioplasty)
ICD-10-CM DX: R07.9 (Pain[s], chest), **I25.10** (Arteriosclerotic, coronary, native artery), **I25.2** (Infarction, myocardium, healed or old), **I10** (Hypertension), **Z98.61** (Status [post], angioplasty, coronary artery)

Facility Services: This is an inpatient stay. The entire record would need to be reviewed before coding. No inpatient codes are assigned in the workbook.

6-5D CONSULTATION

Professional Services: 99253 (Evaluation and Management, Inpatient Consultation)
ICD-9-CM DX: 786.50 (Pain[s], chest), **414.01** (Arteriosclerosis/arteriosclerotic, coronary, native artery), **305.1**

(Tobacco, abuse), **V45.82** (Status [post], percutaneous transluminal coronary angioplasty) **V15.81** (Noncompliance with medical treatment)

ICD-10-CM DX: R07.9 (Pain[s], chest), **I25.10** (Arteriosclerotic, coronary, native artery), **F17.210** (Dependence, drug, nicotine, cigarettes), **Z98.61** (Status [post], angioplasty, coronary artery), **Z91.14** (Noncompliance, with, medical treatment)

Facility Services: This is an inpatient stay. The entire record would need to be reviewed before coding. No inpatient codes are assigned in the workbook.

6-5E CARDIAC CATHETERIZATION REPORT

Professional Services: 93510-26 (Cardiac Catheterization, Left Heart), **93543** (Injection, Heart Vessels, Cardiac Catheterization), **93545** (Injection, Heart Vessels, Cardiac Catheterization), **93555-26** (Vascular Studies, Cardiac Catheterization, Imaging), **93556-26** (Vascular Studies, Cardiac Catheterization, Imaging)

ICD-9-CM DX: 786.50 (Pain[s], chest), **414.01** (Arteriosclerosis/arteriosclerotic, coronary, native artery), **V45.82** (Status [post], percutaneous transluminal coronary angioplasty)

ICD-10-CM DX: R07.9 (Pain[s], chest), **I25.10** (Arteriosclerosis, coronary, native artery), **Z98.61** (Status [post], angioplasty, coronary artery)

Facility Services: This is an inpatient stay. The entire record would need to be reviewed before coding. We will not be assigning codes on inpatients.

6-5F PTCA/STENTING REPORT

Professional Services: 92980-LC (Coronary Artery, Insertion, Stent)

ICD-9-CM DX: 414.01 (Arteriosclerosis/arteriosclerotic, coronary, native artery)

ICD-10-CM DX: I25.10 (Arteriosclerosis, coronary, native artery)

Facility Services: This is an inpatient stay. The entire record would need to be reviewed before coding. We will not be assigning codes on inpatients.

CASE 6-7

6-7A TRANSESOPHAGEAL ECHOCARDIOGRAM REPORT

Professional Services: 93312-26 (Transesophageal, Doppler Echocardiography)

ICD-9-CM DX: 424.1 (Stenosis, aortic [valve])

ICD-10-CM DX: I35.0 (Stenosis, aortic [valve])

Facility Services: 93312 (Transesophageal, Doppler Echocardiography); **424.1** (Stenosis, aortic [valve])

CASE 6-9

6-9A OPERATIVE REPORT, ABDOMINAL AORTIC ANEURYSM

Professional Services: 35102 (Aneurysm Repair, Abdominal Aorta)

ICD-9-CM DX: 441.4 (Aneurysm, aorta/aortic, abdominal)

ICD-10-CM DX: I71.4 (Aneurysm, abdominal aorta)

Facility Services: This is an inpatient stay. The entire record would need to be reviewed before coding. We will not be assigning codes on inpatients.

6-9B PATHOLOGY REPORT

Professional Services: 88304 (Pathology, Surgical, Gross and Micro Exam Level III)

ICD-9-CM DX: 441.4 (Aneurysm, aorta/aortic, abdominal)

ICD-10-CM DX: I71.4 (Aneurysm, abdominal aorta)

Facility Services: This is an inpatient stay. The entire record would need to be reviewed before coding. We will not be assigning codes on inpatients.

Chapter 7

Digestive System, Hemic/Lymphatic System, and Mediastinum/Diaphragm

CASE 7-1

7-1A OPERATIVE REPORT, ANAL FISSURE

Professional Services: 46200 (Fissurectomy)

ICD-9-CM DX: 565.0 (Fissure/fissured, anus/anal), **455.9** (Hemorrhoids, sentinel pile)

ICD-10-CM DX: K60.2 (Fissure, anal), **I84.6** (Hemorrhoids, skin tag, residual)

Facility Services: This is an inpatient stay. The entire record would need to be reviewed before coding. We will not be assigning code on inpatients.

CASE 7-3

7-3A OPERATIVE REPORT, DIALYSIS CATHETER

Professional Services: 36584 (Replacement, Venous Catheter, Central)

ICD-9-CM DX: 996.1 (Complication[s], catheter, dialysis, mechanical, obstruction), **585.6** (Disease/diseased, renal, end stage)

ICD-10-CM DX: T82.49xA (Complications, catheter, dialysis, mechanical), **N18.6** (Disease/diseased, end stage renal)

Facility Services: 36584 (Replacement, Venous Catheter, Central); **996.1** (Complications, mechanical, dialysis, hemodialysis), **585.6** (Disease Failure, renal, end stage)

CASE 7-5

7-5A OPERATIVE REPORT, SIGMOIDOSCOPY

Professional Services: **45331** (Endoscopy, Colon-Sigmoid, Biopsy)
ICD-9-CM DX: 211.4 (Neoplasm, intestine/intestinal, large, colon and rectum, Benign)
ICD-10-CM DX: D12.7 (Neoplasm, intestine, large colon and rectum, Benign)

Facility Services: 45331 (Endoscopy, Colon-Sigmoid, Biopsy); **211.3** (Neoplasm, intestine, colon and rectum, Benign)

7-5B PATHOLOGY REPORT

Professional Services: 88305 (Pathology, Surgical, Gross and Micro Exam, Level IV)
ICD-9-CM DX: 211.4 (Neoplasm, intestine, large, colon, Benign)
ICD-10-CM DX: D12.7 (Neoplasm, intestine, large colon and rectum, Benign)

Facility Services: 88305 (Pathology, Gross and Micro Exam, Level IV); **211.3** (Neoplasm, intestine, colon, Benign)

CASE 7-7

7-7A OPERATIVE REPORT, CHOLECYSTECTOMY

Professional Services: 47562 (Cholecystectomy)
ICD-9-CM DX: 574.20 (Cholelithiasis)
ICD-10-CM DX: K80.20 (Calculus, gallbladder)

Facility Services: 47562 (Cholecystectomy); **574.20** (Cholelithiasis)

CASE 7-9

7-9A INITIAL HOSPITAL SERVICE

Professional Services: 99221-57 (Evaluation and Management, Hospital)
ICD-9-CM DX: 868.00 (Injury, internal, abdomen), **458.9** (Hypotension), **991.6** (Hypothermia, accidental), **780.09** (Unconscious/unconsciousness), **E816.0** (Accident, motor vehicle, not involving collision)
ICD-10-CM DX: S36.90xA (Injury, intraabdominal), **I95.9** (Hypotension), **T68.xxxA** (Hypothermia), **R40.20** (Coma), **V87.8xxA** (Accident, traffic, noncollision)

Facility Services: This is an inpatient stay. The entire record would need to be reviewed before coding. No inpatient codes are assigned in the workbook.

7-9B OPERATIVE REPORT, LAPAROTOMY

Professional Services: 47360 (Liver, repair, wound)
ICD-9-CM DX: 864.05 (Laceration, liver), **458.9** (Hypotension), **991.6** (Hypothermia, accidental), **808.8** (Fracture, pelvis), **E816.0** (Accident, motor vehicle, not involving collision)
ICD-10-CM DX: S36.113A (Laceration, liver), **I95.9** (Hypotension), **T68.xxxA** (Hypothermia), **S32.9xxA** (Fracture, traumatic, pelvis), **V87.8xxA** (Accident, traffic, noncollision)

Facility Services: This is an inpatient stay. The entire record would need to be reviewed before coding. No inpatient codes are assigned in the workbook.

7-9C DISCHARGE SUMMARY

Professional Services: 99238 (Evaluation and Management, Hospital, Discharge)
ICD-9-CM DX: 854.05 (Injury, intracranial), **864.05** (Laceration, liver), **991.6** (Hypothermia, accidental), **458.9** (Hypotension), **427.5** (Arrest/arrested, cardiac), **E816.0** (Accident, motor vehicle, not involving collision)
ICD-10-CM DX: S06.9x7A (Injury, head, with loss of consciousness), **S36.113A** (Laceration, liver), **T68.xxxA** (Hypothermia), **I95.9** (Hypotension), **I46.9** (Arrest, cardiac), **V87.8xxA** (Accident, traffic, noncollision)

Facility Services: This is an inpatient stay. The entire record would need to be reviewed before coding. No inpatient codes are assigned in the workbook.

CASE 7-11

7-11A OPERATIVE REPORT, PLACEMENT OF GASTROSTOMY TUBES

Professional Services: 44615 (Enterotomy), **49440** (Gastrostomy Tube, Placement, Percutaneous, Nonendoscopic)
ICD-9-CM DX: 552.8 (Hernia/hernial, internal, with obstruction)
ICD-10-CM DX: K46.0 (Hernia, abdominal, with obstruction)

Facility Services: This is an inpatient stay. The entire record would need to be reviewed before coding. No inpatient codes are assigned in the workbook.

CASE 7-13

7-13A OPERATIVE REPORT, SPLENECTOMY

Professional Services: 38100 (Splenectomy, Total)
ICD-9-CM DX: 865.04 (Rupture/ruptured, spleen, traumatic), **E816.0** (Accident, motor vehicle, noncollision)
ICD-10-CM DX: S36.09xA (Ruptured, spleen), **V87.8xxA** (Accident, traffic, noncollision)

Facility Services: This is an inpatient procedure stay. The entire record would need to be reviewed before coding. No inpatient codes are assigned in the workbook.

Chapter 8
Musculoskeletal System

CASE 8-1

8-1A OPERATIVE REPORT, APPLICATION OF HALO

Professional Services: 20661 (Halo, Cranial)
ICD-9-CM DX: 805.01 (Fracture, vertebrae/vertebral, cervical, first [atlas]), **805.02** (Fracture, vertebra/vertebral, cervical, second), **E819.0** (Accident, motor vehicle)
ICD-10-CM DX: S12.000A (Fracture, neck, cervical, vertebral, first), **S12.100A** (Fracture, neck, cervical, vertebral), **V49.40xA** (Accident, driver, collision, motor vehicle)

Facility Services: 20661 (Halo, Cranial); **805.01** (Fracture, vertebrae, cervical, first [atlas]), **805.02** (Fracture, vertebra, cervical, second), **E819.0** (Accident, motor vehicle)

CASE 8-3

8-3A OPERATIVE REPORT, DISSECTION AND EXCISION

Professional Services: 11401 (Excision, Lesion, Skin, Benign)
ICD-9-CM DX: 686.1 (Granuloma, umbilicus)
ICD-10-CM DX: L92.9 (Granuloma, umbilicus)

Facility Services: 11401 (Excision, Lesion, Skin, Benign); **686.1** (Granuloma, umbilicus)

8-3B PATHOLOGY REPORT

Professional Services: 88305 (Pathology, Surgical, Gross and Micro Exam, Level IV)
ICD-9-CM DX: 686.1 (Granuloma, umbilicus)
ICD-10-CM DX: L92.9 (Granuloma, umbilicus)

Facility Services: 88305 (Pathology Gross and Micro Exam, Level IV); **686.1** (Granuloma, umbilicus)

CASE 8-5

8-5A OPERATIVE REPORT, TUMOR EXCISION

Professional Services: 27618-RT (Excision, Tumor, Leg, Lower)
ICD-9-CM DX: 215.3 (Neoplasm, connective tissue, leg, Benign)
ICD-10-CM DX: D21.21 (Neoplasm, connective tissue, leg, Benign)

Facility Services: 27618-RT (Excision, Tumor, Leg, Lower); **215.3** (Neoplasm, connective tissue, leg, Benign)

CASE 8-7

8-7A OPERATIVE REPORT, TENDON REPAIR

Professional Services: 26356-F9 (Repair, Hand, Tendon, flexor), **26370-51-F9** (Repair, Finger, Tendon, Profundus), **64831-51-F9** (Repair, nerve, Suture)

ICD-9-CM DX: 883.2 (Wound, open, finger[s], with tendon involvement), **955.6** (Injury, nerve, digital), **E920.8** (Cut/cutting by, cutting or piercing instrument)
ICD-10-CM DX: S61.206A (Wound, open, finger, little, right), **S64.496A** (Injury, nerve, digital, little), **W25.xxxA** (Contact, with, glass)

Facility Services: 26356-F9 (Repair, Finger, Tendon, flexor), **26370-F9** (Repair, Finger, Tendon, Profundus), **64831-F9** (Repair, nerve, Suture); **883.2** (Wound, open, finger, with tendon involvement), **955.6** (Injury, nerve, digital), **E920.8** (Cut by, cutting or piercing instrument)

CASE 8-9

8-9A OPERATIVE REPORT, CLOSED REDUCTION

Professional Services: 26605-LT (Fracture, Metacarpal, Closed Treatment)
ICD-9-CM DX: 815.01 (Fracture, metacarpus/metacarpal, base, first metacarpal), **E885.1** (Fall/falling, from roller-skates)
ICD-10-CM DX: S62.232A (Fracture, metacarpal, first, initial encounter), **V00.121A** (Accident, transport, pedestrian, conveyance, non in line roller skates)

Facility Services: 26605-LT (Fracture, Metacarpal, Closed Treatment); **815.01** (Fracture, metacarpus, metacarpal, base, first metacarpal), **E885.1** (Fall, from roller-skates)

CASE 8-11

8-11A OPERATIVE REPORT, SHOULDER

Professional Services: 29805-LT (Arthroscopy, Diagnostic, Shoulder)
ICD-9-CM DX: 719.41 (Pain[s], joint, shoulder), **782.0** (Numbness), **V13.59** (History of, musculoskeletal disorder NEC)
ICD-10-CM DX: M25.512 (Pain[s], joint, shoulder), **R20.0** (Numbness), **Z87.39** (History, disorder, musculoskeletal)

Facility Services: 29805-LT (Arthroscopy, Diagnostic, Shoulder); **719.41** (Pain[s], joint, shoulder), **782.0** (Numbness), **V13.5** (History of, personal, musculoskeletal disorder)

CASE 8-13

8-13A OPERATIVE REPORT, DEBRIDEMENT

Professional Services: 29877-LT (Arthroscopy, Surgical, Knee)
ICD-9-CM DX: 717.7 (Chondromalacia, knee)
ICD-10-CM DX: M94.262 (Chondromalacia, knee, left)

Facility Services: 29877-LT (Arthroscopy, Surgical, Knee), **717.7** (Chondromalacia, knee)

Chapter 9
Respiratory System

CASE 9-1

9-1A INITIAL HOSPITAL CARE

Professional Services: 99291-GC (Evaluation and Management, Critical Care)

ICD-9-CM DX: 441.4 (Aneurysm, aorta/aortic, abdominal), **518.81** (Failure/failed, respiration/respiratory, acute), **496** (Disease/diseased, lung, obstructive [chronic] COPD), **780.09** (Unconscious/unconsciousness), **787.91** (Diarrhea/diarrheal [bloody]), **458.9** (Hypotension), **780.57** (Apnea/apneic, sleep), **272.4** (Hyperlipidemia), **278.00** (Obesity), **V46.11** (Dependence, on, respirator [ventilator])

ICD-10-CM DX: I71.4 (Aneurysm, abdominal aortic), **J96.0** (Failure/failed, respiratory, acute), **J44.9** (Disease, obstructive, lung), **R40.20** (Coma), **R19.7** (Diarrhea), **I95.9** (Hypotension), **G47.30** (Apnea, sleep), **E78.5** (Hyperlipedemia), **E66.9** (Obesity), **Z99.11** (Dependence, on, respirator)

Facility Services: This is an inpatient stay. The entire record would need to be reviewed before coding. We will not be assigning codes on inpatients.

9-1B RADIOLOGY REPORT, CHEST

Professional Services: 71010-26 (X-Ray, Chest)
ICD-9-CM DX: 518.81 (Failure/failed, respiration/respiratory)
ICD-10-CM DX: J96.9 (Failure/failed, respiratory)

Facility Services: This is an inpatient stay. The entire record would need to be reviewed before coding. We will not be assigning codes on inpatients.

9-1C RADIOLOGY REPORT, CHEST

Professional Services: 71010-26-76 (X-Ray, Chest)
ICD-9-CM DX: 518.81 (Failure/failed, respiration/respiratory)
ICD-10-CM DX: J96.9 (Failure/failed, respiratory)

Facility Services: This is an inpatient stay. The entire record would need to be reviewed before coding. We will not be assigning codes on inpatients.

9-1D PROGRESS REPORT

Professional Services: 99291 (Evaluation and Management, Critical Care)
ICD-9-CM DX: 518.81 (Failure/failure, respiration/respiratory), **458.9** (Hypotension), **578.9** (Bleeding, gastrointestinal), **V46.11** (Dependence, on, respirator [ventilator])
ICD-10-CM DX: J96.9 (Failure, respiratory), **I95.9** (Hypotension), **K92.2** (Bleeding, gastrointestinal), **Z99.11** (Dependence, on, respirator)

Facility Services: This is an inpatient stay. The entire record would need to be reviewed before coding. We will not be assigning codes on inpatients.

9-1E PROGRESS REPORT

Professional Services: 99291 (Evaluation and Management, Critical Care); **99292** (Evaluation and Management, Critical Care)
ICD-9-CM DX: 518.81 (Failure/failed, respiration/respiratory), **787.91** (Diarrhea/diarrheal [bloody]), **790.7** (Bacteremia), **041.89** (Infection/infected/infective, bacterial, specified NEC), **275.41** (Hypocalcemia), **788.5** (Oliguria), **427.89** (Tachycardia, sinus), **782.3** (Edema/edematous), **285.9** (Anemia), **V46.11** (Dependence, on, respirator [ventilator])
ICD-10-CM DX: J96.9 (Failure/failed, respiratory), **R19.7** (Diarrhea), **R78.81** (Bacteremia), **A49.9** (Infection, bacterial), **E83.51** (Hypocalcemia), **R34** (Oliguria), **R00.0** (Tachycardia, sinus), **R60.9** (Edema), **D64.9** (Anemia), **Z99.11** (Dependence, on, respirator)

Facility Services: This is an inpatient stay. The entire record would need to be reviewed before coding. We will not be assigning codes on inpatients.

9-1F PROGRESS REPORT

Professional Services: 99291 (Evaluation and Management, Critical Care)
ICD-9-CM DX: 427.31 (Fibrillation, atrial), **518.81** (Failure/failed, respiration/respiratory), **458.9** (Hypotension), **276.6** (Overload, fluid), **788.5** (Anuria), **790.7** (Bacteremia), **041.89** Infection/infected/infective, bacterial, specified NEC), **V46.11** (Dependence, on, respirator [ventilator])
ICD-10-CM DX: I48.0 (Fibrillation, atrial), **J96.9** (Failure/failed, respiratory), **I95.9** (Hypotension), **E87.7** (Overload, fluid), **R34** (Anuria), **R78.81** (Bacteremia), **A49.9** (Infection, bacterial), **Z99.11** (Dependence, on, respirator)

Facility Services: This is an inpatient stay. The entire record would need to be reviewed before coding. We will not be assigning codes on inpatients.

9-1G DISCHARGE SUMMARY

Professional Services: 99238 (Evaluation and Management, Hospital, Discharge)
ICD-9-CM DX: 518.81 (Failure/failed, respiration/respiratory), **441.4** (Aneurysm, aorta/aortic, abdominal), **427.89** (Bradycardia), **790.7** (Bacteremia), **041.89** (Infection/infected/infective, bacterial, specified NEC), **276.6** (Overload, fluid), **788.5** (Anuria); **V46.11** (Dependence, on, respirator [ventilator])
ICD-10-CM DX: J96.9 (Failure/failed, respiratory), **I71.4** (Aneurysm, aorta, abdominal), **R00.1** (Bradycardia), **R78.81** (Bacteremia), **A49.9** (Infection, bacterial), **E87.7** (Overload, fluid), **R34** (Anuria); **Z99.11** (Dependence, on, respirator)

Facility Services: This is an inpatient stay. The entire record would need to be reviewed before coding. We will not be assigning codes on inpatients.

CASE 9-3

9-3A PULMONARY FUNCTION STUDY

Professional Services: 94060-26 (Pulmonology, Diagnostic, Spirometry, Evaluation), **94720-26** (Pulmonology, Diagnostic, Carbon Monoxide Diffusion Capacity), **94260-26** (Pulmonology, Diagnostic, Thoracic Gas Volume), **94360-26** (Pulmonology, Diagnostic, Resistance to Airflow)
ICD-9-CM DX: 493.90 (Asthma/asthmatic), **V15.82** (History [personal], tobacco use)
ICD-10-CM DX: J45.909 (Asthma/asthmatic), **Z87.82** (History, personal [of], tobacco dependence)

Facility Services: 94060 (Pulmonary, Diagnostic, Spirometry, Evaluation), **94720** (Pulmonary, Diagnostic, Carbon Monoxide Diffusion Capacity), **94260** (Pulmonary, Diagnostic, Thoracic Gas Volume), **94360** (Pulmonary, Diagnostic, Resistance to Airflow), **493.90** (Asthma); **V15.82** (History [personal], tobacco use)

CASE 9-5

9-5A OPERATIVE REPORT, SEPTOPLASTY, TURBINATE REDUCTION, AND TONSILLECTOMY

Professional Services: 30520 (Septoplasty), **30930-50-51** (Turbinate, Fracture, Therapeutic), **42826-51** (Tonsillectomy)
ICD-9-CM DX: 470 (Deviation, septum [nasal]), **478.0** (Hypertrophy/hypertrophic, turbinate), **478.19** (Obstruction/obstructed/obstructive, nasal), **474.00** (Tonsillitis, chronic)
ICD-10-CM DX: J34.2 (Deviation, septum), **J34.3** (Hypertrophy, nasal, turbinate), **J34.89** (Obstructive, nasal), **J35.01** (Tonsillitis, chronic)

Facility Services: This is an inpatient stay. The entire record would need to be reviewed before coding. We will not be assigning codes on inpatients.

CASE 9-7

9-7A OPERATIVE REPORT, ETHMOIDECTOMY AND ANTROSTOMY

Professional Services: 31255 (Ethmoidectomy, Endoscopic), **31255-50** (Ethmoidectomy, Endoscopic), **31267-51** (Antrostomy, Sinus, Maxillary), **31267-50-51** (Antrostomy, Sinus, Maxillary), **31287-51** (Sphenoidotomy, Excision, with Nasal/Sinus Endoscopy), **31287-50-51** (Sphenoidotomy, Excision, with Nasal/Sinus Endoscopy)
ICD-9-CM DX: 473.9 (Sinusitis, chronic), **471.8** (Polyp/polypus, ethmoidal [sinus]), **470** (Deviation, septum)
ICD-10-CM DX: J32.9 (Sinusitis, chronic), **J33.8** (Polyp, sinus, ethmoidal), **J34.2** (Deviation, septum)

Facility Services: 31255-50 (Ethmoidectomy, Endoscopic), **31267-50** (Antrostomy, Sinus, Maxillary), **31287-50** (Sphe-

noidotomy, Excision, with Nasal/Sinus Endoscopy); **473.9** (Sinusitis, chronic), **471.8** (Polyp, ethmoidal [sinus]), **470** (Deviated, septum)

CASE 9-9

9-9A OPERATIVE REPORT, BRONCHOSCOPY

Professional Services: 31615-50 (Tracheobronchoscopy, through Tracheostomy), **31622-50** (Bronchoscopy, Exploration)
ICD-9-CM DX: 786.3 (Hemoptysis)
ICD-10-CM DX: R04.2 (Hemoptysis)

Facility Services: 31615-50 (Tracheobronchoscopy, through Tracheostomy), **31622-50** (Bronchoscopy, Exploration); **786.3** (Hemoptysis)

9-9B PATHOLOGY REPORT

Professional Services: 88104 (Cytopathology, Fluids, Washings, Brushings)
ICD-9-CM DX: 786.3 (Hemoptysis)
ICD-10-CM DX: R04.2 (Hemoptysis)

Facility Services: 88104 (Cytopathology, Fluids, Washings, Brushings); **786.3** (Hemoptysis)

Chapter 10
Urinary, Male Genital, and Endocrine System

CASE 10-1

10-1A OPERATIVE REPORT, NEPHROSTOMY TUBE EXCHANGE

Professional Services: 50398-LT (Nephrostomy, Change Tube)
ICD-9-CM DX: V55.6 (Attention to, nephrostomy), **591** (Hydronephrosis),
ICD-10-CM DX: Z43.6 (Attention [to], nephrostomy), **N13.30** (Hydronephrosis)

Facility Services: 50398-LT (Nephrostomy, Change Tube); **V55.6** (Attention to, nephrostomy); **591** (Hydronephrosis)

10-1B RADIOLOGY REPORT, NEPHROSTOGRAM

Professional Services: 50394-LT (Nephrostogram), **74425-26** (Urinary Tract, X-Ray with Contrast)
ICD-9-CM DX: V55.6 (Attention to, nephrostomy), **591** (Hydronephrosis)
ICD-10-CM DX: Z43.6 (Attention [to], nephrostomy), **N13.30** (Hydronephrosis)

Facility Services: 50394-LT (Nephrostogram), **74425** (Radiologic supervision and interpretation) **V55.6** (Attention to, nephrostomy), **591** (Hydronephrosis),

CASE 10-3

10-3A OPERATIVE REPORT, URETHROPEXY

Professional Services: 51840 (Urethropexy)
ICD-9-CM DX: 625.6 (Incontinence, urine, stress [female])
ICD-10-CM DX: N39.3 (Incontinence, urine, stress, female)

Facility Services: 51840 (Urethropexy); **625.6** (Incontinence, urine, stress [female])

CASE 10-5

10-5A OPERATIVE REPORT, STENT INSERTION

Professional Services: 52332-LT (Ureter, Endoscopy, Insertion, Stent), **74420-26** (Urography, Retrograde)
ICD-9-CM DX: 592.1 (Calculus/calculi/calculous, ureter)
ICD-10-CM DX: N20.1 (Calculus/calculi/calculous, ureter)

Facility Services: 52332-LT (Ureter, Endoscopy, Insertion, Stent), **74420** (Urography, Retrograde); **592.1** (Calculus, Ureter)

CASE 10-7

10-7A OPERATIVE REPORT, BIOPSY

Professional Services: 54505-50 or **54505** and **54505-50** (Testis, Biopsy)
ICD-9-CM DX: 606.0 (Azoospermia)
ICD-10-CM DX: N46.01 (Azoospermia)

Facility Services: 54505-50 (Testis, Biopsy); **606.0** (Azoospermia)

CASE 10-9

10-9A OPERATIVE REPORT, PROSTATECTOMY

Professional Services: 55845 (Prostate, Excision, Retropubic, [Radical])
ICD-9-CM DX: 185 (Neoplasm, prostate [gland], Malignant, Primary)
ICD-10-CM DX: C61 (Neoplasm, prostate [gland], Malignant Primary)

Facility Services: This is an inpatient stay. The entire record would need to be reviewed before coding. We will not be assigning codes on inpatients.

CASE 10-11

10-11A OPERATIVE REPORT, THYROIDECTOMY

Professional Services: 60220-RT (Thyroid Gland, Excision, Partial)
ICD-9-CM DX: 226 (Adenoma, thyroid)
ICD-10-CM DX: D34 (Neoplasm, thyroid, Benign)

Facility Services: This is an inpatient stay. The entire record would need to be reviewed before coding. We will not be assigning codes on inpatients.

Chapter 11
Female Genital System

CASE 11-1

11-1A CONSULTATION

Professional Services: 99252-57 (Evaluation and Management, Consultation)
ICD-9-CM DX: 627.1 (Bleeding, postmenopausal), **574.10** (Cholelithiasis, with, cholecystitis, chronic), **204.10** (Leukemia/leukemic, lymphocytic, chronic)
ICD-10-CM DX: N95.0 (Bleeding, postmenopausal), **K80.10** (Calculus, gallbladder, with, cholecystitis), **C91.10** (Leukemia, lymphocytic, chronic)

Facility Services: This is an inpatient stay. The entire record would need to be reviewed before coding. No inpatient codes are assigned in the workbook.

11-1B OPERATIVE REPORT, HYSTEROSCOPY

Professional Services: 58558 (Hysteroscopy, Surgical with Biopsy)
ICD-9-CM DX: 627.1 (Bleeding, postmenopausal), **621.0** (Polyp/polypus, endometrium)
ICD-10-CM DX: N95.0 (Bleeding, postmenopausal), **N84.0** (Polyp, endometrial)

Facility Services: This is an inpatient stay. The entire record would need to be reviewed before coding. No inpatient codes are assigned in the workbook.

11-1C OPERATIVE REPORT, CHOLECYSTECTOMY

Professional Services: 47562 (Cholecystectomy)
ICD-9-CM DX: 574.10 (Cholelithiasis, with, cholecystitis, chronic)
ICD-10-CM DX: K80.10 (Calculus, gallbladder, with, cholecystitis)

Facility Services: This is an inpatient stay. The entire record would need to be reviewed before coding. No inpatient codes are assigned in the workbook.

11-1D PATHOLOGY REPORT

Professional Services: 88304 (Pathology, Surgical, Gross and Micro Exam, Level III)
ICD-9-CM DX: 574.10 (Cholelithiasis, with, cholecystitis, chronic)
ICD-10-CM DX: K80.10 (Calculus, gallbladder, with, cholecystitis)

Facility Services: No inpatient facility services provided.

CASE 11-3

11-3A OPERATIVE REPORT, STERILIZATION

Professional Services: 58605 (Ligation, Fallopian tube, Oviduct)
ICD-9-CM DX: V25.2 (Sterilization, admission for)
ICD-10-CM DX: Z30.2 (Encounter [for] sterilization)

Facility Services: This is an inpatient stay. The entire record would need to be reviewed before coding. No inpatient codes are assigned in the workbook

Chapter 12
Nervous System

CASE 12-1

12-1A OPERATIVE REPORT, CRANIECTOMY

Professional Services: 61312-LT (Craniectomy, Surgical)
ICD-9-CM DX: 432.0 (Hematoma, brain, nontraumatic, epidural)
ICD-10-CM DX: I62.1 (Hemorrhage, intracranial, epidural, nontraumatic)

Facility Services: This is an inpatient stay. The entire record would need to be reviewed before coding. We will not be assigning codes on inpatients.

CASE 12-3

12-3A OPERATIVE REPORT, RE-DO CRANIECTOMY

Professional Services: 61312-78 (Craniectomy, Surgical)
ICD-9-CM DX: 432.0 (Hematoma, brain, nontraumatic, epidural)
ICD-10-CM DX: I62.1 (Hemorrhage, intracranial, epidural, nontraumatic)

Facility Services: This is an inpatient stay. The entire record would need to be reviewed before coding. We will not be assigning codes on inpatients.

CASE 12-5

12-5A OPERATIVE REPORT, PUMP IMPLANTATION

Professional Services: 62350 (Catheterization, Spinal Cord), **62362-51** (Infusion Therapy, Pain)
ICD-9-CM DX: 340 (Sclerosis/sclerotic, multiple)
ICD-10-CM DX: G35 (Sclerosis, multiple)

Facility Services: This is an inpatient stay. The entire record would need to be reviewed before coding. We will not be assigning codes on inpatients.

CASE 12-7

12-7A RADIOLOGY REPORT

Professional Services: 72020-26 (X-Ray, spine)
ICD-9-CM DX: 722.10 (Displacement/displaced, intervertebral disc, lumbar)
ICD-10-CM DX: M51.26 (Displacement, intervertebral disc, lumbar)

Facility Services: This is an inpatient stay. The entire record would need to be reviewed before coding. We will not be assigning codes on inpatients.

12-7B OPERATIVE REPORT, RE-DO LAMINECTOMY

Professional Services: 63042-RT (Laminectomy)
ICD-9-CM DX: 722.10 (Displacement/displaced, intervertebral disc, lumbar)
ICD-10-CM DX: M51.26 (Displacement, intervertebral disc, lumbar)

Facility Services: This is an inpatient stay. The entire record would need to be reviewed before coding. We will not be assigning codes on inpatients.

12-7C PATHOLOGY REPORT

Professional Services: 88304 (Pathology, Surgical, Gross and Micro Exam, Level III [bone fragments])
ICD-9-CM DX: 722.10 (Displacement/displaced, intervertebral disc, lumbar)
ICD-10-CM DX: M51.26 (Displacement, intervertebral disc, lumbar)

Facility Services: This is an inpatient stay. The entire record would need to be reviewed before coding. We will not be assigning codes on inpatients.

12-7D RADIOLOGY REPORT, MRI LUMBAR SPINE

Professional Services: 72149-26 (Magnetic Resonance Imaging [MRI], Spine, Lumbar)
ICD-9-CM DX: 722.10 (Displacement/displaced, intervertebral disc, lumbar)
ICD-10-CM DX: M51.26 (Displacement, intervertebral disc, lumbar)

Facility Services: This is an inpatient stay. The entire record would need to be reviewed before coding. We will not be assigning codes on inpatients.

CASE 12-9

12-9A ELECTROENCEPHALOGRAM REPORT

Professional Services: 95816-26 (Electroencephalography [EEG])
ICD-9-CM DX: 780.09 (Unconscious/unconsciousness), **794.02** (Abnormal/abnormality/abnormalities, electroencephalogram EEG)

ICD-10-CM DX: R40.20 (Coma), **R94.01** (Abnormal, electroencephalgram [EEG])

Facility Services: 95816 (Electroencephalography [EEG]); **780.09** (Unconsciousness), **794.02** (Abnormal, EEG)

Chapter 13
Eye and Auditory System

CASE 13-1

13-1A CLINIC PROGRESS NOTE, EYE EXAMINATION

Professional Services: 92002 (Ophthalmology, Diagnostic, Eye Exam, New Patient), **76512-26** (Ophthalmology Ultrasound, [B scan]), **96372** (Injection, Intramuscular), **96374** (Injection, Intravenous Push), **J1885_ 4** (Table of Drugs, Toradol, [Additional name: Ketorolac]), **J1120** (Table of Drugs, Diamox, [Additional name: Acetazolamide])
ICD-9-CM DX: 921.3 (Injury, eyeball), **372.71** (Hyperemia, eye), **379.23** (Hemorrhage/hemorrhagic, vitreous), **E917.9** (Striking against, object [moving])
ICD-10-CM DX: S05.8x2A (Injury, eyeball), **H11.432** (Hyperemia, eye), **H43.12** (Hemorrhage, vitreous), **W22.8xxA** (Struck [by], object)

Facility Services: No facility services provided.

CASE 13-3

13-3A OPERATIVE REPORT, ENTROPION WITH MINI-BLEPHAROPLASTY

Professional Services: 67923-E4 (Entropion, Repair)
ICD-9-CM DX: 374.00 (Entropion, [eyelid]), **379.91** (Pain[s], eye), **372.10** (Conjunctivitis, chronic), **370.34** (Keratitis, exposure)
ICD-10-CM DX: H02.002 (Entropion), **H57.11** (Pain[s], eye), **H16.211** (Keratoconjunctivitis)

Facility Services: 67923-E4 (Entropion, Repair); **374.00** (Entropion, [eyelid]), **379.91** (Pain[s], eye), **372.10** (Conjunctivitis, chronic), **370.34** (Keratitis, exposure)

CASE 13-5

13-5A OPERATIVE REPORT, MYRINGOTOMY AND ADENOIDECTOMY/TONSILLECTOMY

Professional Services: 42821 (Adenoids, excision, with tonsils), **69421-50-51** (Myringotomy)
ICD-9-CM DX: 474.02 (Adenoiditis, chronic, with chronic tonsillitis), **474.10** (Hypertrophy/hypertrophic, adenoids, and tonsils), **381.10** (Otitis, media, chronic, serous)
ICD-10-CM DX: J35.03 (Adenoiditis, chronic, with tonsillitis), **J35.3** (Hypertrophic, adenoids, with, tonsils), **H65.493** (Otitis, media, nonsuppurative, chronic)

Facility Services: 42821 (Adenoids, excision, with tonsils), **69421-50** (Myringotomy); **474.02** (Adenoiditis, chronic, with chronic tonsillitis), **474.10** (Hypertrophy, adenoids, and tonsils), **381.10** (Otitis, media, chronic, serous)

Chapter 14
Anesthesia

CASE 14-1

14-1A OPERATIVE REPORT, ANESTHESIA
Professional Services:
PHYSICIAN CODE: 00902-P1 (Anesthesia, Anus)
CRNA CODE: 00902-QX-P1 (Anesthesia, Anus)

Facility Services: No CPT code assignment for anesthesia is made in the hospital setting.

CASE 14-3

14-3A OPERATIVE REPORT, ANESTHESIA
Professional Services:
CRNA CODE: 00920-P1 (Anesthesia, Genitalia, Male)

Facility Services: No CPT code assignment for anesthesia is made in the hospital setting.

E/M Audit Form

A blank E/M audit form is included in this appendix. The coder is to photocopy the audit form for each E/M case in the workbook and for the tests that contain E/M cases. A blank form is also located on the companion web page, http://evolve.elsevier.com/Buck/next.

This Audit Form is based on the 1995 Documentation Guidelines for Evaluation and Management Services.

CHAPTER _____, CASE _____

HISTORY ELEMENTS	Documented
HISTORY OF PRESENT ILLNESS (HPI)	
1. Location (site on body)	
2. Quality (characteristic: throbbing, sharp)	
3. Severity (1/10 or how intense)	
4. Duration* (how long for problem or episode)	
5. Timing (when it occurs)	
6. Context (under what circumstances does it occur)	
7. Modifying factors (what makes it better or worse)	
8. Associated signs and symptoms (what else is happening when it occurs)	
*Duration not in CPT as HPI Element TOTAL	
LEVEL	

REVIEW OF SYSTEMS (ROS)	Documented
1. Constitutional (e.g., weight loss, fever)	
2. Ophthalmologic (eyes)	
3. Otolaryngologic (ears, nose, mouth, throat)	
4. Cardiovascular	
5. Respiratory	
6. Gastrointestinal	
7. Genitourinary	
8. Musculoskeletal	
9. Integumentary (skin and/or breasts)	
10. Neurological	
11. Psychiatric	
12. Endocrine	
13. Hematologic/Lymphatic	
14. Allergic/Immunologic	
TOTAL	
LEVEL	

PAST, FAMILY, AND/OR SOCIAL HISTORY (PFSH)	Documented
1. Past illness, operations, injuries, treatments, and current medications	
2. Family medical history for heredity and risk	
3. Social activities, both past and present	
TOTAL	
LEVEL	

History Level	1	2	3	4
	Problem Focused	Expanded Problem Focused	Detailed	Comprehensive
HPI	Brief 1-3	Brief 1-3	Extended 4+	Extended 4+
ROS	None	Problem Pertinent 1	Extended 2-9	Complete 10+
PFSH	None	None	Pertinent 1	Complete 2-3
			HISTORY LEVEL	

EXAMINATION ELEMENTS	Documented
CONSTITUTIONAL (OS)	
• Blood pressure, sitting	
• Blood pressure, lying	
• Pulse	
• Respirations	
• Temperature	
• Height	
• Weight	
• General appearance	
(Counts as only 1) NUMBER	

BODY AREAS (BA)	Documented
1. Head (including face)	
2. Neck	
3. Chest (including breasts and axillae)	
4. Abdomen	
5. Genitalia, groin, buttocks	
6. Back (including spine)	
7. Each extremity	
NUMBER	

ORGAN SYSTEMS (OS)	Documented
1. Ophthalmologic (eyes)	
2. Otolaryngologic (ears, nose, mouth, throat)	
3. Cardiovascular	
4. Respiratory	
5. Gastrointestinal	
6. Genitourinary	
7. Musculoskeletal	
8. Integumentary (skin)	
9. Neurologic	
10. Psychiatric	
11. Hematologic/Lymphatic/Immunologic	
NUMBER	
TOTAL BA/OS	

Exam Level	1	2	3	4
	Problem Focused	Expanded Problem Focused	Detailed	Comprehensive
	Limited to affected BA/OS	Limited to affected BA/OS & other related OS(s)	Extended of affected BA(s) & other related OS(s)	General multi-system (OSs only)
# of OS or BA	1	2-7 limited	2-7 extended	8+
			EXAMINATION LEVEL	

MDM ELEMENTS	Documented
# OF DIAGNOSIS/MANAGEMENT OPTIONS	
1. Minimal	
2. Limited	
3. Multiple	
4. Extensive	
LEVEL	

AMOUNT AND/OR COMPLEXITY OF DATA TO REVIEW	Documented
1. Minimal/None	
2. Limited	
3. Moderate	
4. Extensive	
LEVEL	

RISK OF COMPLICATION OR DEATH IF NOT TREATED	Documented
1. Minimal	
2. Low	
3. Moderate	
4. High	
LEVEL	

MDM*	1	2	3	4
	Straightforward	Low	Moderate	High
Number of DX or management options	Minimal	Limited	Multiple	Extensive
Amount and/or complexity of data	Minimal/None	Limited	Moderate	Extensive
Risks	Minimal	Low	Moderate	High
			MDM LEVEL	

*To qualify for a given type of MDM complexity, 2 of 3 elements in the table must be met or exceeded.

History:
Examination:
MDM:
Number of Key Components:
Code:

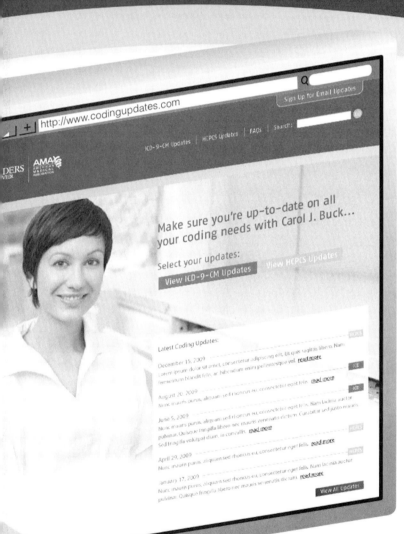

Trust Carol J. Buck and Elsevier for the

resources you need at *each step* of your coding career!

Track your progress toward complete coding success!

Step 1: Learn

- ❏ Step-by-Step Medical Coding 2010 Edition • ISBN: 978-1-4160-6836-5
- ❏ Workbook for Step-by-Step Medical Coding 2010 Edition • ISBN: 978-1-4377-0218-7
- ❏ Medical Coding Online for Step-by-Step Medical Coding 2010 • ISBN: 978-1-4377-0369-6
- ❏ Virtual Medical Office for Step-by-Step Medical Coding 2010 Edition • ISBN: 978-1-4377-1505-7

Step 2: Practice

- ❏ The Next Step: Advanced Medical Coding 2010 Edition • ISBN: 978-1-4377-0441-9
- ❏ Workbook for The Next Step: Advanced Medical Coding 2010 Edition • ISBN: 978-1-4377-0675-8
- ❏ Advanced Medical Coding Online for The Next Step 2010 Edition • ISBN: 978-1-4377-0442-6
- ❏ Online Internship for Medical Coding 2010 Edition • ISBN: 978-1-4377-0819-6

Step 3: Certify

- ❏ CPC® Coding Exam Review 2010: The Certification Step • ISBN: 978-1-4377-0817-2
- ❏ CCS Coding Exam Review 2010: The Certification Step • ISBN: 978-1-4377-0815-8
- ❏ The Extra Step: Facility-Based Coding Practice 2010 Edition • ISBN: 978-1-4377-1365-7
- ❏ The Extra Step: Physician-Based Coding Practice 2010 Edition • ISBN: 978-1-4377-0767-0

Step 4: Specialize

- ❏ Evaluation and Management Step: An Auditing Tool • ISBN: 978-1-4160-6724-5

Coding References

- ❏ 2010 ICD-9-CM for Physicians, Volumes 1 & 2, Professional Edition • ISBN: 978-1-4377-0208-8
- ❏ 2010 ICD-9-CM for Hospitals, Volumes 1, 2 & 3, Professional Edition • ISBN: 978-1-4377-0207-1
- ❏ 2010 ICD-9-CM for Physicians, Volumes 1 & 2, Standard Edition • ISBN: 978-1-4377-0748-9
- ❏ 2010 ICD-9-CM for Hospitals, Volumes 1, 2 & 3, Standard Edition • ISBN: 978-1-4377-0747-2
- ❏ 2010 ICD-9-CM for Physicians, Volumes 1 & 2, Professional Softcover Edition • ISBN: 978-1-4377-1434-0
- ❏ 2010 ICD-9-CM for Physicians, Volumes 1 & 2, Professional Compact Edition • ISBN: 978-1-4377-1433-3
- ❏ 2010 ICD-9-CM for Hospitals, Volumes 1, 2 & 3, Professional Compact Edition • ISBN: 978-1-4377-1432-6
- ❏ 2010 HCPCS Level II Professional Edition • ISBN: 978-1-4377-0211-8
- ❏ 2010 HCPCS Level II Standard Edition • ISBN: 978-1-4377-0818-9
- ❏ 2010 ICD-10-CM Standard Edition Draft Manual • ISBN: 978-1-4160-2567-2
- ❏ 2010 ICD-10-PCS Standard Edition Draft Manual • ISBN: 978-1-4160-6412-1

Author and
Educator
Carol J. Buck,
MS, CPC-I, CPC,
CPC-H, CCS-P

Get the next resources on your list today!

- • Order securely at **www.elsevierhealth.com**
- • Call toll-free **1-800-545-2522**
- • Visit your local bookstore

PC-10

ELSEVIER